THE RISE OF URBAN AMERICA

ADVISORY EDITOR

Richard C. Wade

PROFESSOR OF AMERICAN HISTORY
UNIVERSITY OF CHICAGO

MODERN CIVIC ART
OR,
THE CITY
MADE BEAUTIFUL

Charles Mulford Robinson

ARNO PRESS

&

The New York Times

NEW YORK · 1970

NA9030
.R7
1970

Reprint Edition 1970 by Arno Press Inc.

Reprinted from a copy in The University of Chicago Library

LC# 79-112570
ISBN 0-405-02473-8

THE RISE OF URBAN AMERICA
ISBN for complete set 0-405-02430-4

Manufactured in the United States of America

MODERN CIVIC ART

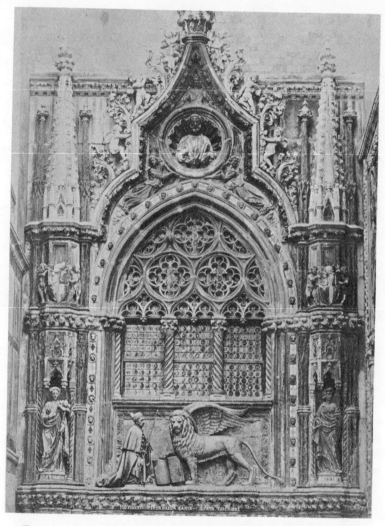

Decoration over an Entrance to the Doges' Palace
in Venice

The doge kneels before the lion of St. Mark in token that
he is servant, not master, of the State.

MODERN CIVIC ART

OR

THE CITY MADE BEAUTIFUL

BY

CHARLES MULFORD ROBINSON

AUTHOR OF
"THE IMPROVEMENT OF TOWNS AND CITIES"

FOURTH EDITION
WITH ILLUSTRATIONS

G. P. PUTNAM'S SONS
NEW YORK AND LONDON
The Knickerbocker Press

The Knickerbocker Press, New York

PREFACE TO THE FOURTH EDITION.

I N rereading this volume fifteen years after its original composition, the author is impressed by two things. One is the endorsement which the lapse of time has given to its principles. For this he can take no credit to himself, since art can no more grow old than beauty. The statement of art principles is as eternal as the truth; and so, if a book enunciates these accurately, as they apply to civic art, it ought not to grow stale.

The reading of the original text has revealed also the progress in municipal art which has been lately made by cities of the United States. In keeping the volume's text up to date, through its several editions, it has been gratifying to note the character of the changes necessitated in the record of fact and condition and in the citation of examples. Many of the hopes (or possibly visions) expressed in the First Edition have become actualities; some observed tendencies toward better things are now established movements; and many specific conditions, which then were criticized, now have been corrected. Of course our cities are still far from perfect; but no one who compares the First Edition with the Fourth can fail to realize that the popular ideal in civic art has greatly risen. This is a more notable advance than simply the widespread organizing which was noted in the Preface to the Second Edition, though in part it may be a natural result of that. At all events, civic-art standards are now such that a lapse into the former conditions of neglect and carelessness is inconceivable.

A word is needed, perhaps, as to the seeming incongruity of a volume on such a subject at a period when modern civilization fights for its life and when cities, that long have been the pride of civic art, are crumbling beneath shot and shell. But was there ever a time when civic art needed more urgently than now that its friends should rally for it, ever a more needed occasion for clearly enunciating its eternal principles than when the builders of cities are facing the despair of a shattered past and the opportunity of an untrammelled future? Surely it is not without significance that during the world war civic art has been the one phase of art which has proved a subject of international discussion. A half dozen committees are concerning themselves, while the war still lasts, to make sure that cities and towns shall be reconstructed in accordance with artistic principles.

C. M. R.

October 1, 1917.

PREFACE TO THE SECOND EDITION.

THAT there has been a call for a new edition of this volume may be understood as meaning much more than the success of a book. It stands for the progress of the Cause for the furtherance of which the book came into existence.

Nothing, indeed, has been more remarkable than the growth of the "civic improvement" movement during the last few years. There must be a strong feeling on the part of an individual before he sets about the organisation of a society to further his purpose; and not until his earnestness has spread to a good many others can he succeed in establishing such an association, if it is to call upon its members for money, work, and self-sacrifice. And yet upwards of twelve hundred local "improvement" societies in the United States alone are now recorded. They range from the club in that village which has wisely substituted a wish to be attractive and beautiful for the old vain dream of bigness, to a society in one of the second-class cities that has 3000 members. The clubs have begun to come into touch with one another through national organisations; and they are, in a wish to learn, reaching beyond their own neighbourhood and even beyond their own country. Cities of like size and class, wherever they are, have similar problems. New York learns something from Paris, and Paris from New York. The illustrations in this volume, of which not one is without general pertinence, happen to be drawn from five different nations, and in the United States they range from the Eastern coast to the new North-west. It is because suggestion can be thus widely and helpfully drawn, that a literature of the subject is possible, and is called for, and can be international.

The best phase of the movement is not, however, its extent, nor even its vigour and growing efficiency, but the dependence it puts on the ideal. By selecting here and selecting there, the dreamed " City Beautiful " becomes a reality, is made a tangible goal. Nobody now laughs it to scorn. Boards of Trade work for it; Chambers of Commerce appoint commissions to consider the local development; to do one's part, in association or individually by gifts, to bring nearer its consummation, has become the test of public spirit and philanthropy; corporations acknowledge its claim to consideration, and politicians have respect for the popular faith in it. It is the one definite civic ideal now before the world.

When, only three years ago, the author published *The Improvement of Towns and Cities*, no one had dreamed of making a book out of the records of scattered and still largely sporadic efforts for improving the aspect of cities and towns, and the requirement was for a small volume that should be a practical handbook for general use by those who were working for town and village improvement. This manual came into larger use than had been anticipated, and the phrase *Modern Civic Art*, which would not at the outset have been understood, was chosen as the natural title for a more comprehensive work devoted chiefly to the artistic side of the subject. The army of workers for bettering material conditions in community life had become conscious of its own worth and was beginning to realise its power for influence. A new, or at least a revived, ideal had found itself. Not merely the philanthropic, "the good and poor," but the rich and cultured were giving thought to the matter. The current periodicals, quick to note the trend of popular thought, became full of the subject ; and their proof of the facility with which it can be illustrated has created the demand that the new edition of *Modern Civic Art* should contain appropriate designs.

Regarding the book itself, the author will avail himself of this opportunity to say only a word. The first two chapters have been occasionally misunderstood. It has been sometimes forgotten that they form only the " Introduction," and that so little can the book and its exposition be judged from them that, as far as it is concerned, the reader could omit them. Of course, the author sincerely hopes that he will not. They have their purpose and were written to be read; but because, necessarily, they speak of the subject as a whole somewhat abstractly, it is not to be concluded that the volume lacks in concreteness and definiteness. For the rest, he would express the warmest gratitude for the extreme cordiality, kindness, and appreciation extended to him by both reviewers and public.

C. M. R.

September, 1904.

CONTENTS

INTRODUCTION

THE CITY'S FOCAL POINTS

IN THE BUSINESS DISTRICT

IN THE RESIDENTIAL SECTIONS

ix

Contents

THE CITY AT LARGE

ILLUSTRATIONS

INTRODUCTION.

CHAPTER I.

A NEW DAY FOR CITIES.

THERE is a promise of the dawn of a new day. The darkness rolls away, and the buildings that had been shadows stand forth distinctly in the gray air. The tall façades glow as the sun rises; their windows shine as topaz; their pennants of steam, tugging flutteringly from high chimneys, are changed to silvery plumes. Whatever was dingy, coarse, and ugly, is either transformed or hidden in shadow. The streets, bathed in the fresh morning light, fairly sparkle, their pavements from upper windows appearing smooth and clean. There seems to be a new city for the work of the new day. There is more than even the transformation that Nero boasted he had made in Rome, for night closed here on a city of brick, stone, and steel; but the morning finds it better than gold. Sleep had come to weary brains and hearts, and had closed eyes tired of dreariness and monotony; the day finds faculties alert and vigorous; and eyes are opening

upon beauty. As when the heavens rolled away
and St. John beheld the new Jerusalem, so a vision
of a new London, a new Washington, Chicago, or
New York breaks with the morning's sunshine upon
the degradation, discomfort, and baseness of modern
city life. There are born a new dream and a new
hope. And of such is the impulse to civic art.

Cities grow in splendour. There are new standards of beauty and dignity for towns. The science
of modern city-making is being formally laid down
as its principles are discovered and its rules enunciated. For the true ideal that spurs to useful endeavour must be that which is based on study and
facts. But as the dawn transforms only real cities,
so can this "new day" come only when the town
of familiar experience has purposed to become what
it should be and might be. In one place this may be
soon, in another late ; in one place there is already
long progress toward it, in another there are only
the yearnings and painful beginnings. Yet everywhere a desire to some extent is present ; often there
are earnest efforts to attain to the beautiful in city-
making ; and there is proud remembrance of such
urban glory as the past may claim.

Out of this irregular progress a law appears of
municipal evolution. Though the development be
slow and tedious, it is sure ; and if the course be
marked, the law noted, the vision at the end described,
doubtless something will have been done to hasten
an advance that was never so swift as now, however

laborious to the impatient the process seems. Considered merely as a morning picture, the new day for cities has its earliest promise in the tower and steeple gleaming in the sunlight. Its later social pledge is in the light that, glancing on the dew-bathed flowers and grass of the people's parks, studs them with jewels as sparkling and as precious to a city as were the gems in the prophet's vision of the new Jerusalem. Again we see it in the beams that, falling athwart the open space, change it to a bright oasis whither pallid multitudes flock from dreary homes, and where little children play, the sun upon their hair.

Progress toward a better day for cities owes more than might be guessed to the impetus of dream and hope and high resolve. These furnish the inspiration to practical achievements. Merely as a measure of the advance, however, the latter alone have first to be considered. Observe how much the modern city is indebted not merely for comfort but for dignity and beauty to recent discovery and invention. The dark streets through which the pedestrian formerly made at night an uncertain way, with his individual lantern, now glow at midnight as at noon. The refuse once poured from upper windows to the streets, in proudest capitals, flows now in subterranean streams, unknown. The pavement, that at best in other days was a racking way of cobblestones, is now made hard and smooth. Streets, once so crowded by enclosing city walls as even in capitals of empires to be narrow, treeless slits between the buildings, now — alike in the humblest and most thronged communities—widen broadly, permitting the traffic to move with ease, and still leave room for grass and trees, and ever and again for flowers. Water is had in abundance to clean the pavements and lay the dust. The mesh of wires that inventions brought with them as a temporary urban evil are now assembling in orderly strands beneath the ground; and there is promise that the smoke, which has hung in a dark cloud above the modern industrial community, is shortly to be dissipated by the ingenuity at work upon the problem.

All these are powerful factors. They lay a strong and suitable foundation upon which a superstructure of civic art may be consistently built up. If, indeed, our cities be spacious, well paved, and clean, with the touch of God's fingers in open space, park, and street, to what mingling of comfort and nobility may there not be aspiration in these days of municipal resource and power? From such a foundation it must, inevitably, be possible to build statelier cities than ever before. So arises modern civic art.

Of all the prerequisites to this progress the most potent is the extension of cities over a greater area. That the normal city can increase vastly in population, with no proportionate increase in congestion, is a condition of supreme importance. This is the aid of rapid-transit to the cause of city beauty. We are not even yet realising fully what it is to mean, for it has brought with it at first a financial and constructive embarrassment in the greater burden of public property to be cared for, extending and multiplying sparsely built-up streets that have to be paved, lighted, provided with sewers and water, and guarded from crime and fire. And this embarrassment is one which many cities have gone half-way to meet through the extravagant extension of their boundaries, so that it has early had an undue proportion of the emphasis. But the net advantage of widening the area available for city expansion remains very great. Therein rests the solution of many problems of city development that have to be solved before the new science of city-making can advance any claim to thoroughness in results ; and if we have hastily gone half-way to meet the one great disadvantage, striving first of all to overcome that, we already know the worst and may expect in the fast coming years to reap a profit which will then appear to be almost wholly net.[1]

And what is this profit to be ? Of its immediate and superficial benefit, in such broadening of thor-

[1] In the United States where, through multiplicity of examples, the first results of the extension of city boundaries can be most conveniently observed, a newspaper took a census at the opening of the twentieth century of "the greatest needs" of a score of the *larger and older* cities. Overwhelmingly they were : (1) pavements ; (2) extension of water- and sewer-pipes ; (3) additional water supply. Such practical wants in old and rich communities would have been inexcusable, and undoubtedly of nothing like this predominance, had not the city's area been recently extended greatly in every case. The census was taken in a period of national prosperity, and as this was prolonged great urban expenditures were undertaken to supply the wants. A compilation made by the *Municipal Journal* two years later put the anticipated expenditures for municipal improvements in that one year in the United States at upwards of a billion dollars. This included $24,000,000 by New

oughfares that there is room upon them not only for the traffic but for the soft and brightening touch of nature, there has been already a suggestion. The change can be better appreciated in the old world than in the new, for there the razing of the walls marks distinctly the transition from the ancient method of city-building to the modern. Within a stone's throw we may find the old, narrow, treeless chasms that did for streets, and the broad new boulevards with trees and turf. But without the provision of some means of urban transit that should be cheap, swift, and frequent, this razing of the confining walls could have accomplished little. Happily, however, one promptly followed the other. The town, having been given the opportunity to expand, found the means to do so. Thenceforth, in the United States, and wherever the self-confident commerce of late years has built new cities, the towns have begun expansively.

The advantage, however, far exceeds an outward and purely æsthetic gain. It promises to check that sad phase of urban development in which, heretofore,

York, mainly for subways, bridges, paving, and water ; about $20,000,000 by Philadelphia, mainly for the improvement of the water system ; and, as an example of the effort by smaller cities, the laying of at least one hundred thousand square yards of paving in St. Paul. These estimates, it should be remembered, were simply on work to be actually done within the twelve months. The commitments for the future represented a far greater sum. In New York, for instance, the rapid-transit tunnel alone was to involve a total cost of $35,000,000. To this more than half a dozen millions were to be added by the tunnel under the East River. Three new bridges, on which work was in progress, were expected to add $60,000,000—a total in these items of more than a hundred millions. Then there were bridges over the Harlem, development of the Bronx district, new street openings, paving, etc., to a very great amount. Clearly, the new obligations were courageously attacked.

the increase of population has meant a closer huddling of the poor. For this there could have been no relief while city walls lasted; it must have gone from bad to worse and have made in the misery of the poor a horrible mockery of the efforts for city beauty; and these walls, we need to remind ourselves, did not have to be of stone. Much more relentless than embattlements of masonry are those gateless walls that time and space throw round about a city. Until rapid-transit lowered these, municipal art held out no promise to the poor.

The tenement we have with us yet, and it seems too much to hope that we shall ever be without it; but it may be an improved tenement, with a playground for the children very near it and a lovely park not far away. Thanks to rapid-transit, modern civic art can now hope to banish "the slum," thus to redeem the tenement, and to make its own conquests thorough. For the expansion of the town resultant from good transit facilities acts in two ways upon the slum. It lessens the pressure from within by making possible the removal of some of the surplus population; it lessens the pressure from without by permitting the increase of the town's accommodation to be by concentric rings. What this means to the community can hardly be appreciated in the bare statement; but the greatest of our humanitarian opportunities lies within it.

That, now, the civic renaissance to which we tend must include an entirely new art of city-making is clear from the character of the factors which have been already considered. Not one of them was operative in the most superb city of ancient times. The opportunities that are offered by recent invention and discovery, the levelling of restricting city walls with the consequent lessening of pressure within the town, an outward movement from the centre for the express purpose of improving industrial surroundings — so robbing the great rise of modern industry of its menace to civic æsthetics, all this is a recent development. It is a happy adjustment to new conditions, seeming to make possible the creation of a city beautiful on lines that are not antagonistic to any development which may be essential to modern urban greatness, and on lines also that should be more permanent and splendid than any civic creation of the past, if the science of city-building be carefully evolved and adhered to.

But there remains one factor more. To describe an art movement in the industrial phraseology of the day, it is as if we had a clear track for our locomotive and an engineer eager to draw the throttle. We need only the steam. If this be conceived of as the power derived from wealth, the gauge should now be marking an extremely high pressure. We are rich enough to-day, not in the United States alone, nor in Great Britain alone, nor in France or Germany. For, whatever may be the per-capita wealth of nations or cities, this is the day of great individual fortunes, which is to say of vast opportunities, and more and more it is the fashion to use these for the public good. It is the day also of ready communication, so that the treasures of the world, the various materials, and the taste and ingenuity of man lie at the hand of him who can pay for them. The city that would make itself magnificent has the whole world to draw upon.

And in this connection, note these thoughts: Bayet in his *Précis d'Histoire de l'Art* observes of the Renaissance cities of Italy that "the accumulation of wealth by these enlightened communities made for artistic progress."[1] The statement is interesting as a historical justification of the claim that in an age of enlightenment wealth does make for art. Art, dependent on slow painstaking, must have its patron who can pay. Bayet again speaks of the Italian cities as republics "which by their commerce and industry became prosperous and rich, and in which political life was especially ardent." This is of interest as showing that the eager feverishness of municipal politics does not necessarily hamper the development of civic art. Nor is it perfectly clear that such art has to develop in spite of, rather than

[1] Ernest Gilliat Smith in his *Story of Bruges* notes an exactly similar phenomenon in the Flemish Renaissance. During the prosperous fifteenth century, when the Renaissance was at its zenith, he remarks that aside from the splendid work done by the great city companies and by the nobles, the movement toward civic art became truly popular. He says: "The new men who had recently amassed fortunes vied with the old aristocracy in the magnificence and luxury of the mansions which they now built; plain, well-to-do merchants were everywhere constructing those roomy, comfortable abodes, which, with their high-stepped gables and their façades encircled with stately panelling and Gothic tracery, still render the streets and squares and waterways of Bruges the most picturesque in Europe."

because of, such interests. For where political life is
ardent, the civic consciousness is strong; the impulse
toward creative representation is fervent; and state,
government, the ideals of parties, are no longer
abstractions, but are concrete things to be loved or
hated, worked for, and done visible homage to. The
strain and stress of city politics to-day are not, then,
a factor essentially antagonistic to civic art.

The final thought is this : Engineering, upon
which the æsthetic aspect of cities is so largely dependent, differs from pure art in that it need not
be the child of inspiration. It is an exact science
and, as such, wealth can buy it, can even import it,
bringing to the city the engineer who can make the
municipality splendidly correct, if among its own
citizens there be no lover who has that power. Here
again in the modern effort for the physical improvement of cities there is singular good-fortune. The
science of city-building does not wholly depend upon
high impulse or inspiration. For its plainer and yet
essential victories the intellect is sufficient. And
yet, over and above this requirement which we can
hope to meet so easily, there are the high motives
that must surely give birth to inspiration.

Thus the modern, dawning, civic art appears as
the latest step in the course of civic evolution. The
flowering of great cities into beauty is the sure and
ultimate phase of a progressive development. It has
represented the crown of each successive civilisation. If decadence has followed it, if the storied

beauty of Babylon, if the splendour of Carthage as Turner painted it, if the chaste loveliness of Athens and the magnificence of Rome marked in each case the culmination of an empire, it has been through no effeminacy and weakness inherent in the development itself. Rather has it been because the glory showered upon these cities was a concentrated expression of the highest civilisation and the highest culture of which the empire was capable.

All that is best the city draws to itself. As magnets acting on filings of steel, the cities attract from their dependent fields whatever there be of learning, culture, and art. The adornment that was lavished upon Venice, Florence, and the minor city-republics of Italy, and again upon the Flemish cities, represented, not weakness, but the virility and rich abundance of those qualities of mind and heart which expressed themselves in the Southern and Northern Renaissance. Had the cities been less beautiful, the Renaissance had been less notable. They mutually interpret each other ; and cities begin to bud and flower in beauty only when learning, culture, and art are flowering around them.

The development will differ in aspect, of course, as the civilisations differ in character. The art of Greece was sculpture, and the glory of Athens in her golden age was the chiselled art of the Acropolis. Rome was imperial, and her glory found expression in construction that was colossal and magnificent. The art, again, of the Southern Renaissance was painting, and we find in frescoes and in the more delicate, more pictorial, phases of architecture the triumph of the Italian republics. To-day, the spirit of the time is commercial and industrial, and our modern civic art reveals itself in forms that commerce and industry comprehend. That our civic art must differ from that of other times does not mean, therefore, that it is not art, or that the new day for cities will be less brilliant than of old. Rather, if it be truly the heir of the past, it must be the new glory of a new time.

Commerce and industry now express themselves, in the realm of city æsthetics, in great highways, in commercial palaces, in bridges, and wharves, and stations. The love of nature, the lately aroused consciousness of what may be called sentiment for landscape, brings vegetation into the busy city to soften and brighten ; and then the spirit of practical philanthropy — so evident to-day — locates playgrounds, builds schools, and insists that modern civic art shall pervade all quarters of the town, remodelling alleys as well as avenues.

Now, if civic art be a phase of urban evolution, it should be possible to trace the steps by which it is approached. Let us consider what these have been in the rise of modern cities: There came first the aggregation. Where no city had been the people flocked — the reason need not now concern us — until there was a city. The aggregation continuing led quickly to congestion, at least in parts of the

St. Paul's, London, from the Thames.

community, and close upon congestion came squalor. We had now a large city, a crowded city, and a miserable one. Out of misery came corruption, debauch of the popular conscience, and—from such favourable conditions—political knavery. These, swiftly, are the steps of the downward course. But all the time there were forces at work for good. The very evil into which affairs had passed created a disgust that vastly aided the reform endeavours. So reform efforts gained gradually in importance.

Ideals were put before the people, and to some extent assimilated. There had already been evidences of æsthetic aspiration, first noted in those quarters in which was congregating wealth—that wealth which had begun to accumulate in accordance with the laws the foreseeing of whose operation had induced the growth of the town. But such is the force of good example that æsthetic aspirations spread broadly. Elementary construction, also, had begun. At first this was for the sake of the traffic and of sanitation ; but by degrees it had a more distinctly æsthetic purpose. Of these forward steps, some, of course, were taken coincidently with the backward, for the community did not march first one way and then the other. Two forces were pulling in opposite directions; and if political knavery turned constructive efforts in the public works to its own evil purposes, the physical condition of the town in its turn gained something from the official eagerness to rob it and the stupid dormancy of the popular conscience that afforded the opportunity for such outrage in constructive work. Thus the early improvements were purchased at an immensely extravagant price ; but — there were improvements and they were hastened.

With varying celerity the conscience now awakened. The reform efforts enlisted individuals, and then associations of individuals, who were concerned in bettering not alone the government, but the aspect, of the town. Where officials were distrusted and individuals and associations tried to act by themselves, or where the trust in officials was misplaced, there followed necessarily much waste, extravagance, and positive injury by poor taste. As the like result followed either of these choices, we find its expression, indeed, almost universal. Then appears another phase in the civic development. This is perception of the waste, extravagance, and lack of artistic judgment, and willingness to seek their correction by submission to expert guidance. With this come co-operation, eagerness to learn the experience of other places and to profit by it, and dependence on those authorities whose knowledge, genius, or talent is broadly recognised. With this new chapter, wherever it is now entered upon, begins modern civic art as distinguished from merely the improvement of cities.

In the broad field of cities, examples can readily be found to illustrate the successive steps in this general evolution. The phases will differ slightly

here and there, as national and local peculiarities
stamp the development; but the course is clear,
essentially uniform, and leading surely to civic
æsthetics as its visible crown. So civic art properly
stands for more than beauty in the city. It represents a moral, intellectual, and administrative progress as surely as it does the purely physical. It
stands for conscientious officials of public spirit,
and where the officials are elective it is evidence
of an aroused and intelligent populace.

Perhaps the steps of this civic evolution will
show more clearly if we turn from abstractions to
the concrete.

The census bulletins of the United States declare
that in that country during the nineteenth century
there came into existence five hundred and thirty-
three communities of eight thousand or more inhabitants each. If we call them all by the name
that doubtless four-fifths of them claim, we shall
group them as cities; and can say, in the census
phrase, that in 1800 the urban population was contained in twelve communities and represented four
per cent. of the total population, while in 1900 it
constituted five hundred and forty-five communities containing more than thirty-three per cent.
of the total population. This is a group of statistics
that illustrates conveniently that nineteenth-century
phenomenon which is known as the " urban drift,"
and which was no more marked in the United States
than in other nations — most notably in Germany

2

and England. This, as representing the "aggregation," constitutes what we have called the first step
in the civic evolution.

To find some of these communities that are yet
in the earlier stages of the subsequent development,
we may turn with best assurance to the Western
States. In the newer towns congestion will not,
happily, be revealed; but that is a spectacle too
familiar in cities of all nations and all times to need
illustration, and wretchedness has not waited for
congestion. We find the town growing on lines
determined partly by accident and partly by the
push of enterprising real-estate holders, not at all
according to artistic design. There is little that can
be reasonably called architecture. If a man wants
a store, a barn, or a house, he goes to the carpenter,
and the carpenter puts up the long, single-gabled,
frame structure that is the simplest and cheapest.
Possibly, if the owner be a merchant and ambitious
to have his emporium impressive, a square front,
built to the height of the roof peak, may be put
before the skeleton structure; but this, misleading
no one, hardly serves to change the type. If there
be no time to build attractive houses, certainly
there is none in which to lay out gardens. People
have not come to live in the place because it is
pretty, but because they want to make money; and
they have not learned yet to love the town. It will
not even represent "home" to them for several
years. Clearly, civic æsthetics are at the antithesis

of this phase; we are yet at the beginning of urban development. In fact, such public spirit as there may be is so crude and sordid that it counts anything — even a water-tank — as growth. The moral, intellectual, and political conditions in this dreary town need not here concern us. They cannot be high.

We may pass now to those thriving cities of about thirty thousand inhabitants which, met so frequently in the more closely settled portions of a country, well represent another stage in the development. In the United States they are frankly industrial communities. Political affairs are in that condition when, out of the sore need of reform endeavours, there is a more or less continuous series of spasmodic reform efforts. But the physical improvement of the town has gone steadily, though expensively, forward. The town is well lighted, most of the important streets are paved, and there are rather more sewer- and water-pipes than perhaps are needed — or, if the aggregate be not excessive, their location is not of the best, for they have been extended on some streets that may not be built up for a decade at the expense of others that are populated. The industry of the town has begun to roll up the expected private gain. The old type of building has given way again and again to something ornate, garish, and showy. Iron is favoured because it can be made to suggest stone, while being cheap.[1] There are stores with cast-iron fronts; there

---

[1] Concrete is taking its place with iron, for the like reason.

are lawns with red iron deer; there is a soldiers' monument of iron. It is the iron age. The houses are now of all kinds. From the extreme of monotony the town has reacted, seeking the extremes of originality. But the residential streets are lined with trees, the square in front of the court-house is kept in order, and most of the houses stand in little gardens that add much to the attractiveness of the place. The people have begun to love their city. It is their home, and they like to have strangers call it "attractive." There are distinct yearnings toward better things. Æsthetic ambition has been born.

The next step in the evolution develops rapidly. A park is laid out. If it is done somewhat apologetically, with a pushing forward of philanthropical reasons, no one is deceived as to the relative importance of these. Gifts are made to the town. The memorial fountain is really stone, for the iron age has passed; and the new public library is so unmistakably a thing of beauty that, although it did not cost as much as the post-office, it is shown to the visitor with no less pride. The new public schools are not barracks within and do not resemble factories on the outside. The factories themselves are improving; and public sentiment has so crystallised that a society has been formed to insist that rubbish be not thrown into the street, that the station grounds be improved, that flowers be generally grown, and that the waste places be taken care of.

This improvement effort is, however, unguided.

There is immense scope for the poor taste of untrained individualism. And as the city grows larger
and its resources increase, the public works become
more spectacular and permanent, so that mistakes in
them last a long time and are striking. The need of
artistic guidance, both in public and private construction, is more keenly felt; the extravagance and
wastefulness of duplicated effort are realised; the
value of an authoritative æsthetic control is perceived,
and it is appreciated that to make true advance in
civic art — which is now frankly a goal — there is
needed something more than means and impulse.

Various efforts are made to provide the required
artistic supervision. If these are reasonably successful, the city — now rich, self-confident, ambitious
for its higher life and its development in beauty —
has reached an advanced and healthy phase in its
evolution. Without much regard as to what the
means are, so long as they are successful, there
dawns a day of civic art.

The plan may be to elect as administrative officers
of the city persons whose education, refinement, and
culture — as well as executive ability and business
sagacity — are a guarantee that the right things will
be done and done well. This has been for the most
part the outcome of the civic reform efforts in Great
Britain, and has hastened the dawn among British
cities of a civic art based on business principles. In
France, under the leadership of Paris, the method has
been to summon to the service of the municipality,

in an advisory capacity, the best experts and artists of the city; and the result has been the development of civic æsthetics on thoroughly artistic lines.
In the United States, where the effort has included
the appointment of "art commissions," the banding
together of cities and of conscientious city officials in
leagues, the association for the public good of artists
and architects, and an immense amount of effort by
popular improvement societies,—with the usurpation
by them of critical functions,— the tendency, so far
as there may be said to be a tendency, is toward
federation, co-operation, and the exchange of experi-
ences, to the end that there may be evolved so
precise a science of city-building that henceforth no
community need be ugly.

The German theory of city administration is based
still more emphatically on scientific principles, almost
to the exclusion of other considerations; but it differs
from the American in that its dependence is not so
much upon a science as upon scientists.   The burgomaster and his magistrates are the best experts procur-
able, and the council of the latter does not pretend to
be citizen-representative, but is made up of honoured,
highly paid, professional, and permanent employees,
trained to the work of city administration.   In Germany, therefore, civic art takes on something of the
thoroughness and exhaustiveness of German science.

The varying national developments of this late
phase of urban evolution are thus interesting mainly
as emphasising the fact that the modern movement

toward civic art is truly international. They reveal,
too, that, however the exact course of the evolution
may vary in different places, municipal æsthetics—
the flowering of cities into beauty—is the ultimate,
the highest, step. It is the phase toward which all
the other urban changes tend. In our day it has
been at once hastened and elevated by many ad-
vances in science, by discovery and invention.

To recapitulate: The first light of dawn is on tower
and spire. There, in the early days, the civic renaissance halted on the great buildings. Now it
embraces much more. Cities are spreading out, and
there is the wish that crowding shall give way.
There is the wealth that wrought wonders of old;
there is an intercourse that levies tribute of the genius
of all the world; there have been taken in orderly
sequence the steps that are precedent to a new municipal beauty; and over all is the widespread modern
spirit of social service. That breathes life into civic
art. That puts the flowers and children into open
spaces—a deed that is typical of many; and makes
our modern civic art not aristocratic, but democratic;
Christian, not pagan. What in detail it will be, just
what is the promise of the new day now dawning
for cities,—this is to be our study.

CHAPTER II.

WHAT CIVIC ART IS.

THE question properly arises as to what municipal art is. Granted that the progressive modern city develops gradually in beauty and splendour, is this normal improvement, which is yet more or less haphazard, civic art? Is the term, after all, a relative one; stands this art alone among all the arts in having nothing absolute, nothing sure? Is there civic art, or merely progress toward civic art, when macadam is laid where no pavement was, or when a bit of waste ground along a river bank is secured by the municipality in order that it may be never used for private ends to the exclusion of the public? If that be civic art, what shall we say if the town, having secured the plot, never develops it; or if, in an effort to "improve," it follows wrong counsels and degrades with tastelessness what might have been a charming feature? Shall we let the spirit of the thing count and still cry "Hail" to civic art?

In other realms of art there must be a joint worthi-

The Arc de Triomphe, Paris.

ness of impulse and execution, else the act is not recognised as art. The child, or untaught man, who would paint a Sistine Madonna and succeeds in making only a daub, is not greeted as a master, nor hears the work called "art," though his impulse be of the highest and most artistic. So in the plastic art and the tonal art, there is something absolute—a standard below which no handiwork is art, whatever be the impulse; above which beauty is surely recognised and where the highest art of all is possible— the coupling of worthy execution to high resolve and noble impulse.

So it is not enough that we should see the progressive city tending normally toward physical improvement, and should lay down therefore a dictum that civic art is a late step in civic evolution. We may well pause to ask ourselves just what is municipal art, and whether we mean only a continuance of improvement, an extension of sequence with never a conclusion, when we talk of civic art as a goal.

Perhaps the common trouble is that our minds are not fixed upon perfection in this art, so that we forget that there may be perfection in it. For most art, it may be noted, serves a useful purpose incidentally, finding in its own perfection, in its own beauty, such justification that often men seek art for art's sake alone; while with municipal art the utilitarian advantages and social benefits become so paramount that they are not forgotten, are not overlooked, in straining for the sensuous pleasure and for that full rounding of positive attainment which in itself may be the artist's goal. Here, then, in this distinction, comes a suggestion for the first qualifying clause in the definition of municipal art. And how natural this first step of definition is! This art, which serves so many social ends, is *municipal,* in the sense of communal.

It is municipal first of all. If men seek it they seek it not for art's sake, but for the city's; they are first citizens and then, in their own way, artists jealous of the city's looks because they are citizens. We do not find men and women banding themselves together to create a public sentiment and fund in order that some sculptor may do a noble bit of work to the glorifying of his field of art. But they so band themselves and so commission sculptors, painters, artists, and landscape designers, for the glorifying of civic art — not just because it is art, but because it is civic. They are not asking the town to help art, but art to help the town ; the artists, not to glorify their art, but by their art to glorify the city.

This, then, is the first consideration, and it is worthy of more emphasis than might appear. It does something else than conveniently differentiate civic art from any other art. It explains why its disciples may care little for artists though giving commissions, why its clientage should be all the urban world — the art ignorant as well as the cult-

ured ; why it must be delayed in coming until
civilisation is at its flower, since not dependent on
individual and selfish ambition ; and why, when
coming, it will magnificently make all other purely
art endeavours but handmaids to its one great effort
— because this is social and the public is behind it.

Thus is civic art first municipal, and has ever
attained its largest victories when cities were mighti-
est.   For in so far as it is art, its principles are
eternal as the truth, and its conquests must be at
least as old as cities.   Down through the Middle
Ages, poets and painters dreamed of the " city beautiful " ; the Irish Gaelic poets sang of it ; barbaric
Nero strove to realise it ; the inspired apostle transcribed his vision in its terms ; Greek philosophers
drew inspiration from the measure of Athens's attainment of it, and the great prophet named Babylon
as "the glory of kingdoms."   As anciently as the
dawn with its golden radiance has transformed cities,
there has been a dream, a sigh, a reaching forth,
with civic art the goal.

And what precisely shall be the definition of this
art, ancient as all the arts, but distinguished from
them by its contentment to be servant, not mistress,
in the glorifying of cities?   What is any art but the
right, best way of doing a certain thing ?   This art,
which is so utilitarian in its purposes as to be civic
first and art afterwards, may be defined, then, as the
taking in just the right way of those steps necessary
or proper for the comfort of the citizens — as the

doing of the necessary or proper civic thing in the right way. Thus is its satisfaction quite as much intellectual as sensuous, and for popular appreciation it must wait — because of its very practicalness — upon popular education.

So civic art is not a fad. It is not merely a bit of æstheticism. There is nothing effeminate and sentimental about it,— like tying tidies on telegraph poles and putting doilies on the cross-walks, — it is vigorous, virile, sane. Altruism is its impulse, but it is older than any altruism of the hour — as old as the dreams and aspirations of men. We talk much about it now, because we are living in a period that has witnessed more building and remodelling of cities than any period of history, and therefore in a period that compels us to turn our thoughts to the best ways of making improvements and to the principles that ought to guide in building the modern city. And those are the laws of civic art, of the great art that is of the people and for the people, that is closest to their lives, and that draws more than half its charm from the recognition of perfect fitness in its achievements. There is much said now of civic art because it has become at last a popular goal — this art of doing civic things in the right way, which is ever the beautiful way. Because this is true there is a civic art.

As an art that exists not for its own sake, but mainly for the good of the community, first for the doing of the thing and then for the way of doing it, there can be only one successful civic art. This will be one which joins utility to beauty. Cities are not made to be looked at, but to be lived in; and if in the decoration of them there be any forgetfulness of that, no successful civic art will follow and the effort will defeat itself. Realising this, we should try to discover some general rules for guidance, and if we succeed, by noting the requirements and the various means that have been tried to satisfy them, we should be able to that extent to translate our art into a civic science that will be more or less exact — into the science of city-building, which is the text-book of civic art. Where the art fails, the cause has been neglect of the rules, through forgetfulness or ignorance.

Precedent, of course, to transcribing the science, there are to be considered the functions of civic art. If the end be to clothe utility with beauty, and in providing the beautiful to provide also that which will add to the convenience and comfort of the citizens, we shall best find its opportunities for usefulness by studying what has been happily called the anatomy of cities. In this there appear three groups of requirements: Those that have to do with circulation, those that have to do with hygiene, and those that have to do distinctly with beauty. No hard lines separate these classes. If in the street plan, for instance, we find the convenience of circulation — *i. e.*, readiest adaptability to the traffic — the most pressing point, we come in the broad open space, shaded with trees and planted with grass, to a problem that is to be approached still from the side of circulation — since convenient short cuts may be offered—and yet from the side of hygiene, and from that of æsthetics. But the classification remains convenient, for in seeking urban welfare and comfort we must act in one or more of these groups. It may be briefly asserted, therefore, that the function of civic art is the making of artistic — which is to say, of æsthetically pleasant — provision for the circulation, for hygiene, and for city beauty.

It is important to note that beauty itself is the object in only one of these three departments of effort, and even then, as in the case of a bit of sculpture, which certainly belongs under neither hygiene nor circulation, other considerations, educational or commemorative, may easily modify the artistic aspiration. Thus the greater part, if not the best, of civic art is that which first does something else than please the senses. And that is why public-spirited men of all interests, striving to ameliorate civic conditions along many lines, find in municipal art one desideratum upon which they all agree, and for the furtherance of which they all — by many paths — are working.

Having observed the purposes of civic art, we come to the means to be employed in gaining them. Here we must seek rules for guidance and may take up art principles. These are not new nor are they novel. They are as old as beauty and as broad as art. They are the three dominant chords on which is built up the melody of all art. They are unity, variety, and harmony.

If our civic art will not stand its double test — first, the civic test, as to the urban good it does; and then the æsthetic test, it fails. And this latter test is a more rigorous requirement with civic art than it is with any other, for municipal art cannot stand alone, to be judged without its environment—and the field in which it stands is so broad to have unity, so varied to have harmony, so much the same in parts to have variety. Consider how easily civic art may fail with this test applied: a thrilling statue on an unkempt street is not successful civic art, because its surroundings are not harmonious; a park, lovely in itself, may fail, from this broad standpoint, for want of that unity in the city plan which would lend to its location seeming inevitableness. Building restrictions designed to insure harmony, but made too severe, may lose their artistic effectiveness by the repression of variety to the verge of monotony. But if it is easy to fail, as surely it is, success is better worth the winning; and where a city, or part of a city, is built up from the ground plan to the street furnishings and construction with regard for these three principles of art, how beautiful, consistent, and intellectually satisfying is the result!

The desirability of obtaining such a thorough, general, and artistic plan of improvement for every community is evident. The chance to plan a city on paper before it is built comes but rarely nowadays,

and the best we can do is to see to it that the cities
grow artistically, that their extensions at least are
beautiful, and that every change in the city itself shall
bring it one step nearer to the ideal. The trouble with
most improvement effort is that it is planned all by
itself, that the benefit to the neighbourhood is studied
rather than that to the community, and that the first
half-dozen years after the improvement is made stand
out with more prominence and importance — receive
more consideration from tax-payers and tax-spenders
— than all the years that are to come thereafter. But
in wise city-building we would consider not five
years, nor ten years, but posterity. And to do this
would be cheaper in the end.

In an effort for civic improvement, therefore, the
first step is to secure a comprehensive plan. This
is almost the only step that can insure the highest
type of modern civic art, since requirements are
greater now than when artists and master builders,
dressing with beauty the narrow streets of Italian
and Flemish cities, created the civic art of five centuries ago. In those cities urban hygiene and circulation made no demands on civic art. Nowadays these
things are fundamental, and unless there be a well
thought out, artistically conceived, general plan to
work on, our civic art will go astray, with lack of
completeness or continuity. So it will fail, because
isolated and spasmodic ; because it will mean a fine
park, some patriotic statuary, three or four good
streets, and a few noble buildings rather than a city

dignified and lovely as a whole — where the open space does not stop with balancing the slum, but redeems it.   We have set for ourselves a more complex problem than was dreamed of by the Renaissance, and unless our modern urban art can solve it, the result will not satisfy.

It is no reproach to the present that so much has been done without the guidance of general plans.   It merely shows that our art impulse outran our art intelligence — a very common procedure.   The architect, the artist, the landscape gardener, — all enthusiastic, — have gone too fast for the civil authorities, who represent the people ; and so the underlying principles, the great laws that should determine the laying-out and the up-building of cities, have not been set down and studied, as they should be, from all sides.   Many a good thing costs more than it ought to, or has to be done over, and often the people have the common-sense argument — though the ideals of the artists are true and high and their dreams need only a little pruning and a little injection of worldly wisdom to be made thoroughly practical.   The great thing, the significant thing in its promise for the future, is that there are such dreams, for it is easy to prune, and worldly wisdom is ever cheaper than inspiration.   If, out of the abundant experience now available, out of the many costly experiments of the recent years that have witnessed in so marvellous a degree the rise and growth of cities, we can now find enough lessons that are pertinent and suggestive

3

to formulate a sort of science of city-building, we shall
have something to guide the artist and something to
awaken the interest and enthusiasm of him who cannot dream.   It will be not the gospel — which is in
the heart — but the law and the prophets of modern
civic art.

That, in fact, is one of the great theoretical wants
of the day.   The dreamers of the city beautiful, the
countless artists and laymen who are working for the
improvement of cities, towns, and villages, want a
theory of civic art to which they can turn.   Practically, the need of the day is the local application of
this general theory to every interested community.
It is the attainment of this end which is sought in
urging that the first step in bringing civic art to a
town should be the provision of a general plan of
development and improvement ; of a complete and
consistent plan, to the end that henceforth every step
taken should be a sure step of progress.

To the greater part of the population, also, the
plan that is thus set forth will represent a new ideal,
and one which they will find readily comprehensible
because concerned so plainly with the conditions
before their very eyes, to the avoidance of abstractions.   The value to the community of a civic ideal
scarcely needs exposition.   Since realisation of this
ideal is dependent ultimately upon the public's appreciation, it will be brought a great deal nearer by
the public's perception of it.   Of course an immense
responsibility will be thrown upon its makers.   The

best expert advice should, unfailingly, be obtained ;
but if the laws of city-building have been put on
paper, it will not be hard to measure the suggestions
by these laws ; and the very prominence of the work
will give to it a publicity broadly inviting criticism,
while the fact that the progress toward the ideal must
continue through a long series of years will demand
that the plan proposed be able to bear the changes
in special interest and point of view which lapse of
years will bring.   The plan once secured, the public
spirit and artistic sense of the community can hardly
fail to insist that it be adhered to.   Educationally, it
may be parenthetically remarked, knowledge of this
plan, which is the perception of a concrete ideal, will
offer a short cut, doing in a few months what can be
accomplished only very slowly by the efforts to
inculcate in school children civic pride and æsthetic
appreciation.   These efforts will be continued, but
they will be given direction and practicalness.

The provision of this ideal, the setting before all
the people of a tangible vision of their own possible
city beautiful, will have other value than merely that
of popular education.   It will offer them inspiration.
Nor will this inspiration be material only, but as
clearly moral and political and intellectual.   The pride
that enables a man to proclaim himself "a citizen of
no mean city" awakens in his heart high desires that
had before been dormant.   "To make us love our
city we must make our city lovely" was taken as its
motto by the Municipal Art Society of New York

when it was organised, and he who loves his city is a better citizen and a better man.

There will be other than merely general inspiration, for the dream of what one's city should be, and may be, and even some day must be, will be a special inspiration to all those professions of the fine arts upon which the beauty of the city ultimately depends. There is not an architect of spirit who will not feel a new incentive when he thinks that he is planning buildings that are to be part of the city of the future; not a landscape gardener who will not plant with greater care because of this vision ; not a sculptor who will not throw himself more devotedly into the modelling of the civic monument that is to be one of the new city's ornaments. And down from the professions to the workers, and from those who execute the commissions to those who give them, will be felt the spur of the dream, the hope, the goal.

"I do not want art for a few," said William Morris, "any more than education for a few, or freedom for a few"—and civic art is essentially public art. It has been likened to "a fire built upon the market place, where every one may light his torch; while private art is a fire built upon a hearthstone, which will blaze and die out with the rise and fall of fortunes."

THE CITY'S FOCAL POINTS.

Embankment and Bridge, Place de la Duchesse Anne, Nantes, France.

CHAPTER III.

THE WATER APPROACH.

NO work of art is satisfying and vigorous if it have not definiteness of expression. Unless it has something to say as to its own character, and says it, not here and there, but with such harmony of its parts that each adds its voice to the others in united expression, the result is not pleasing. That, in fact, is the goal in mind when it is said that the three underlying principles of art are unity, variety, and harmony.

Considered from the standpoint, then, of civic art, a primary fault with most towns and cities is the lack of definiteness in the impression they make as one approaches them; and it is the unconscious perception of this want which explains why the approach by night is generally so much more satisfactory than by day. At night the glow in the sky, and then the countless lights gleaming in serried rows, and every string of golden beads standing for a street, mark the town clearly, with

no conflict of expression, and with irresistible appeal
to the imagination. Pinned thus against the lone-
liness and blackness of the night, the composition
has a single message — that of warmth and life,
of the juxtaposition of comfort with ceaseless effort
and burning desire — which is the true message of
the town.   There is no jar, there are no distractions.
The picture suggests a single thought and its voice
is unmistakable and beautiful.

And as a work of art, the municipality has a right
to be considered in this impressionist way.   Sociologically, indeed, the details alone are important;
but artistic details never make an artistic whole
unless they harmonise; and if we propose by modern civic art to rear the city beautiful, the picture
is to be considered as a unit.   As we see it first,
afar off, we may study it as a composition; and
then, as we come nearer, we shall see details — but
the first impression counts.

Does this seem to be a fantastic, æsthetic idea ?
Remember the often painted and million times lov-
ingly remembered view of Florence from San Miniato
heights — Brunelleschi's dome and Giotto's tower
making the centre of a composition which is an
urban picture never to be forgotten.   Do you know
the view of Rome from the Campagna, with the
dome of St. Peter's rising high over the Church's
city; do you remember the sea view of Venice, the
water lapping the walls of its palaces; have you seen
New York from the Upper Bay, its tall buildings

clustered like a forest of silver birches, gleaming in the brilliant light and marking the town with unmistakable personality ? Ask yourself if these strongly marked pictures have no value to the communities that form them ? Are they a worthless asset in civic love and civic pride ?

On a road leading out of Boston into the suburbs there is a view through an arch of trees of the gilded dome of the State House on Beacon Hill; from a point on the Thames there is a loved view of St. Paul's with central London clustered about it — a vignette that stands for much. Upon just such little things as this is fixed the citizen's love for his city; its towers and domes pin his affections, and the more because in every case the composition has inevitably a meaning, a clearness and accuracy of significance, that makes it more than merely a pretty picture. It is a work of that art which speaks not to the eye alone, nor to the head alone, nor to the heart alone; but, unitedly, to senses, brain, and sentiment. And what elements go to make this picture of the city! What a story it tells of human progress or human fall — with broken hearts or blasted lives among its shadows, and its spires and towers that gleam in higher light the proofs of efforts that have succeeded, of dreams that have come true! Think what you look upon when you see a city, and reflect that if it has definiteness of expression, if it says to you one beautiful and appropriate thing clearly and distinctly, it is the greatest work of art that man can create.

What the thing that it says shall be, therefore,
— whether a huge advertisement dominates the
scene, whether great black chimneys, or towers and
spires rising above the trees, determine the picture's
character,— is a question that may well make pause
those who have a voice in the selection. It is not a
question only of civic art, unless that art be involved with broad and heavy responsibilities. It
is a question in part of civic pride, and so of good
citizenship; and its solution is like the solution of all
such questions. It depends on the willingness of
the individual to surrender a little of his private
liberty; to build, not exclusively for his own profit,
or even under the dictates of his own artistic sense,
but with a feeling for the resulting whole.

The most favourable place from which to view a
city is usually, as even the cited examples suggest,
the water. There no distracting element intrudes
between scene and seer. The waves are a neutral
foreground, sufficiently detailed, and yet with no
detail to arrest the eye; and beyond — with distance
to idealise and harmonise — the city rises in a contrast sharp and urban. The water view is one that
civic art, then, cannot overlook. Happily, from the
æsthetic standpoint, the city is rare which is not
located upon water; and yet there is scant thought
of the water-front appearance, scant regard for the
possibilities of the urban picture where it should be
seen most advantageously. The shore must long
and perhaps always be one of the community's focal

points, but the tendency is to appear to turn the back upon the water. At the water's edge the town began, and pressing inward and climbing higher the beginning is forgotten or ignored, as if a cause for shame. But rather is it cause for pride, and as the city grows the water gate is still the entrance, the view across the waves the first picture still for growing numbers. If civic art is anywhere to be jealous of results, there is no point that can more fittingly demand attention than this — the picture of the city from its river, its lake, or sea. Whatever the body of water, it will bear its multitude of observers, for if the narrow river would seem to have fewer than the port of sea or lake, remember that the farther shore, and every bridge that spans the stream, affords the water view.

As to details, civic art, as the effort to make cities beautiful, cannot afford to let slip the opportunity of a bit of natural open space in such location. For here, at last, however close the buildings press upon it, the breezes play at will and the sun shines in unbroken radiance. No expression of nature is so welcome in a city as is water, with its care-free, gay, and tireless playfulness. Even in the street fountain it is a ceaseless pleasure and in the park's artificial pond or stream a constant joy. No city with so great an æsthetic asset at its feet should fail to utilise- it, or part of it, for æsthetic purposes, though there be ever so foolish an indifference to the picture that the city itself may make when seen across the waves.

This accepted as a primary principle of civic art, it is to be understood that there is no need for such use of the water-front to interfere with that commercial or industrial use of it which was a cause of the town's location there. If the stream be swift enough to furnish power, it has a natural beauty that requires only a place for observation ; if the body of water be large enough for navigation, the craft afloat upon it will furnish life and picturesqueness to add the charm of variety and human interest to the natural majesty of the scene. To give up, then, the practical use of the water would be even to rob it of some of its urban attractiveness. In fact, because the city represents essentially man's conquest of nature, the water within its confines and which induced men to settle there may most fittingly appear as "harnessed," to do men's work, or as bridled, to bear their burdens. Æsthetically, we should not demand the abandonment of the use of the water — only a place whence, with all its activities, it may be seen, for civic art assumes that the stream on which a city is located will not be transformed into an open sewer.

But the problem of the water-front, which is so fascinating in the concrete example, since a scenic effectiveness can be certainly added to convenience and utility, gains in an abstract consideration almost baffling complexity. There are so many kinds of shore line, both as respects the topography and the use to which the shore is put, that in general discussion only the broadest rules can be suggested. On this point, more than in any other problem of modern civic art, there must be a feeling of concrete incompleteness and of total inadequacy in the abstract consideration. For all the time there must be the consciousness, so discouraging from this point of view,—but so inspiring from another,—that for the particular water-front that may be most in the mind, there is possible a thrillingly noble solution which here is hardly touched upon and to which much even of what is said has the scantiest pertinence.

Among the varieties, then, of town and city water-front there can be few qualities that are universal ; but generally it can be assumed that there will be an accessible space somewhere along the shore that is not required for docks or wharves or mills. This should be reserved for the public enjoyment of the community's chief æsthetic asset — not relinquished to individual exclusiveness. But if there be no inch of shore that commerce and industry do not demand, there still are the upper floors of the piers, and generally — the banks rising from the water's edge — an opportunity for a drive or promenade so elevated that the demands of commerce must be satisfied below the level of this pleasure ground, since its needs have to be met at the water's margin. Finally, if our water be a stream, with broad mud-flats on one or either side, which only the freshets or incoming tide conceal, the solution generally is to confine and quicken the current within

the town by walls of masonry, so that with more
rapid movement it shall scour its bed and shall carry
off the surplus waters of the freshet without a flood,
or with the flowing tide shall rise harmlessly within its walls. Then the flats can be reclaimed and
changed to park lands ; and the new value of the
adjacent property, and the shortening of the bridges,
involving reduced cost of building, will offset much
of the expense involved.

But to return to that first picture of the city as it is
seen across the water by the approaching voyager,
to that view which—in so far as civic art is art—may
logically demand the first consideration, and which,
as the first revelation of the city, is to mean so much,
what is the character that it ought to have ?   We
have seen that scenically it should be the best view.
The sloping or terraced site, the orderly edging of the
town, the neutral foreground—all these are conditions
very favourable to an urban picture that will please.
But in the reality the scene that should be so splendid
is too often mean; the edge of the town that should
be orderly is ragged and bedraggled; where cleanliness
should be easiest, filth is common; where relative
age should give an appearance of permanence and
stability, there still are temporary structures.   The
town has turned its back on its best feature, and
again and again whatever of it is most shabby, mean,
and sordid crowds upon this natural vestibule.   The
explanation will vary with different localities.   Here
it is the greed of commerce and a hasty surrender to

its demands; there the railroad came in, to the destruction of some of the usefulness of the water, and the town, turning away in disgust, gathered around the station, forgetting until too late that what had been a source of commercial wealth and power might be still a source of beauty. But long before the wretchedness of details impresses the voyager, he must usually look in vain for definiteness of character.

What is the definite impression he ought to gain? Here is the water gate of the city. He should see before him the special, not merely the general, character of the place. The latter will be inevitably revealed by the clustered buildings—be they the hotels and villas of a resort, the warehouses and dominating chimneys of an industrial community, or the surmounting minarets and domes of an Oriental seaport; but the stamp of national and local characteristics should not suffice. The thing to be sought is the relation of this town to this body of water—the special meaning of its own particular water-front.

In most cases the function of this is to be a vestibule. It is an entrance to the city, and generally the entrance that means most to it. There should be, therefore, dignity, nobility, and prominence. To the portal suggestion of the term " water gate " there should be given structural expression; of the importance of this focal point there should be topographical evidence. The voyager should be made to realise, as he comes nearer to the apex of the curving shore-line, that he is coming to the entrance of the town.

To the architect, the occasion offers a rare opportunity, not merely in a personal sense in the setting
of his building and the certainty that it can be ever
seen in perspective; but in a civic sense, to the
degree that a chance is well-nigh changed to a duty.
To the landscape gardener, if there be some of the
water-front that commerce can spare to beauty, the
opportunity is equally noble. He has here, and
at last, a canvas that can be studied in its whole as
well as in parts. And finally the municipality itself
finds on the water-front a condition to which civic
duty clearly pertains—in the opportunity so to construct the public works that they shall enhance the
attractiveness of the city and shall do justice to its
importance.

These, clearly, are the general principles that
should guide in the treatment of the urban water-
front. Specifically, the problem is more abstruse
owing to the many kinds of water-front and the
many uses to which it may be put. Even in the
same community the problem may have many
sides.

The city of New York, for instance, has about a
hundred miles of water-front; but it is fortunate
in having at the Battery a spot that is clearly the
centre of the composition—from every standpoint.
Here, inevitably, it was proposed to place the naval
arch and to make the formal entrance to the city.
The structure was to be of great size, and it was
intended that the treatment of the sea wall, basin,

beacons, steps, etc., should not merely harmonise
but should form a very important, and by no means
the least beautiful, part of the design. The project
was interesting as a concrete development of the
principles and theory of water-gate treatment. It
thus reduces to a splendid specific illustration what
had been an abstract argument, just as does, on a
smaller scale, the harbour treatment of Bordeaux,
of Genoa, and of a few other foreign ports. It pictures what a city ought to have.

In the miles of docks and flimsy pier sheds, in
the meanness of the long water-front streets, New
York,[1] like most American seaports, teaches what
should not be done, rather than what should be
done. European cities must be sought for examples
on a large scale of adequate commercial treatment
at the water's edge. The raised promenade of
Antwerp or, better yet, of Algiers, and the constructive orderliness of Hamburg, for instance, are
suggestions that have not failed completely of application. The need is not so much to appreciate
wretchedness where it exists, nor to point out
means of improvement, as to translate aspiration
into action. New York itself, as a city, has begun
with the necessary elementary construction of new
docks and widened streets, but with a hundred
miles of water-front there must still be spaces that
commerce can spare to pleasure; some areas, more
accessible and greater than have been yet dedi-

[1] There has been considerable improvement since this was written.

cated to public use, where the ceaseless beauty of the waves, the free breezes, and the tireless panorama of the shipping can be popularly enjoyed. But even now, with the scanty provision of these spaces, the water-front problem of the greater city is one of many typical phases. The universal problem, however, can be best considered doubtless by examining examples of various types of water-front treatment wherever these may be found, without regard to a single city.

Paris, with the quays along the Seine, and London, still more successfully, with the ambitious Victoria Embankment, represent an elaborate, formal treatment almost common in Europe when a river bisects a town. Examples of such treatment gradate from the simple quays of Florence and Pisa and the brick walls of Amsterdam's placid canals to the long promenades and broad walled-gardens of Budapest, or even to the sea-front, as at Nice. Passenger travel by light steamers is easily cared for under these conditions, and from the standpoint of modern civic art the formal, the architectural, and the urban character of the treatment, with its engineering excellence and hygienic merits, is wholly to be commended. It has, as the best civic art must have, the beauty of utility. It is dignified and harmonious; it fittingly sets off the architecture that lies beyond it; it builds the city to the water's edge with orderly stateliness; it offers the desired vantage-points for observation. It is an old form of treatment, but in its spirit and in the

The Thames Embankment, London, at Somerset House.

results accomplished it is thoroughly modern. Boston has made good use of it for the Charles River, and a recent State law of Iowa—passed at the request of awakened communities—gives to towns bisected by meandering streams the right thus to narrow the channel and save æsthetically (as also economically) the reclaimed land.

Upon the quays there will be a shaded promenade and, if they be long enough and broad enough, a drive. Beyond this, which itself may be beyond a strip of turf,—when that can be provided,—will come the buildings. The quays will not straighten the shore-line, but will follow its pleasing curves, so gaining new points of view and vistas that had else been lost, and new points of observation whence to study the façades. The device may thus be called an urbanisation of the always pleasant rural shore-road. It is that road extended, where space is too precious to permit the river to wander freely and flood its banks at the whim of storm or season—that road made formal and stately, to harmonise with the construction that presses upon it, and made becoming the wealth and resources of a city. It is adapted to all the variations of conditions where town and shore-line meet. Here there may be broad planting at its side and villas set far back; there it will take its devious way before lofty buildings and at the head of crowded streets, now rising to a viaduct that commerce may flow beneath it unhampered by its invitation to luxurious indolence; and now,

circling the tenement district with a necklace of
lights, it broadens here and there into a playground.
Where the shores are low, and there is not space for
a broad park on the water-front, and where the level
of the river falls and rises sharply, this is quite the
ideal treatment.

In the case of a stream, bridges must form a very
important feature of the water-front development,
merely considered architecturally and scenically. The
bridges that spring from the quays of Paris seem an
inseparable part of the construction. It happens that
they are separable, and rarely coincident in date with
it; but this does not appear. The bridge that begins
and ends in the quay must harmonise with the quay;
and the quay must provide, in broadened plaza and
hospitality to converging streets, a bridge approach
that shall be at once suitable and convenient for the
travel. The surface appearance of the bridge belongs to another discussion. We are here considering
the town's water approach, where only a lateral view
of the bridge is offered — the one view, however,
that adequately gives the structure's architectural
value; and with its art importance alone is there now
concern. Engineering merit is assumed.

Stone construction, or at least stone piers, are
obviously invited strongly by the masonry of the
embankment in order to secure harmony. Beyond
this, the charm of the bridge will lie mainly in long
horizontal reaches. Perpendicular motives will not
be necessary; and though it is quite the fashion, in

the rare cases of an effort to make bridges monumental, to put a tower, or towers, in the centre, there
is always a danger that these will have an isolated
appearance. The place for the monumental treatment is at that point on the shore which is to be
emphasised as the water gate; but the bridge, if designed conscientiously as a work of art that shall be
permanent, as cities go, and always very conspicuous, may be made a thing of beauty with no such
piling on of ornamentation. Of course at times the
necessity for a centre draw justifies, and even requires, perpendicular motives; but these need not be
deliberately invited to make the bridge imposing.   If
they are invited, the ideal place for them is at the
structure's end.   There they may easily emphasise
the portal significance which all bridges have when
the water which they span forms the boundary of the
town.   Interesting examples of this effect are offered
by, for instance, the Karl Bridge at Prague, and the
railroad bridge at Mayence.   In fact, of the latter it
has been remarked that while the bridge is of the
very ordinary truss type, the architects have saved it
æsthetically by providing "a handsome and imposing, not to say romantic, entrance, which not even
railroad tracks can ruin."   Further than that, it is an
entrance, we may note, that has meaning.

   There are other principles which will be useful as
guides in choosing bridge designs that are likely to
please. Not only should the structure harmonise, as
far as possible, with the quays and with its general

setting, not only should its beauty be sought mainly in long horizontal reaches,— to the distrust of perpendicular effects, using the latter at the bridge ends if at all (when this is possible),—but it must be remembered that the beauty of the bridge as a whole depends most on its main lines. Any attempt to deceive as to the nature and position of these by concealing them with ornament can only fail, being false to every principle of art. To beauty of form in these main lines, there must then be added symmetry. Imagine a stone bridge of several arching spans. It is not enough that the lines of these spans be lovely. There must be symmetry between the spans themselves, so that, for example, on either side of the centre they shall be equal in number and size — an obvious matter, and yet one often ignored. And the bridge must seem to harmonise with its natural setting and its purpose as well as with its constructed terminal. This applies to the degree of its massiveness, to the character of the scenery, or, if it be in the midst of a city, to the style of the architecture amid which it stands.

Let it be recalled that while the purpose of the bridge is utilitarian there is no other structure in the city that has greater permanence, or as great a prominence, for good or ill. There is nothing that should be built with more consideration for the artistic result. Indeed, is it not true that a bridge across the Thames in London is upon the same plane of monumental and architectural importance as is St.

Paul's itself, and so makes demand for the like skill and taste to design and to embellish it? The Romans, who were the great bridge-builders of antiquity, had no higher title to bestow than the term "Pontifex Maximus"—greatest builder of bridges. And to-day, in an industrial age, it may be remarked, the bridge and viaduct are to us about what the town gate was to the builders of ancient times, so that it behooves us to demand not merely strength but dignity and a civic splendour, in their construction. Every city bridge is an opportunity; and as to the smaller towns, how charming a memorial a beautiful bridge might be! The triumphal arch can be made effective only at great expense. It is a vain-glorious type; while in the bridge the arch is at the service of humanity.

Of the river-front façades, as seen from the water or across the quay, it is difficult to speak as fully in general terms. But it can be said that where the buildings stand close, a degree of uniformity in height, and harmony in style at least, will add very greatly to the appearance of solidarity—a desideratum in the water view of a city. And it has been already suggested that if the shore-line be permitted to retain its curves, the façades will be thereby rendered more effective, their planes changing to conform with the curves of the shore.

Finally, it should be pointed out that of the famous cities of the Old World that are situated on rivers, many owe a large part of their splendour to the æsthetic use of the water-front.   Examples are: London, of which the chief monumental features are the embankment and the bridges; Paris, where every inch of the river bank is utilised; Rome, with its vigorous bridges and new development of the river course; Budapest, which finds in the river the key to its whole scheme; Prague, where the æsthetic interest is largely centred on the embankment and fine bridge; Berlin, where the bridges are made monumental, though the unimportant river is slighted; Dresden, which has pointed the way for many a smaller place; and Munich, with its Quaistrasse.

When the land terminates in bluffs that can be planted, at the top at least; or when — even with a low shore — opportunity is offered for a water-side park, however narrow, we may have a chance for the pleasantest kind of water-front treatment. There is no need to go into specifications here, for it is the charm of landscape gardening that it is as infinite in its varieties as the earth itself, being an adaptation to topography and all natural conditions. But to bring nature to nature, so to dress this important part of the town that looking into the water it sees mirrored there laughing nature, is a more pleasing art than formal building to the water's edge. There is needed only a trained mind and eye to make much of the possibility, and so fair is the result — of such blessing to the city — that it may reasonably be urged that all the stream banks of a town that are not actually required for commerce should be put in the hands of park commissioners, to be defended, in natural beauty, from rubbish heaps and spoliation. Even if the stream be one which furnishes power, the banks may be reserved. We shall refer to this again, under " Parks."

And there is another thought in regard to the water-front. When the body of water is navigable, here is an appropriately beautiful site for many a civic pageant. Nowhere does music make more sensual appeal than on the water; with far more beauty than on the street can the pageant that goes by water be invested, and in greater variety can it be dressed. The very fact of holding the pageant here will tend, too, to emphasise the value of the waterway as a thoroughfare, and will make the public ownership of the banks, whence its beauty may be seen, of a value better understood and esteemed.

So, to recall the points observed, modern civic art requires for the water-front, all too commonly neglected, primary consideration. It would consider first the far-off picture, of the town as a whole; then the nearer view, when we seek for definiteness of character, and look along the shore for something to indicate the significance of this portal to the city; then the details when, drawing yet nearer, we estimate the city's importance and wealth and genius by the way it is built to the water's edge, and if there be bridges, by the beauty of these. What is the city's attractiveness; are its public works beautiful; has it regard for sanitation; have its people free access to the shore and a chance for enjoyment there, or, as if in bondage have they allowed greed to huddle them into the inland streets?

Modern civic art, as one can guess by these questions, is never a mere æsthete. Loving beauty, it loves humanity yet better. It wants the surroundings of men to be clean, wholesome, and uplifting, as well as pleasant to see. Personified, modern civic art appears as a sort of social reformer, for if the eye be that of the artist, there yet is surely in it the tear of the philanthropist.

CHAPTER IV.

THE LAND APPROACH.

THE city that has only a water approach is too rare to be taken into the calculation. Civic art has to consider quite as certainly the requirements and possibilities of the approach by land, and it finds in the problem not only great importance but an interest that might hardly be anticipated.

This problem had in the past a worthier treatment than had the approach by water, because when the cities were walled it was necessary to make a special and formal provision for the land entrance. But this worthier treatment ceased after a time, for when the walls were razed, or when towns were built without surrounding walls, the problem became too diffused for visibly concentrated solving. The city was suffered simply to "taper off" on the land side, with no mark of its end or beginning — unless it were a light, a pavement, or a curb. There was no adequate recognition of so important a matter as the city's threshold.

The period was one of transition in the development of cities, but it was one of vast importance. It meant a better day for them, for more æsthetic possibilities were involved in the change than could at once be grasped. The city now had room to grow, to spread out in all directions, to shake itself loose, after long compression, and, like a plant restored to its natural environment, to thrust out its streets as tendrils binding it to the earth again. This was the first, almost involuntary, effect, and every country-leading thoroughfare became an " entrance."

Not only were these land entrances to the city too numerous now for elaborate topographical or structural designation, but their location was constantly changing as the tendril-streets grew longer and reached farther, while the whole impulse of the movement — in reaction from the previous huddled condition of cities — was toward an obliteration of the line that had once divided town and country. This was to be effected, not by the urbanisation of the country but by the ruralisation of the town, by the breaking down of barriers so that the country might flow with unrestraint through city streets. Thus there was scant wish to mark formally the inland entrances to the town.

With the coming of the railroads conditions again changed. Passengers by rail had a single definite point of arrival and departure, which for practical purposes was to them the town's entrance. Here they left the city to enter the train, or left the train to emerge into city streets. Their senses had here the first opportunity for a "time exposure" in which to secure a lasting picture of the town. From the moment of passing the city boundaries until the station was reached there had been at best a chance for no more than " snapshots," the first serious view proving that obtained as they issued from the station portal. And to add importance to this new civic entrance, the passengers by railroad became far the greater portion of all those who entered or left the town by land. In its railroad stations, therefore, the town had suddenly new, permanent, and formal entrances.

This urban significance, with its architectural opportunity,— not to say obligation,— was hardly grasped popularly. Here and there an architect comprehended it, and made his design in accordance — perhaps with a good deal of personal satisfaction but with so little public appreciation that the efforts appear sporadically. That so obvious a significance could be overlooked, must be attributed in part, no doubt, to the circumstance that the railroad in succeeding the stage-coach was long regarded as merely a development of the latter. In Europe the cars are still made in semblance of the body of a coach, and in England they are still called "carriages." So the railroad station was thought of as an inn or roadhouse in highly advanced form, and very often to-day the station proper — the waiting rooms and platform — is made only secondary and incidental to a hotel, the architect throwing the outward structural emphasis on the latter function.

Much of the neglect of the station's real meaning is due, then, to that distraction and confusion consequent upon the mistaking of incidentals for essentials. In this confusion a factor of some influence appeared in the entirely natural development of a portion of the station structure as a clock tower. The necessity of punctuality on the part of the citizens when going to the station invites the fixing here of a clock that can be widely seen, and so in station after station the clock tower is found. There is nothing in this construction incompatible with a portal expression, if only the wish to make the latter be kept in mind [1]; but what with the use of an important part of the building for offices or for a hotel, with this arrangement of a clock conspicuously on its exterior, and the recollection that the railway itself is the successor of the stage-coach, — the permanency of whose right-of-way was never fixed, — there is many a temptation to forget that the station is the gate of the town. The costly new Paris terminal of the Paris, Lyons, and Mediterranean Railroad, for example, has about its ornate and Frenchy façade, from a corner of which a decorated clock tower is tossed jubilantly into the air, no suggestion whatever of the portal of a city.

Yet, we have said, portal significance is not en-

[1] Witness: The Gross Horlage in Rouen, or the Clock Tower in Bern.

tirely ignored. Not only do architects occasionally appreciate it and indicate it deliberately, but
the very sweep of a train-shed's arched roof in the
terminal station is so suggestive of an entrance that
many times the structure quite inevitably assumes
that character when there is offered no opportunity
to screen the curve, while the architect who desires to emphasise the portal idea finds therein a
strikingly good chance.[1] Again, the very volume
of the travel here, reaching in its convergence and
dispersion all parts of the town, has invited for
practical convenience the provision of a broad open
space before the station and the centring to it of
radial thoroughfares — all this lending that topographical importance which would naturally charac-
terise the gateway of a city. So the railroad station
became, not merely practically, nor merely theo-
retically, but to a large extent also visibly and in
spite of structural distractions, the new land portal
to the city. And as the consideration of municipal
art and of what has been called the science of city-
building becomes more thoughtful, this civic relation is better appreciated and is becoming better
recognised in the planning of stations and streets.
It gives a key to the civic significance to be expressed in station and square.

The utilitarian point of view must, of course,
have first thought in civic art, but from a conception which is all utilitarian it is no long step to
the thought of the importance of treating artistic-

[1] The single train-shed is rapidly ceasing to be typical.

ally a point that is to mean so much to the city.
For as far as the citizens are concerned the station
is a focal centre, and as far as the rest of the world
is involved it is the point from which the first
serious impression of the town is gained. It should
be, then, one of the first and most important points
to be considered in making a general plan for the
development of the city on thoroughly modern
and rational lines, and for its beautifying. It is the
first point that logically should be thought of after
the water-front, if it be proper to regard the latter
as the natural entrance. Nor will the railroad company find an addition to the attractiveness of its
station less to its interest than will the town. If
by a pleasing station and an attractive setting for it
travel is apparently shorn of some of its repellent
discomforts, the railroad company gains as much
by the greater willingness of the townspeople to
travel as the town gains by the more urgent invitation thus extended to travellers to stop there. Perhaps this advantage to the railroad seems theoretical
and problematical, a bit too dependent on sentiment
to merit expenditure by a "soulless corporation."
If it does, we should recall that as yet a majority
of the cases of station improvement, as regards the
surroundings no less than the station itself, have
owed their initiative to the railroad companies and
have been mainly or wholly paid for by the latter.

The character of the station, whether terminal
or way, should of course determine the treatment

to be adopted in its approaches; and the advantages
of attractiveness in the station and in its setting
apply as certainly, if somewhat less obviously, to
the course of the road through the town. Thus we
come to the natural divisions of the definite discussion.

Let us take up first the character of the station.
The common failure to grasp the really civic significance that pertains to it,—the failure to look at
it, as civic art must, from the standpoint of the
municipality instead of merely from that of the railroad which owns or rents the structure,—has led
to the addition of a third type to the two kinds of
construction that strictly railroad conditions must
have suggested. There are not only the terminal
and the way station,—the two inevitable and wholly
appropriate types,—but because the roadhouse and
inn theory still lingers, finding an excuse in some
practical convenience, and because the company's
claim upon the structure even to the decision of
its style is held to be paramount to that of the community, there is developed, as we have seen, a type
which may be called "the disguised." In this the
architect screens the train-shed, putting before it a
structure that is sometimes a hotel, as often in Great
Britain, and sometimes an office building, as often
in the United States, and from which all visible
significance as a portal has vanished. He doubtless
does this at the behest of the company; but in so
doing he not only gives civic art cause to mourn,

he robs the station of that importance, of that appropriate character, and even of the accurate railroad significance with which frank treatment as the city portal might have stamped it.

The terminal Gare du Nord in Paris as seen from the short street leading up to it, the station at Hamburg with the turrets flanking its castellated main pavilion, the many-portaled front of the Gare de l'Est in Paris, and the station in Genoa with its enclosing arms are striking examples of the portal treatment. Of the suburban, or way, station conception, the new station at Cologne is an example on a large scale; the station at One hundred and twenty-fifth Street in New York is a familiar illustration; and the type may be found in innumerable towns in all countries — perhaps in no villages more prettily and appropriately than in those suburbs of Boston where a series of structures designed by H. H. Richardson are framed in bits of landscape that owe their charm to the genius of the elder Olmsted. Of the "disguised" type, the familiar St. Pancras in London may stand for the hotel, and the Philadelphia stations of the Pennsylvania and Reading roads for the commercial.

Upon the amount of space available, the travel offering or likely to offer, and upon the character of the station — as it conforms with one or another of these types — must depend, if there are to be consistency, harmony, and good sense, the treatment that the city will give to the space before the station.

St. Pancras Station, London. A familiar type of European station in which a hotel, screening the train-shed, disguises the true significance of the building. Only the clock tower suggests possible connection with a railroad.

And this problem, originating as it does with modern civic art, is one which can be taken up with a more hopeful confidence of results than that with which the choice of the style of building is considered. The latter depends upon matters that are far removed from civic art, while the development of the station square is essentially a problem in that art, and a most interesting one.

Turning, then, to the community's own treatment of the land entrance, we find that stations always should, and not uncommonly do, front upon open public spaces. They should be thus situated, first, — to place, as ever in civic art, utilitarian advantages foremost in the discussion, — that the large and hurried travel of a busy centre may be commoded; second, that the station, of which the importance to the community can scarcely be exaggerated, may have all the topographical prominence that it deserves, and that the city may thus emphasise and dignify the structural value of its chief land portal; third, for the gain in the city's æsthetic aspect. First impressions are notably virile and lasting, and the stranger must form his first impression of the city from the view which meets his eyes as he passes out of the station to enter the town. A square will be pleasanter than a street, if only for the space it gives.

Some years ago the city of Genoa set itself to improve the area in front of the railroad station. There it placed, appropriately, the statue of Columbus, and in surrounding this with turf and flowers it did so "in order," as the Genovese authorities expressly declared, "that the first impression of strangers coming to our city may be favourable." The like course has been followed for a like reason, though not always so frankly confessed, by a great number of towns and cities. Thus it is that in "station squares" we come upon a distinct and important group of problems — of "portal square" problems—which it is appropriate to discuss apart from other open spaces.

This square in front of the principal railroad station in Genoa is an unusually well arranged example. Architecturally, the building exemplifies a city portal conception, and very markedly. Its walls are turned in a concave around a corner of the square, so that they seem to enfold the town, and over two adjacent streets converging from beyond the station are thrown conspicuous gate-like arches, joined to the station as if a part of it. The station portal which is in the centre becomes, then, one of a series of three perfectly apparent entrances to the town that are united in one elaborate triple gateway. Before the station there is an open space which is larger than needed for business, and the municipality has gone to work to give to the incoming traveller a pleasant first impression. The town is at once individualised and set in its proper niche of history by the memorial to Columbus, placed here that it may appropriately be the first sight to greet the traveller's

A Civic Centre in Berlin. The buildings from left to right are: The Altes Museum, the new Cathedral with the Lustgarten before it, the Royal Palace, and the Kaiser Wilhelm I. Memorial. The monumental bridge in the foreground is the Schloss Brücke, over the Spree. Note the imposing effect of grouping the structures.

eye. This is a reminder that, other conditions being favourable, the square before the station is an exceedingly appropriate place—second only to the area before the town hall — for a distinctly civic statue. With some room still to spare after erecting the statue, the Genovese authorities gave to it a park setting, though the area nearest the station was not planted, that it might be free whenever needed. By this device, also, the statue was set far enough back for good perspective. Turf, shrubs, and trees were planted, that it might have verdure for background; and yet there was retained a thoroughly formal treatment, consistently urban in suggestion. The result is that the arriving traveller's first impression is of a city rich and handsome, while not too large for the softer graces of vegetation ; and of a town of the historical interest of which he has full understanding and assurance. The departing traveller, on the other hand, has reminder that he is deliberately leaving the delightful city when he enters the portals of its station, that it is no urban jaunt he is to take for he is passing through the city gate.

It has seemed worth while to note thus, with some detail, the station square at Genoa, not merely for its own merit as an example of a bit of distinctly modern civic art, but for its suggestiveness to innumerable towns and cities of like or smaller size. At the extremes, however, of population, for cities that are much larger and for villages that are much smaller, other treatment will often be advisable.

We may easily find hints. Mere room does not mean success.

Hamburg, which has done much on lines of civic art, failed lamentably in the treatment of the space before its new station. The square was of inviting opportunity in its area, and the city began well by making liberal provision for the travel which, converging at a station, was especially likely to esteem time as a factor of importance. There are broad walks and a very wide expanse of pavement, and the roadways lead directly to the door, and yet large areas remained for planting. A good thing was done in providing amply for illumination, and the electric-lighting apparatus is frankly decorative. But the wide flat spaces that are given to planting are grass plots enclosed by low wire fences, with their monotony almost unrelieved, the few flowers, that ought to have been shrubs, proving inadequate for the broad area. There is, indeed, an effect of spaciousness; but the spaciousness of lawn that a city can show in front of its railroad station is not very impressive to those who have just been travelling through the open country, and if this effect be ignored there is nothing left. The space has no character. Along with this failure we may recite the well-known and pitiful failures of New York before the big Pennsylvania Station and of Boston before its North and South Union stations. The trouble in these cases is that there was not even an attempt at worthier treatment. The arriving

traveller in New York, passing with gratitude out of
the tunnel, although impressed by the station structure, can feel only disappointment at adjacent civic
developments. Boston, which has been a leader
in the United States in many phases of civic art,
relinquished to the ugly elevated railroad the broad
spaces of precious opportunity before its stations.

In great cities the treatment of the area in front
of the station must generally be strictly urban. The
open space exists at this point first for the facilitation and convenience of traffic, and only secondarily
for æsthetic purposes. Except, therefore, where the
available area is very large in proportion to the
travel across it,— and the value of the land rises exactly as the need for the open space increases,— the
practical problem is rather that of treating utilities
artistically and of making the æsthetic best of a
probably bad situation than of deliberate effort by
gardening. In this connection the space in front of
the Gare de l'Est in Paris has suggestion. It is not
so much a square as a broadened bit of boulevard
that has been yet further widened by converging
streets. Trees have been planted, giving height to
the flat area,— an important æsthetic principle,— but
except for this Paris, with all her love of beauty and
fondness for display, has here held herself strictly in
check. Tram communication with various parts of
the city centres here, as it very properly may, and
the transfer- or waiting-room for the trams is
almost the first edifice that the arriving traveller

sees when he leaves the railroad station. Without permitting such barbarity as Boston, Paris has here made the accommodation of travel her first consideration. The earliest impression of the stranger is that of a populous, busy city — but, withal, one arranged with singular convenience, and one in which the abundant trees prevent too violent a contrast in the swift transition from rural to urban scenery.

Where, we may observe, there must be this contrast, it should be made so marked that there will be no danger of comparison. The area should be so handsome, so superbly architectural, as to suggest civic wealth and splendour. The Senate Committee on "A Plan for the Improvement of the District of Columbia" (Washington) thus formally describes in the preliminary report its scheme for the new Union Station [1]:

The plans call for a station longer than the Capitol, the building to be of white marble, the façade to be Roman in style of architecture. . . . Facing the Capitol, and yet not too near that edifice, the new station will front on a semicircular plaza, six hundred feet in width, where bodies of troops or large organisations can be formed during inaugural times or on other like occasions. Thus located and constructed, the Union depot will be in reality the great and impressive gateway to Washington.

Again, of the plaza it says : The proposal is that it shall be

six hundred feet in width by twelve hundred feet in length, ornamented with fitting terrace, basins, and fountains. This

[1] Fifty-seventh Congress, first session. Senate Report No. 166.

great station forms the grand gateway of the capital, through
which everyone who comes to or goes from Washington must
pass; as there is no railroad entering the city that will not use
the station, it becomes the vestibule of the capital. . . .
The three great architectural features of a Capitol city being the
halls of legislation, the executive buildings, and the vestibule, it
is felt by the railroad companies that the style of this building
should be equally as dignified as that of the public buildings
themselves.   Therefore it is that the design goes back to pure
Roman motives.

The central portion is derived directly from the Arch
of Constantine, and into subordination to this the
wings are brought, so emphasising the portal conception.

If great cities can rarely make the station square
a component of the park system, smaller communities may, obviously, quite often develop it in this
way.   In fact, as one goes down the scale of population, the point is reached at last where the railroad
itself, by the improvement of its ample station
grounds, can supplement the community's efforts to
give an invitingly park-like character to the entrance
to the town.

In these smaller communities the station has
rarely the appearance of a terminal, being one neither
in fact nor aspiration.   Really a way station, it is
consistently treated as such; and the edifice, both in
its architecture and its setting,—which, as a bit of
landscape work, will not be out of harmony with the
structure,—follows the lines of a shelter or transfer
building in a park.   Of this type there are, as has
been said, hardly lovelier or more satisfying examples

to be found in the United States than in the little structures and station grounds on the line of the Boston and Albany Railroad upon what is called the Newton Circuit, just out of Boston. Here well designed stations, built of stone, and so adding to their grace suggestions of stability and permanence, rise from parks developed in the natural style, to fit pleasantly into an environment of nature as seen by the traveller who is hurried through wood and field. The bloom of hardy perennials in masses of flowering shrubs here takes the place of the stiff beds of summer flowers seen in many station grounds that pretend to be improved. In groups, they wed the building to the grounds, they frame with waving lines the patches of lawn, or hide the too-near corners, while the changing foliage, the masses of many-coloured stalks and twigs, and the green of the conifers prolong through all the year that colour and attractiveness which in carpet gardening is too often seized for only the brief weeks of summer.

The new station at Cologne offers architecturally an interesting example, because on a large scale, of the city development of this way or suburban type of construction. As such it is indeed noteworthy. Both in itself and in the approach to it which the municipality has arranged, it has suggestion; for the type — though not as flattering to cities as the terminal, or even as the disguised — is inevitably common with them. In appearance the Cologne station is suggestive of an exposition building in permanent

Railroad Station at Waban, Mass., on the Boston and Albany Railroad. A suburban station in a parklike setting.

materials. It is the immensely amplified ornamental
shelter of a park. Constructively, the train-shed's
location parallel to the street iterates the fact that
this is not a terminal; and though in the direct, near
view this effect is slightly negatived by the great
arch of the main entrance, still it may be said that
the impression on the whole is that of a splendid
way station, rather than of the meeting of town and
road at a gate. There is a very long façade, as relatively there must always be in the way-station type,
and the city, in considering the demands of the
traffic, finds that length instead of breadth can accommodate all that centres here. The open space
before the station is laid out, therefore, as a broad
parallel street with cross streets leading up to it —
a plan which can generally be followed with the
way-station type of structure. The spaces between
the cross streets — the corners rounded for the convenience of the travel — are set out as grass plots,
adorned with shrubs and flowers, and so making a
pleasant introductory to the town. Just inside these
enclosures, where their suitably flaring bases make
no trespass on the pavement, are placed the ornate
electric-light poles. The whole arrangement is well
fitted to the given conditions.

But it is proper to ask how the conditions might
have been improved. The tracks entering the station
at Cologne are elevated, so that the natural place for
the main floor would be above the level of the street.
The architects to solve their difficulty adopted the

high-basement plan of façade. Instead of doing
this, the station might have been built at the track
level, and the space before it have been terraced.
This arrangement is one that may be often and
happily adopted, now that the abolition of grade
crossings is so widely demanded, and it need not inconvenience the travel. The carriage approach can
be lifted by grade to the level of the main floor; and
if the van approach, with unchanged level, be carried
under the terrace to the real, though concealed, base-
ment, there will be a considerable gain from various
points of view. To this lower approach, also, the
city surface cars might come. The arrangement relieves the area before the building, and adds to the
comfort of travellers in enabling them to change from
steam to urban transit without leaving the building.
As to civic æsthetics, the joint dignity of town and
station at this meeting-place—not a little endangered
by the "glorified shelter" conception—can thus be
fully assured, for in terraces there is conspicuousness, and urban art has rich opportunity. The station at Providence, Rhode Island, illustrates such
a site.

But before the arriving traveller has emerged from
the station he has generally gained some sort of an
impression of the town. If his views of it have been
as "snapshots," they have been serial; and if the
opportunity for deliberate judgment has been lacking, a prepossession at least has been gained. The
railroad must enter the town in one of three ways,

or in combinations of them. It must enter on the level, or on an embankment crossing the streets by an elevated structure, or in a cutting. The last way is comparatively rare, being costliest, and either of the others offers a general survey. But the view is not flattering. Building sites are chosen in proximity to the railroad only out of necessity — for the facilitation of business, as in the case of warehouses or other large receiving or shipping establishments, or because the land not needed for these purposes is cheap. Manufacturing plants and warehouses are seldom beautiful, and on the cheapest land the cheapest residences are built, while in any case the smoke and dirt of the railroad would tend quickly to blacken all structures within their reach. So it happens that the city turns its most forlorn side to the railroad, edging the route with the dingy and prosaic.

To do something toward ameliorating this condition, which can give no pleasure to the traveller, is within the power of the railroad corporation. There may be planting along the borders for long distances, and mere neatness will do much. The result is as well worth effort as the improvement of the station grounds, and certainly it means so much to the town that the latter should require the railroad, as a condition of its entrance, to keep in order and sightliness the whole of its right of way within the city limits.

It need hardly be stated here that there ought to be no grade crossings. They are characteristic not of the modern city, but of a transition stage out of which the modern city—which, if we have not built, we can at least foresee—is developing. It were far better and cheaper, both for the railroad company and for the town, that the need of abolishing the grade crossing were recognised at the start, as law is now more and more insisting that it shall be. Once recognised, there would be laid down in advance a complete and definite plan. The railroads would enter on the line that offered fewest engineering difficulties to the avoidance of grade crossings; they would have a union station, conveniently situated, suitably approached by converging streets, and with before it an ample area that could be appropriately developed. So the land entrance to the town would be, as a whole, pleasing, impressive, and dignified, and at the station the architect scarcely could fail to recognise and express its real significance.

In the matter of elevated construction along the permanent right of way, there would be insistence on something more than that the embankment be turf-covered, or the retaining walls handsomely faced. There might be some gardening on the banks, with well placed shrubs where opportunity offers—even that can now be occasionally seen; and there should certainly be a demand that so important a structure as the bridge by which the railroad crosses a thoroughfare be designed on artistic lines. These bridges which the railroad is permitted to throw across the streets close the vistas of the streets and have such civic prominence as few structures in the town possess. It is of the utmost importance that they be not hideous, and there is no reason why they should be. Nevertheless, too few towns or cities have made serious protest against the ugliness of the bridges that the railroad has hung so conspicuously over their streets.

Thus the problem of the land entrance to a town spreads out into problems of approach as well as of terminal. And because there must be considered the prospect from both road and town, because it is impossible that there should be any unsought natural beauty about this entrance, and because again the whole reason for the construction is utilitarian and profit-making, to the end that it is vain to depend unreservedly on æsthetic impulse, there arises many a perplexity and embarrassment. The purely ideal can hardly be expected. But it is clear that certain good things that make for modern civic art can reasonably be looked for.

It will be to the advantage of the railroad as well as of the town to have a worthy entrance; but it remains for the town to insist upon this. If in its first plotting there are laid down the lines and proportions of the local main street, how much more appropriately now may there be determined the best lines for the through travel, the course and station of the railroad that is to build up the town and to give to the world its view of the town! If in the community's growth the water entrance be developed by the municipality, is there less reason that it should provide for the busy inland entrance approaches that shall be dignified, worthy, and convenient? If in constructing the bridges that carry its own streets the municipality exercises artistic care, shall it be negligent in the matter of the bridges that, crossing its streets, present lateral views so striking and far visible? If it constructs parkways, demands well kept streets, and requires its citizens to preserve the orderliness of their gardens, shall it fail to enjoin less care on that permanent right of way on which the railroad is permitted to bisect the town and from which the travelling public gains its view of the community? Civic art must surely rise to recognition of the importance and true significance of the modern railroad route and station as the land entrance of the modern town; and, recognising it, there must be demand for a treatment that shall be worthy because at once sensible, appropriate, and artistic. It should be the worthy portal of a worthy city, and for this end the community and railroad must work together.

CHAPTER V.

THE ADMINISTRATIVE CENTRE.

LIKE an artist choosing the central figures of his group before he begins the composition, or as a landscape designer notes the dominant natural features of the given site before drawing his plans, we, in the study and practice of modern civic art, must pass from the portals of the city, from the entrances by water and by land, to the administrative centre of the town.   This is the point that should naturally demand our next attention, for this should be the heart of the town.   Its municipal life should be centred here, and it should be a distinct and definite point.

To the buildings of the government, which would go to constitute the architectural elements of an administrative centre, there ought to be given not merely a central location, which will be invited by considerations of convenience even more strongly than by those of sentiment, but all the additional emphasis and conspicuousness that site can offer.   No

other structures are so appropriately entitled to the
best position that the town can afford, convenience
and appearance being jointly considered, as are those
that officially stand for the town.   And this being
true of the leading public buildings, they are gregar-
ious.   They belong in about the same location, the-
oretically, without regard to (because above) the
temporary matter of land values and the claims of
individual real-estate interests.   And not only do
these structures belong together, but each gains
from the proximity of the others.   There is, for
example, a utilitarian gain, in the concentration of the
public business and the consequent saving of time;
and there is a civic gain, in the added dignity and
importance which the buildings seem to possess.
Collectively, they appear to make the city more
prideworthy; they suggest the co-operation of
departments rather than that individual sufficiency
which separate buildings recommend and which is
at the root of so much administrative evil; they make
the municipality, in this representation of the mighti-
ness of its total business, seem a more majestic thing
and one better worth the devotion and service of its
citizens.   They make it seem better worth living for
and working for, as of larger possibilities for good,
than could the same buildings when scattered about
the town and lost in a wilderness of commercial
structures.

    It scarcely needs to be said, further, that a group-
ing of these buildings may be as advantageous æsthe-

tically, for all of them and for each of them, as it is in
a civic sense and utilitarian sense, and as from those
points of view it would seem to be natural. A prominent architect, in discussing this matter at a national
gathering of his profession, has maintained that
" isolated buildings of whatever individual merit are
insignificant in comparison to massed constructions,
even if these latter be comparatively mediocre in
quality." This is a very strong claim, but even if it
be pared down—as the architects did not require that
it should be—there remains enough of undoubted
truth powerfully to endorse on æsthetic grounds the
grouping of the public structures. Granting this,
consider what a waste of opportunity there is in the
erection of monumental buildings for a city—whatever the landlord represented by each—that are so
separated as to make it impossible to see them
together. Probably without additional expense,
certainly without addition proportioned to the resulting gain, they might be put together, and to
every building there might thus be given something of majesty by its mere setting among its
neighbours. So there would always be created, if
natural laws were followed, a civic, or administrative,
centre in each town.

But the buildings represent various landlords—
national, state, county, and urban—and even those
that are municipal represent various sections of
the city government—executive, legislative, educational, or judicial—that usually are too independent

of one another to pool their interests in choosing sites. So it has repeatedly happened that the post-office has been erected in one place, the court-house in another, the city hall in a third, and the public library and high school in yet others, even when — as in the typical New England village — there is reserved a public area unbuilt upon in the heart of the town (the "green" or "common"), upon which the official structures would most appropriately face. To be sure, in the old towns of New England the earliest church was erected here; but that circumstance merely testifies to the appropriateness of the site, for there was no real grouping of public buildings.

The objection may be made that the vicinity of the city buildings would be a poor place for a school, or even for the library. A good deal depends on the character of the officials. With politics at low ebb morally and intellectually, the city hall may not be the most desirable of neighbours. In Birmingham, on the other hand, where politics have been on a higher plane than in most American cities, the art gallery and the council chamber were long under one roof, with the town hall across the street on one side and the new art school across the street on the other. Even the new gallery is separated by no more than a street's width from the council chamber. But speaking generally, we may say that the educational structures can be fittingly separated from the executive and legislative and from the judicial, for in these days cities have grown too large to crowd into a single space quite all that is important. In the physiology of cities it is not accurate to-day to speak of "the heart" of the town; but, rather, of a series of nerve centres. Thus it is possible to have, with no contradiction of terms, more than a single centre. There may be, for instance, an administrative centre and an educational centre, just as we have already found collecting and distributing centres — all of them focal points of the town — at the water gate and the land entrance. A peculiarity, it may be noted, of the beautiful street plans of Washington and Paris is their topographical provision for a great number of such nerve centres.

It is possible and convenient to discuss under a single head the administrative and educational foci, because they are alike in being, in each case, a group of public buildings. The same laws bring the structures together, the same principles of civic art commend their concentration and suggest the governing of it. Alike, they are architectural aggregations, probably, before in practice they are topographical foci, and the arrangement of the streets that lead to them, or of the streets or squares upon which they front, — all the generous provision for a large circulatory requirement, — will be determined by the location of the structures, instead of itself determining this. Here, then, is one of the few points in city-building where the topographical procedure may be perfectly rational, a result of forethought rather than of chance—even, if necessary, to the rebuilding of that portion of the town. As the public's interest is greater than the interest of any individual or set of individuals, the ideal alone should be considered in the placing of the public buildings. Let us consider what the ideal placing would be.

Most of the structures of a city are arranged in rows, fronting on the streets. This is an extremely undesirable arrangement for public buildings. Needless to say, they might form a very stately series; and there are a host of examples — notably the handsome row of public structures on the Ringstrasse of Vienna—that could be named to endorse such a location. But Vienna's Ringstrasse is to be counted out for the present, and of the other cases in which public buildings are collected into a group arranged along the side of a street, it may be doubted whether there is a single one in which the effect would not have been better with some other disposition. The main objections to location on a street, even assuming that there be no commercial interruption of the series, are: (1) the endangering of what is called the scale of the buildings; (2) the lack of opportunity for perspective owing to the narrowness of the street; (3) the loss of apparent relative importance.

If the side of the street opposite to the public buildings be not built upon,—if it be a park or other reservation,—the buildings, as far as civic art is concerned, face not on a street but on the reservation, which is quite another matter. If the street be built up on the opposite side, private ownership of that land puts in jeopardy the beauty and dignity of the public structures through the possibility of mingling inharmonious architecture, of making a squalid and unworthy outlook, or of destroying scale by the erection of a "sky-scraper," or any colossal building, that would dwarf the public structures. The danger that threatens on the farther side of the street threatens also at either end of it, except that there the possibly unworthy outlook becomes an unfortunate approach. If, on the other hand, both sides of the street be reserved for the public buildings, so that they face each other in two series, the space between becomes simply a court. This, clearly, would serve the buildings better if it were wider than a street and were not open to all kinds of traffic — if, in other words, it were really a court and not a street.

The narrowness of a street, again, is a serious matter because of its denial of opportunity for perspective, the public buildings being deliberately monumental. The architect should not be discouraged by a thought that the beholder of his work for the municipality can get no more than eighty or a hundred feet from the base lines. Such discouragement would be a sad thing for the city; and if there were no disheartenment, and lovely buildings were still erected, their beauty would be well-nigh wasted by the necessity of having to look straight up their

walls to see them. In the case of Vienna's Ringstrasse, the street is extremely broad — so broad as
to become at any point, with its trees and turf and
"parking," a little park; while its great width is
further enhanced by the curve of the street, that
renders possible long and changing oblique views of
the façades. That is why the majestic Ringstrasse
is not to be taken as an example of the normal
street. It is hardly fair to call it a street at all, for it
is more like a long, curved plaza. Finally, if the
public buildings be crowded along the edge of a
street, what is there to distinguish them from the
other structures of the town, to give them character,
prestige, and the surpassing dignity and conspicuousness that should be theirs? To set them back
from a street elsewhere built up closely would be
even to conceal them further. For all these reasons
together the street is the least satisfactory location
for the public buildings of a community, a fact that
is even emphasised by the circumstance that it is the
usual position for buildings of other kinds.

Location on the water-front is in many cases to
be strongly urged. It will frequently happen that
this is not a geographically central location, as when
the water forms the boundary of the town. But
even when that is the case — and often, on the
contrary, a bisecting stream will fix the town's geographical centre more surely than could an arbitrarily chosen site — the water-frontage is likely to
be, nevertheless, extremely central in a commercial

Railroad Station at Wellesley Farms, Mass., on the Boston and Albany Railroad.

sense, the population and business of the community crowding close upon it.   If such a site be, in fact, sufficiently central to satisfy the convenience of the community, there is much to commend its selection for the location of the public buildings.

The advantages are double, as they should be, —the site benefiting the appearance of the city as a whole and the aspect of the public buildings considered by themselves.   As far as the city is concerned, the grouping of the public buildings along the water-front offers an opportunity for that harmony of water-front treatment, that visible permanence of construction, that stateliness of architectural facing, that may mean so much to the town in the water view.   As far as the buildings themselves are concerned, the water outlook is something more than pleasing.   It safeguards them from the interference of private construction; and it invites carefully treated approaches with an irresistibility which makes them unquestionably fitting.   The very rise of the bank, with its suggestion of terraces or sloping ascents, adds to the dignity and seeming importance of the buildings.

From a picturesque standpoint the site is, then, an entirely favourable one.   A drawback is that the government buildings—excepting a possible custom-house—have little essential connection with the water.   Utility does not demand their location along its edge, as it does demand the location of many other kinds of structures, and for this reason the municipality is likely to need its water-front space for other purposes, if the body of water has commercial or industrial value. But even in those cases there is to be urged the setting aside of some area for enjoyment, and upon this public reservation if it be large enough, or at least to front upon it, the municipal buildings might often be arranged with advantage. So would be served a twofold purpose. The public buildings would face upon the water-front, and a portion of the water-front would be preserved for public enjoyment. The artistic treatment given to the plot would constitute a beautifying of the buildings' approach or site at the moment that it was also park development.

With scarcely less certainty than the possession of a water-front, most communities have an eminence. If it does not command the whole town, it yet commands a considerable area, so that whatever structure is reared upon it possesses a conspicuousness above that of the town's other buildings. Various considerations urge the reservation of this site for a public pleasure ground. The urgency of the considerations grows as the height of the eminence increases, for a far view is a precious possession; but when the height is not very great, when the ascent is neither so long nor so steep as to interfere seriously with traffic, and when the summit, if centrally located, is given over to building,—as it is likely to be under this combination of conditions,— then it would be difficult to find more fitting tenants than the structures that house the government of the city.

There they would visibly dominate the town. To them the community would look up, seeing them lording over it at every turn, as, in fact, the government ought to do. The buildings would appear, to that extent, as a free people's appropriate creation in succession of the castle of the feudal lords. And, apart from this sentiment, the height of the location would emphasise the relative importance of the buildings, without making too great a demand upon the architect or involving too high a cost for construction. They would gain in seeming importance and in dignity, merely because of their situation; and here once more there would be invitation for those balustrades and terraces that may do so much to place a building to advantage. In the distant view of the city the buildings of its government would be, fittingly, the first and most striking objects of the scene. The Capitol at Washington suggests itself immediately as a familiar example. Of its location, an English critic, Frederic Harrison, has declared:

I have no hesitation in saying that the site of the Capitol is the noblest in the world, if we exclude that of the Parthenon in its pristine glory. . . . Londoners can imagine the effect if their St. Paul's stood in an open park, reaching from the Temple to Finsbury Circus, and the great creation of Wren were dazzling white marble, and soared into an atmosphere of sunny light.

As to the advantages that grade itself offers to

buildings, the "Papers Relating to the Improvement of the City of Washington"[1] contain these very important reflections:

Abrupt changes of grade are not obstacles, but opportunities. We have been abundantly satisfied if our buildings were planted, not set; that is, if the surface were levelled for them and they had no apparent connection with the ground on which they were placed. . . . There is nothing more attractive than walls, steps, terraces, balustrades, and buttresses, which are integral parts of most (public) buildings abroad, and which, when the natural grades have not given excuse for their existence, have been deliberately created as necessary setting to the buildings.

The monumental treatment of grade may, then, very greatly enhance the imposing effect of a building. As the paper continues, this work is of immense variety:

It can be made to soften too great austerity of design and to dignify too great license. In many cases the approaches to a simple, inexpensive structure exalt it above a pretentious but undeveloped neighbour, and in any scheme for the embellishment of a city, too much stress cannot be laid on these important accessories to the higher architectural achievements.

Finally, and more prosaically, the very site safeguards the public buildings from the intrusive elbowing of private structures that might dwarf them, that might screen them from view, or might shut out their light. As was assumed at the beginning of this chapter, no site can be too good for the structures that officially represent the town. Here again,

[1] Senate Document 94, Fifty-sixth Congress, second session. Paper by C. Howard Walker.

as on the water-front, if it be impossible to secure some of this advantageous situation to public enjoyment by means of a park, the end may be indirectly gained by dedicating it to the public buildings.

But many communities, having neither a suitable eminence nor an available bit of water-front on which to locate their public structures, are compelled to make choice along the existing ways — be they the streets, parks, or squares — of the city. This, because the question has been long neglected so that the best natural sites are pre-empted, is the common problem; and when it does arise, it is taken up too often with no courageousness of spirit or comprehensiveness of plan. Then there is secured no grouping of the buildings; but, one by one, as necessity occurs, the question of situating single public structures is dealt with half-heartedly — at how great a loss to the total impressiveness, beauty, and majesty of the city! Even, however, amid these discouraging conditions, it is possible to find a rule that will help immensely in obtaining results which, though far from the ideal, are yet comparatively favourable for building and for town.

We have said that the street, using the term in its ordinary sense, is the least satisfactory location for the public structures. The reproach may be modified and an exception made, when a site is chosen that puts the building at the axes of important thoroughfares. From the standpoint of the town, the building then suitably closes street vistas;

and from the building's standpoint, it may then be seen
in perspective and has as great a conspicuousness as
a relatively built-in site can give. The location, if
not equal to the water-front or an eminence, is, all
things considered, fairly good. In the original street
plan of Washington much stress was laid upon the
axial position of governmental structures. In Paris
there is given to such monumental constructions as
the Opera House, the Arch of the Star, the Made-
leine, and the Hôtel des Invalides axial treatment by
causing a convergence of streets to them and by
making their location complementary to similarly
massive construction at the vista's other end. In
the new street planning of London, Washington,
and countless other cities, this axial position for
important buildings is again endorsed, both for the
building's sake and for the street's. It not only
terminates with a satisfactory mass the street vistas
that were only wearisome if not thus closed, but it
prevents the buildings of special prominence and
size from destroying the scale of ordinary structures
or from thrusting themselves too intrusively upon
the street.

To recapitulate, then, the government buildings
should be grouped. That is, there ought to be a
civic centre. If grouped, they should not be strung
along a street. The street position is on the axis
at a focal point. When grouped, they belong at the
edge of squares or plazas; or, best of all, if the site
be sufficiently central, on an eminence or upon the

water-front. If the public structures be educational institutions, the water-front might well prove unduly distracting. The ideal neighbour of an educational centre is a public reservation suitable for the play of little children, and inviting, by its quiet and leisure, the reflection and study of adults.

But the requirements of civic art in the grouping of the public buildings are not exhausted by these considerations. We have noted only the relations of the buildings to the town as a whole. They have relations to one another. A number of these are comprised in what the architect calls scale — the adoption of a certain module to which all the buildings must strictly adhere, as they can with no loss of individuality. If they so adhere that no building clashes with its neighbour, we may hope to attain that beauty of harmony and repose of which so many non-professional persons gained a new concrete conception in the "Court of Honour" at the Chicago Fair. If they do not adhere to it, the grouping will prove of doubtful æsthetic value.

Oftentimes it will be possible, also, to emphasise the group plan, or to appear to group existing buildings that are really somewhat scattered, by joining them by means of arcades or colonnades or — if they be too far apart for that — by formal avenues of trees, with balustrades and sculpture. This is a course that may do much for civic art, not only in the end to which it leads but by the means it uses to reach that end.

Of the relations of the now really or apparently grouped buildings to the structures near them, something has been already said. Here requirements of scale are hardly less pressing than in the group itself. In European cities building regulations which determine not merely the height of the structures, but of the cornice line, are so common that the matter of scale can be easily governed. In America, however, there is danger. Boston imposed a special restriction as to height upon structures erected on Copley Square, with a view to safeguarding the beautiful buildings of a public character that had gathered there. In New York, where the chaste little City Hall occupies the centre of a green that has not been thus protected, dozens of millions of dollars have been expended upon structures that edge the square and that shut it in with lofty walls which utterly dwarf the municipal building. The same huge sum of money might have secured a series of structures that would have been civic ornaments. Those that have risen, while fairly good of their type, do not include a single one that is an art possession, such as would have been appropriate around the edge of this little park which is the centre of the municipal life of the chief city of the United States. The apparently lost opportunity points to the lesson that it is well to go one step beyond the grouping of the public buildings, and to assure the maximum success by regulating the character and size of the buildings that bound the group.

It should here be said that the Municipal Art Society of New York appointed a committee in 1902 to consider the possibility of securing an administrative, or civic, centre in New York, by grouping public buildings in a central location. After careful study, the committee reported in favour of making the present City Hall Park the centre of such a scheme. It recommended that the park be cleared of all buildings except the beautiful City Hall, which is in the middle of it, and that the municipality proceed to acquire all of the property (a portion of which it already owned) facing the park directly on the north. On this area, and on a block to be acquired on the east, it should then erect new administrative buildings. These, it was pointed out, with the Post-Office on the south, would furnish at least a partial frame that might be dignified and fairly harmonious. The committee added that the transformed park, "attractive and spacious to an extent that can now be scarcely imagined," would be "a fitting site for generations to come for every class of adornment that may make beautiful the place, or commemorate historical events or characters." Even though the suggestions of the report, which were presented in a persuasive financial as well as æsthetic light, are not to be carried out, they possess an interest as showing a keenly felt need.[1]

Though conditions be ever so discouraging, as certainly they appeared to be in New York, modern

[1] New York subsequently undertook the creation of a civic centre, great in scale, on an adjacent site.

civic art will not be content to forego dreams of their betterment. It will yet have that civic centre vision which was the climax of the civic art of the Flemish and the Italian Renaissance. The dream of New York is surpassed, as conditions warrant, by a plan in Chicago for grouping public buildings on the lake-front; and in Springfield, Massachusetts, and Cleveland, Ohio, where circumstances have given exceptional advantages, the "group plan," on a square that leads to the water-front, is being actually secured. In each of these places, also, it is the earnest popular interest which has rendered possible this result.

Finally, it may be suggested as a fitting conclusion, that the architectural grandeur of Athens, Florence, Venice, Budapest, Moscow, Antwerp, and Paris,— to name but a few examples,— is due largely in each case to the concentration of the chief buildings. Imagine its chief buildings as separated and isolated, and the beauty of each of these cities departs.

IN THE BUSINESS DISTRICT.

CHAPTER VI.

THE STREET PLAN OF THE BUSINESS DISTRICT.

MODERN civic art, having fixed certain definite foci, having determined that here shall be the formal entrance to the town by water, there its entrance for those who come by land, and that in such a place its public business shall be transacted ; having laid down the principle that an open space is desirable at each of these "nerve centres," and that important streets should converge to them,— civic art, having established these bases and gone so far, is ready to take up the larger and more intricate problem of the street plan of the business district. The problem is important, interesting, and difficult. In the anatomy of the city there is no point at which the circulatory demands are so great, so insistent, so impatient, or where failure to provide adequately for them is so injurious. In the existing city there is no portion where it is more difficult to make changes, nor is there any district that has been allowed to grow with so little scientific planning.

In the typical town in the United States, ever a most attractive field for the student of community development, the broad, straight Main Street of the village has become in fact, as it already is in name, the main thoroughfare of the town. From it the business has overflowed into a series of narrow streets that cross it at right angles, and on the broader of these it may extend some distance. The arrangement, stretching the business along two sides of an uncompleted triangle, is the most inconvenient possible, involving greatest loss of energy and time. Or the business, having found no cross street of especial invitation, may extend equally along a series of them and then spread over a thoroughfare that, paralleling the main street, connects them. So it will overflow a rectangle, and perhaps a series of these, until there is a large business district tending to be rectangular. In no other equal area is space so precious, or time and distance more important factors; yet, to go from any point on one street to any point on one that is parallel, two sides of the triangle must be traversed. Furthermore, the traffic, far larger than had been intended for these streets, doubtless chokes them. Every slowly moving truck impedes every vehicle behind it. The great business houses, barely seen from the mean and narrow thoroughfares, lose their dignity. Rapid-transit facilities, crowded on to one or two broad highways, contract these for general traffic and, consequently, the attempted rapid-transit is delayed. In London where, thanks to excellent police regulation, the traffic moves with relative celerity, a calculation has been made that "every omnibus and cab that uses the main streets of the 'City' and its approaches is delayed on an average half an hour each day through blocks and partial blocks." Could the money loss of this to passengers in cab and motorbus be estimated, consider what would be the aggregate!

A problem that, for all its difficulty, so urgently invites solution has not lacked for thought. There are such practical requirements that civic art must have had pressing claims to be heard among them; and yet it is heard, for if the centre of the city be not imposing, if there be here no handsome sites, no stateliness, no majestic thoroughfares, and the convenience of the business be not consulted, the modern city has lamentably failed to realise the ends of civic art. The courage with which this hardest of all the problems has been attacked in the world's great cities is one of the most interesting and inspiring, as it is one of the most suggestive, episodes in the history that relates the rise of the new ideal for cities — that ideal born of new conditions and which cannot therefore be a fruitless dream.

This essential newness of the problem is well illustrated by one of the most striking attempts that have been made to solve it. On Christmas day in 1857, as a result of preliminary agitation, Emperor Francis Joseph of Austria issued a decree addressed to the Minister of the Interior, requiring that "the enlargement of the inner city of Vienna, for the purpose of its suitable connection with the suburbs, should be undertaken as speedily as possible." It was suggested that the surrounding fortifications and ditches, which are always the great opportunity of the cramped old Continental cities, be removed, and that at the same time there be made adequate provision of sites for a new war office, a city marshall's office, an opera house, imperial archives, a town hall, and the necessary buildings for museums and galleries. The decree required that there be opened a competition for plans for the improvement, the jury to consist of a commission of high officials representing various interests, these commissioners before making the awards, however, to "submit the plans to a committee of specialists appointed by them." Three designs were to be selected for prizes and the premiums were to be two thousand, one thousand, and five hundred gold ducats. This was the opportunity, the perception and courageous seizure of which have since made Vienna so superb and famous. Eighty-five designs were submitted, and though none of the premiated plans was literally carried out, they gave suggestions and set the standard for the final scheme. But this, as the decree required, dealt rather with the enlargement of the inner city and its convenient connection with the suburbs than with a remodelling of the district itself.

Thirty-five years later, in the last decade of the nineteenth century, the municipality took up the latter problem, inviting the architects and engineers of the world to compete in the submission of plans for the remodelling of old, central Vienna. There were two prizes of ten thousand florins, three of five thousand, and three of three thousand florins. For "part designs which do not comprise the whole city, but consider only a few questions of the improvement, or means of communication," there were prizes of three thousand florins and under; and finally prizes were promised for plans that were good in parts though not satisfactory as a whole. The jury was composed mainly of professors, leading architects, and engineers; and far-off Vienna proved again that she had nothing to learn either as to modern municipal ideals or civic spirit from Berlin or Paris or Rome or from the hurrying cities of England and America.

The early days of Philadelphia and New York offered exceptional opportunities for a scientific planning of the business districts in communities which, as could be even then foreseen, were destined to become great cities. That the outcome in each case is a failure, an example of what not to do, shows how little progress had yet been made in the physical science of cities. There was, however, consciousness of the problem and its thoughtful consideration. For Philadelphia no less a personage than William Penn made a plan. Its feature was a long series of rectangles that were almost squares, the straight highways unrelieved by curve or diagonal, with two of the streets, which crossed at right angles in a big open space nearly in the middle of the tract, considerably broader than the others. If there was little of art or science about the design, there was enough forethought to appreciate the value of frequent open spaces for the admission of light and air to a crowded section, for the provision of good building sites on the ground facing the public areas, and for relieving the monotony of the district.   Penn's plan shows five such spaces, each half as large again as an ordinary block, in a district only five blocks broad by twenty-two long.[1] Had the same proportion been secured for the closely built-up sections of the city when it extended beyond this district, as the Consolidation Act of 1854 directed should be done, there would have been two hundred and eighty small parks in the city plan of Philadelphia at the beginning of the twentieth century instead of the forty-five that were actually there. But there was not enough public appreciation of the importance of the problem to secure the adoption of even the one redeeming feature of Penn's plan.   The straight streets and rectangular blocks, unrelieved by frequent open spaces, extended over the growing city and were adopted as a model by the thirty or more outlying towns and villages that have since been incorporated in it.

When New York came to wrestle with the problem, in 1807, the public held it serious enough to

[1] The area between Vine and South streets and the Delaware and Schuylkill rivers.

demand the consideration of a formally appointed commission. This laid down — tradition says with a mason's hand sieve — the familiar gridiron plan. The one irregular thoroughfare was Broadway, already a road of too much importance to be molested, and to that happy chance New York owes the only opportunities for civic stateliness or beauty afforded in its street arrangement. Broadway has developed, too, as the great business street, just as the diagonal Ridge Avenue in Philadelphia has become, in spite of its narrowness, a street of shops. If, as wisely remarked, " the shop-keepers go where the travel is," the value of the diagonal thoroughfare for circulatory purposes is attested.

But there are other faults in the rectilinear plan. Frederick Law Olmsted has put some of them well in saying of the commission's work :

> Some two thousand blocks were provided, each theoretically two hundred feet wide, no more, no less; and ever since, if a building site is wanted, whether with a view to a church or a blast furnace, an opera house or a toy shop, there is, of intention, no better place in one of these blocks than in another. . . . If a proposed cathedral, military depot, great manufacturing enterprise, house of religious seclusion, or seat of learning needs a space of ground more than sixty-six yards in extent, from north to south, the system forbids that it shall be built in New York. . . . There is no place in New York where a stately building can be looked up to from base to turret, none where it can even be seen full in the face and all at once taken in by the eye; none where it can be viewed in advantageous perspective. . . . Such distinctive advantage of position as Rome gives St. Peter's, Paris the Madeleine, London St. Paul's, New York, under her system, gives to nothing.

The plan offers the maximum of building area, but the minimum of effect.

Costly failures where there might have been magnificent successes are not confined to the United States. If modern civic art has learned, the world over, a lesson, if it has been taught to recognise the worth of a street plan for the business district that shall consult convenience of travel and stateliness of result, it has done so by dear experience widely distributed. To devise on paper a plan intelligent and comprehensive required no impossible genius; to secure public appreciation of such a plan required examples not only of its success but of the failure of simpler plans. In London after the great fire there was presented an opportunity as thrilling as any that America has had. Here, in the heart of the world's greatest and richest city, a large district could be replanned. There was a genius who saw the chance and contrived a scheme that would have rendered London superb among the cities of to-day; but the design of Sir Christopher Wren was in advance of the age, and you must seek diligently now to find it in the archives of an Oxford college. Four hundred and thirty-six acres had been burned over; a cathedral and eighty-seven churches were to be rebuilt; a site was to be found for a new exchange and for other public buildings; and of about fourteen thousand structures, some of which might have stood in the way of a new planning, not one was left.

But London was rebuilt in the old way, and such

improvements as have since been made, unsatisfactory
as they are, have cost enormously. From 1798 to
1821 ten select committees made reports on particular improvements. In another twenty years, from
1832 to 1851, Parliament appointed eleven or twelve
select committees to take into consideration plans
for the improvement of London and to advise as to
the best means for carrying out the plans. These
committees did little more than report on the causes
of the crowding—which were obvious enough—and
on the difficulty of making changes owing to the
great cost. All this was impressing the lesson. At
last, however, conditions became so serious that vast
expenses had to be assumed. In the thirty-four
years from 1855 to 1889 the Metropolitan Board of
Works expended upon street changes and improvements more than fifteen millions sterling. The net
cost, after recoupments from the sale of surplus land,
exceeded ten millions sterling, while a million and a
half pounds more had been paid out by the board
in grants to local districts, to aid them in bearing the
cost of the smaller street improvements. It was
at about the end of this period that the chairman
of the improvement committee of the London County
Council observed that the streets of London meas-
ured some two thousand miles, and that in the thirty
years ending with 1889 the board of public works
had succeeded, with its great expenditure, in constructing a total length of fifteen and four-fifths miles
of new streets, with an average width of sixty feet.

He noted this with pride; but those who know
Wren's plan, who recall how easily it might have
been adopted, and its lines extended over the whole
metropolitan area as London stretched farther into
the country, can see only pathos in his figures, and
realise more keenly than before the value of care in
original street planning.

The plan of Sir Christopher Wren for the rebuilding of burned London was in accord with the
principles of civic art as they are recognised to-day.
Wren was surveyor-general, so that his masterly
design took a natural precedence; it was accepted
also by the king, and what now seems the mere
accident of a lack of ever so little ready money and
a desire for haste were allowed to prevent the future
splendour and convenience of the great city. The
main features of his plan, which well repays study,
were to be, going from west to east: (1) A circular
space at the top of Fleet Street hill, about on the site
of St. Dunstan's Church. From this eight streets
were to radiate, the eight to be connected with one
another at a suitable distance from the centre by
cross streets, these forming an octagon in relation to
the circle. (2) A triangular space in full view from
Fleet Street hill. This was to widen toward the east
and was to include St. Paul's and Doctors' Com-
mons. (3) An open space in the centre of which
should stand, on its old site, the Royal Exchange,
and grouped around this space were to be the public
buildings. From this point, which was to be the

Sir Christopher Wren's Plan for Rebuilding London after the Great Fire in 1666.

topographical centre, there were to radiate ten streets, each sixty feet wide. Three of these reached directly down to the river, offering from it a noble view of the Exchange. Along the river bank there was to be a broad quay, and opposite London Bridge a large semicircular space with arterial streets radiating outward. Here and there, where radials of different systems crossed, there were established new open spaces and new centres. The plan showed, in brief, that use of broad, straight streets linked together by monumental buildings, that provision of commanding sites for important structures, that use of diagonals, of open areas, and of curving streets with their changing view-points, which the accepted plans of Paris, of Vienna, and of Washington have now made familiar.

The opportunity was allowed to pass, and all the subsequent and costly changes in the London plan have proved inadequate, because it since has been impossible financially to carry out a single comprehensive scheme that should bring every part into direct relations with every other. In all street planning there must be regard for the through lines of travel as surely as for the local, and it is these through courses which scattered improvements generally fail to benefit to great extent. The through travel in its usually heavy volume demands arterial thoroughfares that shall be wide, uniform in their width, straight, of easy gradient, and on the direct line between important foci. These requirements alone involve a considerable dignity of aspect. To gain the best spectacular results, however, civic art must be mindful also of other factors. Perhaps the most notable of these in the business district is the architectural effect.

The relation between the architecture and the street plan is reciprocal. Each can do so much for the other that while, on the one hand, a street may be opened or widened simply that a monumental structure may be the better seen, on the other hand the precise location of a new street may be determined by the position of existing structures that are prominent, according as they would or would not close the vista of the street, and so enhance its beauty. For in a city mere distance is not fine. There should be set up visible limits, or at least accents, and the ideal would be to proportion the breadth of the thoroughfare to the distance between these limits or main accents. We have seen in this connection how Sir Christopher Wren built up his street plan from the focal points offered by important buildings and then on the minor axes obtained variety of treatment. We may observe also how the Arc de Triomphe in Paris is made a topographical centre whence twelve great streets radiate, and how fully again the method is exemplified in the plan of Washington.

A few years ago there was a project on foot in Brussels to prolong a certain street[1] in order to

[1] The Rue du Lombard toward the Rue Saint-Jean.

establish direct communication between two important points. The utilitarian advantages of the proposed street were overwhelming, but the matter was not decided until that national society of workers for civic art, L'Œuvre Nationale Belge, had prepared a report on the æsthetic effect. This report showed what view of the Palais de Justice the new street would reveal, what views it would afford of two churches that were on its line, the character of the new view it would open of the Hôtel de Ville, and finally what would be the general aspect of the street itself and of the lateral streets as seen from it. The incident is a happy illustration of the many points that civic art would have kept in mind when arranging or changing the street plan of a city's centre.

And there are some other requirements even than these. There is to be considered the general line of frontage, or building line, for this may be set back to widen a narrow street; the erection of porticoes over the walk, the projection and height of balconies and awnings, and finally the regulation of building heights if we would have an imposing thoroughfare. In the European cities, where more frequently than in the United States the central authority pushes new streets through closely built-up districts, there are statutes to control all these matters. Though these deal so directly with the architectural aspect of the city that they may be considered more fittingly under that head, it is well to observe here that their special design is to preserve the dignity of the street.

In laying down, then, an ideal street plan, for the business district of a city, there should be first a comprehensive scheme, a skeleton of arterial thoroughfares to provide for the through travel from point to point. These great roads will be direct, broad, straight, and free from heavy grades. At the focal points there will be open spaces and from these the great streets will radiate. Then, in laying down the precise location of any one of them, we shall note what views it opens, what its accents are, and, if possible, we shall proportion its width to its length or seeming length. On the lateral and minor streets, designed for local traffic, we shall obtain a pleasing variety in the street lines — even if it be only that of sudden regularity. Later on we will safeguard the appearance of the street by building regulations; we may even swerve it a little to preserve an historic or beautiful edifice; and we will take care that if it is to pass upon viaduct or bridge, or if a bridge is to be suspended over it, the majesty and beauty of the street shall not be destroyed by a hideous structure. In carelessness of civic art, in haste, in wonder at the prowess of modern industrialism and awe of our cunning with iron and steel, we have suffered a hopelessly unæsthetic truss bridge, cheaply made and quickly put together, to become a common and well-nigh prevailing type. The marvel is not that iron and steel are used, but that we submit to their use in ugly lines. Suppose, it has been suggested, that under the eaves of Notre Dame in Paris there were, instead of the graceful sweeps of the arched bridges across the Seine, a couple of truss constructions—like, for example, the bridge by which rich Chicago has permitted State Street to be demeaned, —how the aspect not of a street alone, but of Paris, would be changed! How much poorer in urban beauty would be the world!

As to the focal points, earlier chapters have suggested what these are likely to be. The government buildings, the entrances to the town, by water and by land—these are sure receiving and distributing centres. Wren's plan has suggested the artificial creation of additional and local foci at convenient points, and the plan of Paris shows how such topographical centres may be located with reference to monumental constructions (as the Arc de Triomphe) that are not in themselves magnets of travel but the conspicuousness of which is desirable on spectacular grounds. That the creation of such local centres may very greatly enhance the commercial value of their building sites, in the business districts of cities, is obvious enough. But the importance of an arbitrary focus can be still further enhanced, so that it becomes more than local.

An interesting example is found in the plan of Dalny, the new city that Russia constructed as a Pacific seaport terminal for its Trans-Siberian Railroad. The street plan of this entire city was made in the office of the Russian engineers before any building was commenced. There are many diagonal arterial thoroughfares, the crossing points of the different systems of radials creating local centres, and in front of the railway station there is a plaza which is an important focus. But in the heart of the town a circular public space had been laid out. Ten long straight streets converge upon it, connected by a circular street that forms the circle's circumference. Built around this, with excellent effect in the plan, there were to be ten structures, each in its separate little block. Yet they included—and it must be remembered that the list was made out in an office, before a house had been put up—buildings of as little individual importance as a private bank (three), a theatre, a club-house, a post- and telegraph-office. Still the aggregate result, the town hall and some government offices being added, locates the heart of the city. It is a valuable suggestion for towns of minor importance.

But the opportunity for new planning on the scale of Dalny may come only once in a hundred years. Such transformations as have been wrought in Paris and Vienna, such extensive changes of street plan and aspect as Berlin and Rome have brought about, and such magnificently comprehensive projects as now accepted for Washington, are possible only under a government that is locally autocratic. Most cities of England, and especially of America, must make their revisions step by step. For this there is no less need of a good general scheme. That every step may count, that every improvement shall bring a lit-

tle nearer to realisation that complete scheme which
would be best, there must be a fixed ideal in mind.
That is why civic art insists so earnestly on the value
of the principles of a general street plan. If we have
not these, we shall be in danger of widening at great
cost a street that comes from nowhere and leads to
nothing, that for all its width will be deserted because the through travel takes a route that is more
direct; we shall be opening spaces to which there is
no convergence of thoroughfares, or we shall make
a mockery of "improvement" by choking a corner
with criss-cross travel through focusing important
streets where there is only a street's width to handle
the converging traffic.

That such dangers are before us always, that the
problem of the street plan even in the business district is not theoretical, there is abundant proof. Consider the changes that London is making, while this
is being written, in the widening of the Strand and
the opening of the great new thoroughfare from Holborn to the Strand. In New York the administration
is having public hearings on the plans for street approaches to the new bridges. In Pittsburg the Architectural Club has lately had a competition of plans
"for the improvement of the down-town districts."
In Toronto the like project is under earnest public
discussion. In San Francisco it has been seriously
taken up. New stations, new bridges, new buildings, and, above all, the growing congestion of an
increasing population — so sadly felt where there is

no scientific plan of circulation — are forcing these problems ever before us.

When the new charter for Greater New York was prepared, the need of rectifying the street system, and of doing this in accordance with a comprehensive scheme that should not be unduly influenced by local considerations, was felt so keenly that provision was made for a general Board of Public Improvements. An accident of politics put on the first board some incompetent men, and in disgust the board was abolished when the charter was revised. But the need remained, and there came to be demanded even the creation of an expert commission, such as that which was working so successfully for Washington. The problem in its universal application is not, as we have seen, merely that of circulation. The traffic is not alone in clamouring for its solution. It is presented also that adequate building sites may be provided — sites that may be large enough for a great building, sites to which impressiveness of effect belong, and to which there may be noble approaches, sites that can offer a frontage on at least three streets without the necessity of owning half a block.

There is, perhaps, too common a notion that the way to secure comfort and convenience for the travel and to bestow on the business district of a city splendour of appearance is simply to widen streets. As well might one think that the one way to emphasise a word in speaking is to scream it, and that therein lay the secret of the art of oratory! The error must be clear from what has been said; but to emphasise it we may note that in Paris the Avenue de l'Opéra is one hundred and twenty feet wide, and the Rue de Rivoli one hundred feet wide, while in London Holborn, Oxford Street, and Bayswater Road have a width of seventy feet (and reach for four miles). Regent Street is eighty feet broad, and Queen Victoria Street seventy-five feet. We may ask ourselves how much of the difference in the impressions that these streets make is due to difference of width. As far as appearance goes, the architectural termini and the relative length are always stronger factors. The width demanded by the traffic alone is not, also, to be determined merely by the traffic's mass. The grade and the speed at which the travel moves must be carefully considered in interpreting the requirements of its volume.

There is, too, something to be said about the choice of the local improvements that are to be undertaken for bettering the urban conditions. There should be remembrance that it is the municipal, as much as the local, condition which it is necessary to improve. The committee of the London County Council which has this matter in charge states that in preparing its annual recommendations to the council it "gives the fullest consideration to the requirements of each district, and accordingly selects, from all parts of London, such improvements as are most urgently needed and which will be of the greatest advantage to the general through travel." This states the rule precisely.

Now, as to securing the radical street changes that may be required, there are in general five methods of procedure : first, the constructing authority may acquire only those properties the whole or portions of which are actually needed for the new or widened street. This is the method usually adopted by the London County Council. Second, there may be secured more land than is actually needed for the improvement, with a view to the gaining of valuable building sites. The plan is suggested in the quoted decree for the improvement of Vienna. Third, property over a large area through which the improvement passes may be acquired, with a view to abolishing a slum district for instance. Examples of this are found in some of the provincial cities of Great Britain and where large land improvement companies have operated. Fourth, the acquisition of only that property which is to be added to the public way and the levying of an improvement charge upon the adjacent lands. This is a familiar American method. Fifth, a modification of the third scheme to the extent that the acquirements are confined to freehold and long leasehold interests, the short leaseholds being allowed to run out. When the acquirements exceed the needs of the new or widened street itself there may be important recoupments by the sale of the sites made so much more valuable through the improvement. When the acquirements are not so considerable as to constitute good sites, or when no land is secured beyond that needed for the street itself,— which is pushed ruthlessly through, regardless of the cutting of lots,—there may be left along its edges building sites so meagre and fragmentary as to be comparatively worthless. In such case the improvement, instead of affording a handsome thoroughfare, results for a long time in only a dismal collection of the backs of buildings and of patches of vacant land. Such an outcome must be anticipated and guarded against in making the new street.

There is one other consideration to influence sometimes the location of new business thoroughfares, or to add to the estimate of their value. It has been found that often there is no better way to redeem a slum district than by cutting into it a great highway that will be filled with the through travel of a city's industry. Like a stream of pure water cleansing what it touches, this tide of traffic, pulsing with the joyousness of the city's life of toil and purpose, when flowing through an idle or suffering district wakes it to larger interests and higher purpose.

There is, finally, this to remember, and it is the especial text of municipal æsthetics. Until there is a good street plan, modern civic art can come to little. A Greek sculptor charged his pupil with having richly ornamented a statue because he " knew not how to make it beautiful." Beauty is dependent on a fineness of line, a chastity of form, the lack of which can be atoned for by no ornament that is superimposed,

by no added decoration.   And this is no more true
in sculpture than in the street plan, which is the
skeleton of the city, the framework of the structure
in the highest and most complex of all the arts — the
art of noble city-building.

CHAPTER VII.

ARCHITECTURE IN THE BUSINESS DISTRICT.

WE have seen that a street which is badly planned can look for little stateliness or even beauty, however meritorious is the construction along its borders or the decoration heaped upon it. Conversely, we have seen that the best planned street requires, for full effect, the safeguarding of its architecture, the establishment of a building line, probably of a cornice line, and the protection of statutes regulating the height of balconies and awnings and the construction of porticoes over the walks. These are all matters that deal indeed with the architecture, but their design primarily is to guard the beauty or dignity of the way. The regulation and the obligations of construction become, then, a distinct phase of civic æsthetics.

This is not merely because architecture is so important in itself that whatever protects it or adds to its imposing character adds immensely to the impression made by the city. It is because the street is so dependent on the architecture for the effect which is offered, that the latter becomes practically a constructive element of the street. Especially must this be true in the business district, where the lots contain no open space before the structures that will divide responsibility for the aspect of the way. In this district particularly, then, would civic art cherish the architecture, and with an equal zeal for the street's and architecture's sake. In this district, too, the architecture is of so distinct a type from that in the residential area as to offer in any event a separate problem.

The most striking modern characteristic of the construction which is to be found in the business districts of cities is height. There are not wanting some indications of a reaction; but for the present at least, and for some years to come, the surpassing height of great office buildings will be the most dominant feature of the business area. More than this, the permanent level of building height for the whole district has been raised so greatly, whatever the possible reaction, as to constitute in itself a clear division between old and modern construction methods.

The influence of this on civic art is pronounced. Tall buildings are concentrators of business. Great office structures, side by side or facing each other across a narrow street, may easily house a daytime population of three to five thousand persons. A population as large as was spread over a square mile or more of these same streets, in the days of the village from which the city grew, is now crowded upon

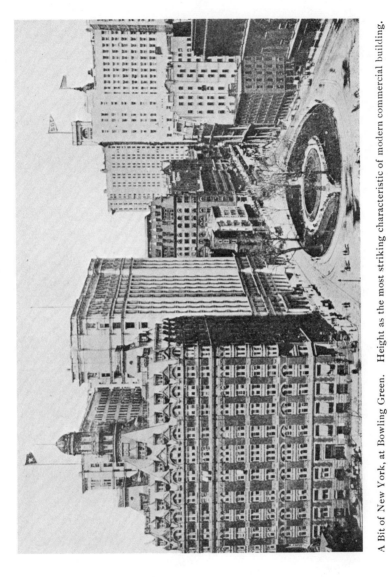

A Bit of New York, at Bowling Green.   Height as the most striking characteristic of modern commercial building.

one block of one street. It is this circumstance which has lately urged, with an insistence that has become compulsion, the widening of many thorough-fares, the cutting through of new streets, and the study of a scientific system of street planning. The tall building requires a wide street quite as much be-cause of the congestion of travel it brings as because it shuts the sunshine out of narrow streets or because it cannot be fitly seen without a perspective sufficient at least to offer an appreciable visual angle. Yet these latter considerations are potent also. They belong more obviously to the field of art. They ex-plain the æsthetic desirability of wide streets where tall buildings are. In the present discussion, how-ever, we are assuming the street and have to con-sider the building.

A degree of harmony if not of uniformity is clearly to be desired in the buildings along the thoroughfare. The business street is essentially formal. There is nothing in the world more artificial, for there is not a stick or stone of it which has not been placed by the hand of man. Orderliness, therefore, is required. We can liken the side of a street to a line of type. The letters need not be of precisely the same height and should not be of exactly the same form and width, but glaring contrasts will shock and offend. A line composed of such a mingling of exclamation points and periods as might well stand (with here and there an interrogation inserted) for many a business street would be a total failure artistically. The same would be true of a line in which colours were hopelessly jumbled. Some regularity, then, in skyline and in lines of balcony and cornice is desirable, with a harmony of tint. The pauses, however, will be clearly marked. These are the accents of the street.

There ought to be an established maximum of height above which no edifice shall rise. A defeat of efforts to establish such a limit can be due only to the strength of private interests. The larger, public interest is altogether in favour of the restriction. Any extensive construction of tall buildings inevitably leads on narrow thoroughfares to a street congestion so unbearable that remedies must be had and these remedies will be extremely costly. The restriction is required, then, (1) for the street's sake, from various points of view; (2) for the building's own sake, since, the ground area being limited, there is a height at which the proportions cease to be pleasant; (3) for the protection of every meritorious structure so that a neighbour, towering immensely higher, may not dwarf it. The first requirement is made the basis of the familiar building statute in European cities, which proportions to the width of the thoroughfare the height of the structures bordering upon it, with a designated maximum limit — moderately increased, sometimes, of course, where the street widens into a plaza.[1] The second requirement is in the heart of the architect, but save in buildings of exceptional

[1] A similar ordinance is occasionally found in the United States — as in St. Louis, for example.

artistic character or in public structures may not have expression. The third requirement is embodied in occasional local legislation, of which the special building regulations enacted for Copley Square in Boston — that a tall apartment house should not dwarf, as projected, the existing examples of beautiful architecture — is a notable illustration.

Equally desirable, and for similar reasons, is the establishment of a minimum building height for any given street, and this need also is recognised by statute in Europe. In fact, it has been seriously suggested in London that when a new street is planned it were well for the committee of the County Council, when formulating the proposal, to invite the views of leading architects and engineers, and on their recommendations to draw up a general scheme providing for the principal feature of the building elevations. In due time the avenue would then have not only convenience but dignity and beauty. If this were done, not in London only but wherever new streets are planned for commercial districts, the progress of contemporary civic art would be more striking.

That the greater height of building, made possible by the modern method of steel construction, will in itself add much to the imposing character of the business district, to its seeming importance, solidity, and impressiveness, if it be so curbed and regulated that there is a degree of uniformity in the rise of the building level, scarcely needs a saying. Between a

street forty feet wide lined with low brick or stucco
structures, and a thoroughfare eighty feet wide with
a border of modern commercial buildings, there is no
comparison, as far as strictly urban effectiveness
goes. But everything must be in scale. The ten-
and eleven-story buildings that make a striking
group around the Old Granary Burial Ground in
Boston, where the law has limited building heights
to one hundred and twenty-five feet, would lose
their impressiveness in New York. There the inter-
polated twenty-story structures would dwarf them.
"Sky-scrapers," however, which rise from two
hundred to two hundred and fifty feet are necessarily
scattered, if only to protect their own light. They
establish a standard to which there cannot be uniform adherence, and the failures to adhere to it look
puny. So there is lost all that impressiveness which
comes from mere order and regularity, while elsewhere
lower structures lose nothing of seeming importance
if there be no higher by which to measure them.

Regarding the size of buildings, and especially
their height, there is, too, another thing to be observed. This is the proportion to be maintained with
respect to the vista in which they come. There has
been note of the value of monumental construction
at focal points. Is there need of the statement that
the construction should be adjusted to the view which
is afforded from converging streets, that it may be
neither too massive nor too small and insignificant?
This will not be an easy thing to adjust by statute.

It also must be in the heart of the architect, or, if the building antedates the street, in the heart of him who plans the latter. The south end of the Treasury, in Washington, as it is seen from the Capitol, has been happily cited as an example. Large as it is, it is too small to count in a view down the length of Pennsylvania Avenue.

The conscientious architect will strive also to establish a relation between the height of his building and the length of its façade; and if his building is at a topographical axis or centre, where prominence is thrust upon it and large size is excusable, if not indeed required, he will see to it that the structure shall still form a definite composition with its neighbours. Finally he will try to put into the appearance of the building something of appropriateness to its purpose, to its location, and its architectural period. When old London Bridge was demolished and a new one made, there was wisely planned a broad approach on the Southwark side. High Street at that time was rich in pointed gables, florid plaster work, diamond casements, and half-timbered overhanging stories. These picturesque features were swept away with the broad approach; there followed a line of monotonous brick fronts — genuine, if homely — and then these were superseded by a row of "Grecian and Italianised façades" that in Southwark could have no meaning beyond a homesick dream or silly imitation. Civic art is in the broad approach and the clearing out of unsanitary rookeries;

9

but there goes with it such a loss, also of civic art, in the style of building which has succeeded, that the beholder does not readily appreciate the existence of a net advantage. These are not, however, matters readily reached by law, unless there be established a commission to pass upon the artistic features of the plan of every projected building as certainly as upon its sanitation. But the thoughts emphasise the many obligations of the architect, and civic art's great dependence on him.

In that remodelling of cities which new conditions make so conspicuous a feature in modern urban development and which is a potent stimulus to municipal æsthetics, it must often happen that in the older communities the location of a new street might endanger some building of historical or architectural interest. But the charm of a street is not dependent on newness. Historical interest is not to be lightly ignored and beauty is ever fresh. The special committee of the London County Council, which in such cases is charged to consider and report on the course of action to be taken; the commissions of experts to which these matters are relegated in French cities; the zealous official guardianship in Italy, Belgium, and Germany,— all this shows that the European cities which have had long experience, and where such opportunities come with more frequency than in America, value highly the chance thus given to secure or preserve picturesqueness, variety, interest, and assured structural beauty

on the street. Modern civic art would not be all
modern in its expression. It is no iconoclast where
beauty is concerned. And therein is one secret of
its power. Speaking merely from the architectural
standpoint, it would draw gladly on the treasures of
the ever lengthening past.

At the same time, every effort must be made to
render the present and future worthy of the best
remnants of the past. In France and Belgium, which
to-day are leaders in the more decoratively æsthetic
features of modern civic art, municipalities offer
prizes for the most beautiful façades. In Paris these
prizes go to owner, builder, and architect, the former
being exempted from half of his street tax and the
two latter receiving highly cherished medals. So in
the new conception of the city beautiful is impressed
the lesson of obligation to the community, the reminder that good taste — love of beauty and ability
to gratify it — should not be so selfish as to hide a
lovely or splendid interior behind a plain exterior,
and that to the city which has made possible a handsome street something in its turn is owing in a visible contribution to the general weal. It is not safe
to leave all this to the results of individual rivalry.
The façades, so long monotonous, in New York and
Philadelphia, and the homely fronts and high garden
walls that often hide beautiful interiors in England,
show the folly of so doing. It is proved again in
the familiar custom of the individual, when leasing
or selling part of a tract, to require that a certain

minimum sum shall be represented in the exterior of the building to be erected. Once such rivalry has, by artificial means, been started, there is needed no great spur to keep it active, but rather that artistic guidance and control which can be given in the building regulations.

In the business portions of a city the effects that are desired are rather those which can be called "stunning" than those dependent on the fineness and niceness of delicate design. In the business street there is inevitably much that is bizarre, blatant, and distracting. It is, further, the very purpose of the business house to attract attention, and civic art has something to be grateful for when, instead of making use of hideous advertisements, or striking colour, or great height, or sudden littleness in a wilderness of "sky-scrapers," the dependence for effect is placed on the dignity of the building's appearance, on the majesty of its proportions, on the impressiveness of its architectural treatment. That is why "stunning effect" can properly be desired in the structures of the business district.

For the topographical conditions that most favour the attainment of this effect there is more and more demand. The public buildings cannot well vie in height with commercial structures, they cannot appropriately attract attention by their diminutiveness, and even a dormant public spirit would awake in protest were it sought to attract attention to such structures by vivid colours or great signs. Hardly

less marked than this need by the public buildings is
the need, for similar reasons, by the banks, by the
clubs, by the homes of the exchanges and commercial bodies, by institutions financial, educational, and
benevolent.[1]   The greater the city becomes the more
urgent is the demand for topographical conditions
advantageous to architectural effect.   The result of
the demand, the available number of such positions
being limited, must be their rapid pre-emption by
this class of structure and their increasingly worthy
development.   That an occupation of such sites by
handsome buildings means much for the aspect of the
town, there is no need of saying.   It means so much
that we must provide many lots of this character
with the certainty that, if so abundant as to be available at last by even commercial structures, such opportunities will be offered to these that many even
of them will seek their effectiveness by artistic
means.

It has been pointed out that the ample provision
of favourable sites is one of the merits of a diagonal
street plan.   It should here be said that where there

[1] Good illustrations of the want of such sites are afforded by the important
buildings that now line narrow Chancery Lane in London, or by the situation of the
new Chamber of Commerce and the new Stock Exchange in New York.   Of the
latter Russell Sturgis has said, in an article in the *International Quarterly* (December,
1902): "There is a building in which for purposes of utility the most has been
made of a lot really too small for its purpose. . . . No courtyard, whether
of entrance (*cour d'honneur*) nor yet central and surrounded by buildings to which
it gives light, no showing in any one direction of the whole building or of any large
mass of it,— two façades on two parallel streets, and nothing else!"   Yet this costly
and beautiful structure is in its design one of the most ambitiously decorative in
New York, and it fails of its full purpose mainly because of the poor chance to see it.

are no open spaces or advantageously placed corners, architecture may yet discover opportunities. In seeking these it will value the broad, curving street, and in itself — as an art — will find no fault with grade. Approaches, also, count strongly with a building. The thing most to be dreaded is the narrow, straight street, with rectangular crossings and every block alike in size and given over to building. That condition is thoroughly discouraging.

There may once have been some reason for a notion that the cities of a democracy could be humdrum in their business districts. Unless we imagine such an idea, how shall we account for the failure to provide noble sites when the plans of the new cities of America were laid down on paper? There must have been a well-nigh universal thought that the splendour of empire and monarchy being over, the need of palaces and of provision for pageantry having passed, and a people having settled down content to be tradesmen without an "upper class," there would be, in the parts of the town where they did their business and with entire equality earned their livings, no need to have one street differ from another — save as volume of travel might require greater or lesser width. But if that idea was ever held, the time has gone when it could be seriously put forward or supported from facts.

The fast increasing wealth of the United States is reflected nowhere more strikingly than in the growing splendour of city structures, and naturally so since toward the cities is the strongly marked trend of population, and they must be always the financial centres. In them, too, there must be massed, in a congestion eminently spectacular, those evidences of riches, luxury, and aspiration that, if widely scattered, might mean as much, but would prove far less striking. When we think that in a single city, for example,— within a space that may be traversed by rapid-transit in half an hour,— there are congregated such evidences of financial wealth as the new Stock Exchange in New York, of commercial precedence as the new Chamber of Commerce, of shipping importance as the noble new Custom House, of business resources as afforded by such private structures as the Equitable Life building or some of its neighbours, of ecclesiastical welfare as Trinity Church, St. Thomas's, St. Patrick's Cathedral, and the Cathedral of St. John the Divine, of magnetic power to wealthy transients as offered by a dozen palatial hotels, of private fortune as shown by the splendour of innumerable individual homes, of the ability to gratify aspirations in art as revealed by the Metropolitan Museum and its noble housing, or educational aspirations as shown by the Public Library and the buildings of Columbia University, or the yearnings of philanthropy as shown in St. Luke's Hospital, or of patriotism as indicated by the Soldiers' and Sailors' Memorial or the Grant Monument, when — to name a very few illustrations of a very few types — there are congregated in small compass such a variety of

noble structures, structures at least upon which the
artistic genius of the day has been lavishly expended
and from which money has not been withheld, it is
clear that cities cannot be, as they never have been,
humdrum.   They make demand for a supply of commanding sites and, these afforded, there will be raised
structures of a pretentiousness and straining for effect
that will insure variety, and of a significance that
will guarantee the interest of the way.

Nor has modern civic art occasion to fear lest
these buildings offer to the architect, in purpose and
requirement, less opportunity or inspiration than did
their prototypes of the golden days of earlier civilisations.   There were never any cities larger than those
of the present time, there was rarely such wealth
massed in them as to-day, there was never before so
long a past from which to draw the lessons of experience, and never a people so familiar with that
past.   There was never so broad a world to be ran-
sacked for treasures as we have now, never so wide
a field from which to select genius, never such a con-
course of spectators as in this travelling time from
which to win applause or condemnation.   Now that
we have suddenly turned our thoughts in this direction, there is not lacking the spur to great achievement.   Of all the huge buildings in the United States
there is hardly one equals a certain city hall, with
its nearly five thousand tenants; and of all the beautiful buildings nine out of the ten that have been ad-
judged the loveliest are public structures.   The vast

city hall happens to have little of art about it, but the opportunity it offered was magnificent. The great cities, now so rapidly re-building, teem with architectural chances; the most favourable sites command highest prices; and civic art is working at no problem with such eagerness, with such assurance of immediately transforming results, as at the reconstruction of cities in the new housing of their activities.

The need of to-day is not so much to incite as wisely to restrain, pointing out that in the long run the height that most counts in a building is the height of the architect's ideal; the richness, that of his fancy; the solidity, that of his self-restraint. The need is that he should realise that his problem is not that of a building only, but of a city.

CHAPTER VIII.

THE FURNISHINGS OF THE STREET.

A STREET consists of more than a passage cleared for travel with a line of building lots on either side. Although assuming, as modern civic art does, a good pavement, even curbs, well-laid walks, and an absence of overhead wires, with pavement and walk kept clean, there still remain other factors to mar the prospect or to adorn it. These are the street furnishings — details, indeed, but in as far as civic art is art it does not dare to scorn them. Rather, it will expend upon them that loving care, that fond attention, which art must ever give to the particulars which fill in and complete the picture after the main lines have been laid down and the dominating features are established. As furnishings of the business street, we may include the necessary lighting apparatus; the street name signs and post boxes that add so much to the convenience of the way; those isles of safety that are sometimes essential at busy crossings; the public-comfort stations, in so far as they are visible; the fire-alarm signal boxes; the trolley poles, if the overhead system be in operation; and, finally, those innumerable and variegated advertisements with which business placards the way.

The opportunity is urgent, broad, and varied. It is independent of merit or demerit in the street plan or in the construction at the street's edge. It may, if ably handled, do much to adorn a street noble in lines and splendid in edifices, but it is not the less pressing where conditions are unfavourable. The problem is, also,— we should note,— strictly modern. With the street plan and the construction at the building line, the civic art of the earliest civilisations had to deal. With the furnishings of the street, as this term is understood to-day, it had no concern.

An interesting illustration of the gradually developed necessity of our street furnishings, and the evolution of their present type, is found in the lighting apparatus. This might well have been, one would think, a problem of the earliest cities. Yet in the beginning it was considered a private rather than a public matter. In the civic Renaissance of Italy, for instance, the street lighting was left to the façades of the abutting structures; and how well the problem, when thus changed, could be handled, that ancient civic art now discloses in the lanterns of the Strozzi Palace at Florence. But the thought of lighting cities had already been long postponed through the fact that those who had to see their way at night were individuals, not the masses. Nor is it strange, since every lamp required separate care before it could be lighted, that when, at last, their provision in the street could be conceived as a civic duty, lights were still made individual charges. If the individual pleased to shirk so publicly his obligation to the community (newly conceived as that duty was), street lamps were omitted altogether.

Mankind began, we should remark, by staying home at nights, taking the hint that darkness meant that day was over; and if his duty or his pleasure did take him forth, he went at his own risk and carried, as he still carries in the country, his own light. The notion that the street before his door might be kept lighted, for his own convenience when he went abroad and at other times for the profit of his prowling neighbours, came, then, very slowly, and it might have been yet longer in arriving if there had not been perception that the fixture for the light could be made a highly decorative feature of the house. So, quite like the balcony, ornamental as well as useful, the street lights were left to the mercy of the builders, and civic art, as civic, took little heed of them.

The public function of the lights was slowly appreciated better as their number multiplied, and when it became possible to lay gas mains through the streets and so to keep all the lamps simultaneously in readiness for lighting — which now required only a touch of flame — the city could appropriately and conveniently take charge by contract of the lighting of its streets, henceforth to run no risk of individual delinquencies. The manifold advantages were apparent; and the oil lamp, though less convenient to manage than the gas lamp, was similarly made a street furnishing, and was cared for indirectly if not directly by employees of the town. By the time that modern civic art began, oil lamps were considered no more than temporary makeshifts, abandoned, for the most part, to outlying and sparsely settled portions of cities, or to small villages. The new art felt little call to give thought to them, and it was just turning its attention to gas lights when electricity appeared. For this reason its conquests in gas fixtures, though here and there important, are yet so widely scattered that the gas lamp of the city street is still usually ugly — multiplied by tens of thousands in the strictly utilitarian shape in which it first came from the factory. The electric light required such an entirely different kind of apparatus as in its turn to present a new problem, and civic art has but lately found time seriously to consider its artistic possibility.

As to the gas lamps, which must still be considered, the candelabra of Paris, arranged for single, double, or grouped lights, are probably the best. Naturally the open spaces, the showy and more decorative parts of a city, have first attention in efforts to bring beauty into street utilities, and we find no examples in Paris more elaborate and ornate than the fixtures on the Place de la Concorde. In Brussels — the "little Paris" in so many things — a prize offered by L'Œuvre Nationale Belge early in its career was for an artistic street light, and was awarded to the designer of a single candelabrum to stand on the Place de la Monnaie, where it was subsequently erected.

The terms of this competition, conducted by a national society organised for the furthering of civic art, had invited the municipalities to "designate those public places" which it was desired to light artistically. A long step in advance was made by such recognition that the site and apparatus had a relation, that the kind of fixture which would be beautiful and artistic in one location might fail in another because no longer in harmony with its surroundings or proportioned to its position. This was a new idea. If there had been any thought of bringing beauty into the lighting apparatus, it had heretofore contented itself with a desire for a better design which should be universally adopted as far as any particular town was concerned. Perhaps even this new expression of an old art truth, that particular environments demand particular treatment, owed something to an economic condition. Certainly a costlier fixture was more likely to be adopted for a showy square, where a few examples could be conspicuously fixed, than on the streets, where a great number would be needed and comparatively little noticed, once their striking ugliness were removed.

To secure, then, for the open spaces of the town especially made designs, that shall fit with certainty into their location; to secure for the business streets a design of lighting post that shall be at least correct in its proportions, appropriate in its style, and graceful in its lines, and its universal adoption on those streets; and then to secure for the residential streets a third and perhaps a fourth design, altered to suit the new environments,—that is ambition enough for most developments of modern civic art. Nor does such a possibility fall far short of the ideal. For such is the formality of a city street in the essential evenness of its lines that regularly recurring light fixtures may properly have a formal likeness of pattern in a given portion of the town where surrounding conditions are similar. If alike graceful and sufficiently conspicuous they will not unpleasantly emphasise the formality of the business street, while the break that is made by the open space will be, in turn, the more strongly marked by the adoption of a different and here better-suited style of apparatus.

It is natural, as noted, that the beginnings of civic art should be characterised by efforts to secure the beauty of the exceptional, but particularly noticeable, light rather than of the ordinary. In New York, the resuscitated Municipal Art Society, desiring to do a popular thing,—which was to say a practical and conspicuous thing,—announced early in 1902 a competition for an electrolier to be placed at

the edge of one of the most important open spaces
of the city — the intersection of Fifth Avenue and
Twenty-third Street. This particular electrolier was
to be combined with an isle of safety, then greatly
needed; but for the present it is enough to note
that the first undertaking was an attempted decoration of the street by providing a beautiful utility, and
that the utility chosen was the lighting apparatus at
a notable point. The competition aroused much attention, both among artists and laymen; and of
the three designs for which prizes were awarded,
one at least was commonly considered to be very
good. The event's art significance, however, lay
not so much in the victory there gained as in the
grappling of the problem, in the elaborate effort to
obtain beauty in a public lighting fixture. The student of civic art cannot fail to be interested in this
occurrence. In what other period in the history of
the world have private citizens banded together and
contributed money that a light fixture on a street
might be beautiful ?

And yet the student, looking closely, must wonder whether the development has reached its end,
whether civic art will not progress beyond the need
of any fixture for street lights; whether, to be explicit, the uprights, though they be ever so ornamental, are not as distinct a transition phase as is
the old wooden post of the oil lamp, even when the
village improvers paint it green. For now there is
hardly a lovelier picture on earth than the night

view of a great city — its thousands of lights twinkling in a mighty constellation. Here is a firmament comprehensible because earthbound, but not the less marvellous for that. Its stars sing together, and their song is of the might of ourselves. The little heaven is rolled out before us, as a scroll. We know its lines well, we can read in our hearts the possible meaning of every star. Their very number is written. And the myriad lights have such beauty, independent of sentiment, that their effect has sunk deep in the hearts of men. We would make our expositions lovely; and lo! with the new-found power of electricity we print on the darkness in miniature the glow of a city's lights. Ever as our mastery of electricity becomes completer, the picture is made lovelier by multiplying lights. The roofs, bases, and corners of buildings are outlined with them. Every cornice, balcony, pinnacle, glows. The darkness of night is turned to the brightness of day, with the addition of a fairyland of mystery. The streets of the exposition are bright almost as in sunshine.

The wonder of the display and the ease with which it is gained make an impression. The cities begin to have buildings outlined in hundreds of lights. Here and there a dome hangs in the sky as if pinned there with golden pins. The strands of a great bridge hang like a necklace of brilliants. A cross of fire among the stars means that a city's church spire there points heavenward. It becomes necessary to enact legislation prohibiting a barbarous

10

use of lights.   The business streets nightly blaze
with them, as never for a festival a few years since.
And civic art ?   Does it wrestle still with the problem
of separate fixtures, placed at regular intervals, occupying precious space and costing much ?   Has it
no dreams of lighting the business parts of cities as
expositions have been successfully lighted ?   It is
doubtful if a harmonious general scheme of such
illumination would cost more than is now expended
privately on the shopping streets.   Certainly it
would cost no more than the total of the public and
private lighting together ; and into what a scene of
beauty and enchantment the business district would
be then transformed at night!   May not this be the
near solution of the lighting problem in that city
beautiful which is the dream of civic art ?

Already, sections of cities have been turned into
such fairylands for gala nights.   The illumination of
the " Court of Honour " in Philadelphia, at the Peace
Jubilee in 1898, when to a section of a business
street there was given the night glory of an exposition ; the transformation of seven blocks of State
Street in Chicago for the Fall Festival of 1899, when
eleven thousand electric lights and nearly four hundred flambeaux flung their radiance on the street ;
the lighting of the public buildings and boulevards
of Paris for the fête of July 14th, in 1900 ; the illumination of Monument Square in Cleveland for the
Grand Army of the Republic encampment in 1901 ;
and the lighting of a district of San Francisco, in

honour of a gathering of Knights of Pythias in
1902, when eighteen thousand two hundred electric
lights were used on the few blocks of the chosen
area, exclusive of the lamps that outlined the colon-
ades and dome of the City Hall, the high tower of
the Ferry building, and a great commercial structure,
— these are typical actual applications of the new
lighting plan in cities, showing its feasibility, its
popularity, and its æsthetic merits.   Merchants, perceiving the commercial advantages of a district
especially attractive because of its night beauty, will
do well to combine to the end that by co-operation
such radiance as now floods parts of Broadway, in
New York, for example, may be made harmonious
and lovely instead of glaring and crude.

The Municipal Art Society of New York in an-
nouncing its competition for an artistic electrolier,
required that it should be fixed upon an " isle of
safety "— by which is meant a raised platform of
refuge where the hunted pedestrian may take breath
in crossing the crowded road.   It is easy to imagine
such a platform without a lighting fixture, but one
will be rarely found.   Both the location and the
purpose invite the fixing of one or more lights upon
it.   Raised but a few inches above the pavement, it
is necessary that there be erected here something of
sufficient height to be seen at a distance, for there is
not only the danger otherwise of driving upon it,
but one of its purposes is to divide the travel into
distinct streams of opposite direction.   As the need

of seeing the tall structure is as great at night as by day, what more natural than that it should be a light ?   Again, the pedestrian who has taken refuge here, has done so that he may wait a favourable chance for the rest of his journey, so that the street isle should be not merely one of safety but also one well fitted for observation.   Finally, the location here of the lighting apparatus removes from walk or pavement a fixture that occupied precious space.   It is natural and common, therefore, that lights should be found on the isle of refuge, and that civic art should make of the two structures a single composition, as the Municipal Art Society of New York required should be done and as Paris has repeatedly done with success.

In Paris and other European cities a clock is often added to the light on the refuge, and the conspicuous fixture is also, especially when at a street intersection, an excellent and appropriate place for the street signs.   In all such cases, the refuge is the pedestal, or base, of one or more superstructures, and artistically is to be treated not as a separate problem but as a phase or part of a larger problem. In its proportions, however, in its relations to the street on which it is, and in the curve of its outline, the artist will find even in the refuge itself a worthy subject.

In regard to street name signs, we have here a street fixture of extreme importance.   Their position on the lighting apparatus of an isle of refuge, while

Isle of Safety and artistic Electrolier placed at Fifth Avenue and Twenty-third Street, New York, after a competition held by the Municipal Art Society.

appropriate, is a comparatively rare event, for street name signs are, or should be, at the intersections of all streets, and the isles of safety even in large cities are few. In addition to their number, the signs have importance because it is essential that they be made conspicuous objects of the way. They must not thrust themselves upon the traveller, but they must be readily found and easily understood when he sees them. A glance must suffice to find and read the sign, for often the traveller will be whirling past his corner at a rapid rate. They must be as clearly visible by night as by day; and, finally, as such prominent objects of the street, civic art must insist that they have the æsthetic attention deserved.

These requirements lay down certain principles: the street name signs should have a regular and uniform location — not necessarily the same throughout the urban area, but always the same under the same conditions. This will enable the traveller, perceiving the character of his surroundings, to look at once to the right place for the name of the street. Again, the system employed in conveying the sign's information should be uniform. If at a given corner the street name should be, for example, printed parallel with the street named, the arrangement should be identical throughout the community. Finally, the name must be so located that there will be a good light on it at night. This requirement has suggested making it a lamp so that a light burning within shall compel its message to be very plain; and it has suggested the fixing of the street names upon the regular lighting apparatus — on the globe, in the case of the gas lamp; and on the pole, possibly with reflectors to draw rays of light down to the sign, in the case of the electrolier. But this need would not interfere with the sign's location on the wall of a structure built flush with the walk, for the corner street lights usually render such location perfectly distinct while it has the further advantages of solidity, relative permanence, economy of cost since it requires no special standard, and economy of precious street space. The main objection to the location is the difficulty in obtaining uniformity. Not only will the height of the sign vary, but frequently there will be no building to attach it to, and in any case different varieties of architecture will suggest different styles of lettering, so that the bewildered traveller will not know exactly where to look nor precisely what to look for. The use by Paris of illuminated advertising pillars, that contain also letter boxes, suggests that the street name sign might be written here and the column, which is really a source of municipal income, be made to serve many useful public purposes besides. American cities, however, are not, as a rule, ready for such municipal business undertakings as the provision, for revenue, of public advertising columns. There is, further, the general objection to putting the street name here, that it will lose its immediate effectiveness in a confusion of lettering.

A need for new street name signs throughout the

borough of Manhattan in New York, and an officially expressed determination that the design adopted should be not only convenient but possessed of as much artistic merit as possible, presented in 1902 an unusual invitation for experiment. This was availed of by the Municipal Art Society, by local improvement associations, and by firms and individuals. Thus a very interesting collection of designs was obtained. Of these it may be said that the most successful added the sign to the existing lighting apparatus, finding in the material of the latter the substance from which to make a suitable frame. As every corner has its street lamp, and the signs may be placed at a regular height, there is secured that uniformity of location which is so essential. The similarity, again, in the style of street light makes possible, without architectural incongruity, that likeness in shape, colour, and size which is necessary in order that the merest glance will leave no uncertainty as to the meaning of the legend borne. It was shown, also, that it is possible to make here again a single composition, the street sign becoming an integral part of the fixture without losing its own identity and sufficient prominence.

Mention of the municipal advertising columns opens one of the most difficult problems of street furnishing. This is the advertising on the public way. It may as well be admitted that there will be advertising. A commercial street, lined with imposing architecture, the façades unmarred by lettering,

no screaming signs, by day no glaring colours, by
night no flashing advertisements, all dignity, repose,
and self-contained placidity,—this would possibly be
the vision of the city ideally fair and stately. But
modern civic art is nothing if not practical. It would
dismiss such a vision as unattainable, and perhaps as
not wholly desirable. As civic art, it would not
crush out of its ideal the whirr and hum of traffic, the
exhilarating evidences of nervous energy, enterprise,
vigour, and endeavour. It loves the straining,
striving, competing, as the most marked of urban
characteristics, and when it advocates broad streets
conveniently arranged, it does this not to silence the
bustle of commerce, but to make the efforts more
surely and quickly efficient. So modern civic art,
coming to the advertising problem, should feel not
hostility but the thrill of opportunity. It will recognise evils in the present methods, but will find them
the evils of excess and unrestraint, and it will perceive
possibilities of artistic achievement by which even
the advertising can be made to serve the ends of *art
dans la rue.*

The first duty would be, doubtless, to curb unrestraint and to check, so far as might be, excessiveness.
The street at least civic art can claim as its own pro-
vince, bidding advertisements stand back to the
building line. No hindrance should be offered to a
clear path for travel by walk or road; no announce-
ment should break the vista of the street, nor thrust
itself before the wayfarer by hanging over the walk

or standing upon it at door or curb. The street should be a clear passage — that is its object in the making; and there is as true a need that every inch of it be open to the sky as that the vista of the way be unbroken. This means that civic art, turning its attention to the furnishings of the street, would frown upon all projecting signs; that it would prohibit all bulletin boards, signs, and transparencies on the sidewalk or at the curb; that it would have no banners hung across the street, nor would suffer any public utility or ornament of the way to be placarded. It would sweep the street itself clean of advertisements from building front to building front.

Does this demand seem too large, the ideal too high to be practical? There is not a particle of it that has not now been somewhere framed in city ordinance — revealing a public approval of each individual item in the count and an imagination that popularly has tried its wings and needs only daring to fly far.

Projecting-sign ordinances are extremely common. Even where these do not entirely prohibit the signs, they make it necessary to ask permission for their erection, and then almost certainly limit the height above the walk at which they may be fixed.[1] In regard to the removal of bulletin boards, signs, and

[1] As far back as the reign of George III. in England this matter of clearing the street of sidewalk obstructions was a recognised necessity. The preamble to an Act of II. George III., cap. 23, 1771, recites that the passage through certain streets in the parish of Aldgate, in the county of Middlesex, was " greatly obstructed by posts, projections, and other nuisances, and annoyed by spouts, signs, and gutters." The enactment is " that all houses and buildings hereafter to be built or new fronted shall, for the effectual and absolute prevention of all manner of projections, annoy-

transparencies from a position on the walk, probably the most interesting case to be cited is that offered by the Merchants' Association of San Francisco. The special interest of this is the circumstance that the prime movers in demanding the enforcement of the existing ordinance and the increase of its restrictive power were merchants, not a few impractical and visionary merchants, but the whole great body of the city's business men, the advertisers themselves; and that the action, taken formally and after long thought, was that of the association which represented them and which is one of the strongest commercial bodies in the United States. *The Merchants' Association Review* summed up the action in these words: "It has been decided by the board of directors, after full consideration, to recommend to the Board of Public Works that all bulletin boards, signs, and transparencies on the outer edge of sidewalks be removed, and that nothing of this character be permitted hereafter." The whole discussion and ordinance are most interesting and suggestive.[1]

ances, and inconveniences thereby, rise perpendicularly from the foundation." In 1834 an act made all signs, sign-irons, sign-posts, barbers' poles, dyers' poles, stalls, blocks, bulks, show-boards, butchers' hooks, spouts, water-pipes, and other projections in front of the houses in Bermondsey liable to removal at the demand of the local commissioners.

[1] The ordinance as finally drawn up presented a compromise in regard to "signs and transparencies on poles," at the outer edge of the walk. These were to be permitted if they were of a design approved by the Board of Public Works and if they bore a clock, — which should be kept accurate,— or lights having a minimum total of 192 candle-power, to be kept lighted every night from sunset to midnight at the expense of the person erecting or maintaining the sign. The argument was that the sign or transparency "would thus benefit the public in exchange for occupying a portion of the public thoroughfare." But this was unsatisfactory, and the final enactment was that only ornamental clocks without name or advertisement should stand at the curb.

In this connection there will be thought again of
the advertising kiosks of many Continental cities,
notably of Paris. Paris has done so much in civic
art that she has gained for herself a reputation that
makes it easier to judge kindly than justly of her
experiments in the furnishing of the street and the
adornment of the city. Could the municipality that
has so bridged the Seine and lined it with noble quays, that has transformed slum districts into
magnificent boulevards, that has made the Place
de la Concorde one of the most brilliant scenes in
the world and yet considers it but an incident in that
belt of urban splendour of which the gardens of the
Tuilleries, the long vista of the Champs Élyseés, the
streets radiating from the Arch of the Star, the Avenue du Bois de Boulogne, and then the Bois itself
are but other parts,— could that city have made a
mistake in permitting the erection of kiosks along
the walks ? How picturesque these kiosks are, and
how much better to concentrate the miscellane-
ous advertising upon them than to scatter it along
the highway ! Little wonder that other cities have
followed the Paris example. But civic art should
have before it a vision of a city beautiful that is no
more Paris, though equally practicable and attainable,
than it is any other particular place. The question is
not, "Does Paris do this ? " but, "Is this the best
practical solution ? " The kiosks are picturesque,
and it is better to concentrate the poster advertising
and put its æsthetic character under control than not

to restrain it. This much may be admitted ; and yet can any one, walking along the Paris streets and giving an unbiassed judgment, declare that these thoroughfares would not be better were all the newspaper kiosks and advertising columns removed ? As a step in the right direction, the experiment is to be commended ; but it is to be considered a step, not a goal. There is, too, a peril in partial advance, lest satisfaction with relative relief grow into contentment. It were better and safer to banish at once all the advertisements from the walk.

Finally, as to banners across the street and the placarding of public utilities and ornaments. The *Review*, published by the San Francisco Merchants' Association, editorially declared, with reference to the first point, in 1901 : "The constant opposition of the association has resulted in freeing our streets from this conspicuous disfigurement." The objection to over-street banners, of which this action in San Francisco is an expression, is common.

What has been said of advertising columns and newspaper kiosks should of course apply with added force to the posting of placards or advertisements on any fixture of the public way,—on any utility, such as the lighting apparatus, or the trolley poles and bicycle racks where these exist. With still greater emphasis, again, must it apply to such decorative furnishings of the street as trees, to the very vitality of which injury may be done by attaching signs, or as statues and public monuments. New York or

London would not permit so atrociously incongruous an act as the posting of bills on the latter, and
yet, it is significantly to be noted, this became so
serious an evil in Paris that a special committee was
appointed to look into the subject just after the Exposition of 1900, when the criticism of foreigners, so
it is said, aroused the French to a realisation of the
impropriety. It is fair to say that an ordinance
already existed which forbade the attachment of
commercial posters to such structures, but the pedestals of statues and the walls and even the doors
of public buildings were plastered with political announcements. So we find even Paris markedly negligent regarding one widely recognised necessity of
civic art. But we have seen that in the broad review
of cities there is now enforced somewhere, though
individually, each item of a list that in the aggregate
would sweep the streets free of advertisements from
building wall to building wall.

These are the restrictive demands. Civic art, it
was said, however, should perceive in the advertising in the business districts such possibilities of good
as almost to forget hostility in the thrill of the
opportunity. For it would not destroy the commercial aspect of the streets, it would not have
them shorn of the marks of enterprise and competition. It would ask only that the public way itself
be free and clear, that irrelevant announcements be
not thrust upon it, and that glaring ill taste and
offensive gaudiness be not shown in the display.

The subject is too large to be gone into here with detail, and the author has treated it pretty fully in another book [1]; but the ideal can be summed up briefly: After the restrictive demands, it would ask, as the positive requirements, that all window announcements be made in gold leaf, neatly and with as few words as may be; that there be encouragement of the rebus sign, in which an arbitrarily chosen device symbolises a trade,—as the three golden balls stand for the pawnbroker's,—so taking the place of considerable lettering; that all advertisements attached to building façades be below a certain height, —thirty feet has been suggested,—and that their size be proportioned to the front surface area under the adopted advertising height-limit of the building to which they are affixed; that all the signs externally attached, and all rebus signs, be made, as far as possible, a decorative element of the structure itself, so harmonising with and entering into the architecture as to increase rather than lessen its effectiveness; finally, that there be a genuine effort to bring art and beauty into the sign, in recognition that it will then gain better commercial results than when hideous.

It is proper here to say that ugly assertiveness secures only an instant's attention and is turned from with disgust; beauty and fitness, which is to say art, are looked at long and with pleasure and are turned to again and again. In most cases, also,

[1] See "The Advertisement Problem," Chapter V. of *The Improvement of Towns and Cities*, G. P. Putnam's Sons.

they can be secured at no greater cost than that involved in providing the strikingly ugly. There has been successful test of this in the competitions conducted by L'Œuvre Nationale Belge, which have lately resulted in the placing of many beautiful signs on the streets of Antwerp and Brussels; and in the exhibition held in the Hôtel de Ville, Paris, in 1902, when some two hundred shop signs were submitted in a competition of artists. It may be objected that the ancient, pictured sign-board rose out of a need, in the illiteracy of the times. When servants and many masters could not read, there was a real urgency that it should be possible to recognise a shop by its picture sign, and that one should be able to direct an enquirer to "the sign of the rose," etc. The reaction came when printed words sufficed. But if now we refuse to read the printed words attentively — as most of us do — there is as good an excuse as of old for a sign that shall not only arrest attention but dwell pleasantly in the memory.

The requirements as a whole are so obviously reasonable, and are becoming so widely endorsed even without their formal statement, that enunciation of them seems almost trite. Many large advertisers are already showing, by their works, their faith in the mild Belgian dictum that in advertising "art is not incompatible with economy and the necessities of trade." A vast change in the aspect of the business street would be caused by faithful adherence to these requirements. Civic art would

have something to be proud of, if it could point
to a modern business street the vista of which was
unbroken by overhead banners or projecting signs,
the walks of which were clear for travel, and on
which, at the building lines, there were harmonious
façades of approximately even balcony and cornice
heights, with no advertising above a certain reasonable limit, and below that all the signs so in harmony
with the architecture as to seem a part of the structures, and beautiful and interesting; while above the
chosen height there were window announcements
only, in gold leaf — self-contained, harmonious, and
dignified. The attractiveness of the street would be
immensely increased, its interest no whit lessened,
and the competition of the merchants still kept
keen, while transferred to a field more rational,
more inviting to their self-respect than now, and
to one very full of promise for art and artists.

There will again be need, however, at the building line of some negative requirements. Gable-
end lettering, and advertising on blank side walls
even below the assumed advertising height-limit,
would have to be prohibited. Civic art would
frown, too, upon sky-signs, which is to say roof-
lettering, if the requirements as to the façades
did not cover this point. When building operations
are under way, it would safeguard the new structure from the depredations of thoughtless advertisers with no less vigilance than it would defend a
completed building, for this is equally a factor in

the aspect of the street. While a fence encloses
the operations, that fence would be kept free from
advertisements. Similarly, the fences in front of
vacant lots and the erection of bill-boards on vacant
property would be made a matter of concern. In
the latter case, the boards should at least be put
back of the building line, so as to be visible only
when one is directly before them, and their erection
should be dependent on the permission of the
owner of the opposite property. Finally, restrictions would be placed on night advertising, especially as regards the use of flashing electric signs; but
this, it is to be hoped, would be better provided for
in the rise of a new ideal of street illumination based
on the new conditions with their new possibilities.

Of all these advertisement requirements, positive
and negative, and of the suggestions that accom-
pany them, there are only two which are not
known to the author as actually now incorporated
in city ordinances, and as enforced, somewhere.
The vision does not seem so remote and unreal,
nor modern civic art so far from the attainment of
the dream.

Some other, though perhaps less essential, furnishings of the business street remain, and are found
with more or less frequency. The poles for the
overhead trolley, the temporary evil of a transition time as there is reason to believe, in business
districts certainly, are still widely existent. The
waste receptacles, the post and fire-alarm boxes, the

public-convenience stations, and the waiting-rooms for surface transportation — all these appear, when they appear at all, as public utilities, and as such furnish fitting means for the decoration of the street.

For it is to be observed that the business street, strictly and solely utilitarian as it is, can be appropriately decorated within itself only by improving the artistic quality of its regular furnishings. There is rarely any excess here of space, for squares and public areas are to be separately considered, and "the business street" is held to refer to that portion alone of the thoroughfare which is given up to business. Almost its sole chance then, within itself, for the finer and more decorative touches of civic art, thus rests on the street furnishings, and from that point of view none of them is so humble as not to deserve — be it post or sign, letter box or isle of safety — real artistic thought and care. Whether the property of the municipality or of private corporations, this artistic character should be equally insisted upon, for in so far as the furnishings occupy space on the public way they are public in the effect that they produce as well as in the function they perform. The use of the street can be properly withheld from a public-service corporation if it will not agree to use the street with adequate æsthetic circumspection.

Municipalities themselves are not beyond the need of such warning. The city of Berlin receives a large income annually from the lease of sidewalk advertising columns or boards, and we have mentioned the kiosks of Paris and the columns for theatrical posters. In New York a few years ago an ordinance was introduced, and promptly smothered, to grant to a private corporation the right to place waste cans along the streets, the cans to be of a certain definite size, "designed and contrived in a suitable manner," maintained at all times "in a neat and sanitary condition," and without expense to the city — in fact to the city's profit, the company agreeing to pay into the treasury twelve and one-half per cent. of the gross income received from the lease of the advertising space. It was estimated that the lease of the advertising would easily be worth a half-million dollars, and might be worth a million, a year. The terms which the company offered reveal that it would be very profitable, and had they been made generally public must have caused many a town and village — and, sadder, many an improvement association of town or village — to blush for the privilege it has thrown away for nothing, except the setting up of the cans. It must have made them ask themselves whether they had gained anything even in securing these, if for rubbish concealed there was substituted a new stream of advertising on the walks. The incident measures also how great is the artistic potentiality of even the humblest street fixtures. What furnishing of the way would be so little noticed as the can for waste? And yet it was calculated that

business men would pay perhaps a million dollars a
year in New York to get their names upon the cans—
a proof of their estimate of the visual importance of
these receptacles.

But this chapter's discussion has been vain, if it
has not made clear that economy of space is a first
requisite in planning the street furnishings. Nothing
will do more to improve the street's appearance than
the avoidance of a multiplicity of fixtures. The
complexity of modern urban life and the highly refined character of its requirements necessitate the
provision of much apparatus for which the modern
business thoroughfare can ill afford the space. The
first requisite, then, is to dispense with all that is
not absolutely essential to the greatest convenience
of the street—as sidewalk advertising; and of the
remaining furnishings to combine as many as may be
in single fixtures. Finally, the fixtures thus arranged
should be rendered as appropriately decorative, which
is to say as artistic, as possible. There is much to
recommend that those which belong to the municipality should bear the city's crest.

The public-convenience station is best underground. That the trolley pole and probably the
lighting apparatus may ultimately be removed from
the business street there is reason to hope, and the
pole for overhead wires is assumed to be banished.
Meanwhile the isle of safety and the lighting apparatus (until the latter also disappears) invite combination; and the street name sign, the waste can, the

fire-alarm and letter box may be conveniently added to the post that supports also the light. The economy of providing the single fixture—instead of the several that now support these utilities separately—would leave ample funds with which to secure and execute a beautiful design. Thus we would have a business street much freer than now for traffic, not less conveniently supplied, and of greater dignity and completeness of effect. A street of noble lines and handsome buildings may quite lose its splendour if marred by conspicuously numerous and ugly furnishings; and since these are such small details, so easily controlled by the single governing body to which the streets belong, failure here is particularly sad.

Street furnishings have been acquired one by one, by such gradual evolution as noted in the case of the lighting apparatus, and each has been—with its separate owner—a separate problem, handled by itself and so constructed. It remains for modern civic art to weld them, to grasp the problem as a whole, sift out the non-essentials from the relevant and necessary, and, treating the street as a canvas to be thickly peopled, to concentrate the furnishings that remain in a beautiful and single composition. The furnishings of a street, like the furnishings of a room, should add not only to its convenience but to its æsthetic aspect.

CHAPTER IX.

ADORNING WITH FOUNTAINS AND SCULP-
TURE.

IN the building and dreaming of beautiful cities there is happily no need that civic art put all its dependence, even in the business district, on the street crowded with travel. The decorative quality that can be given to the public utilities is only a detail. The potential splendour inherent in a scientific street plan will have little notice, if attention be not drawn to it by a bold seizure of the opportunities for urban embellishment which it affords. The basic lines of the city may be faultless, the furnishings of the street may be as concentrated and as beautiful in fixtures as is consistent with their use, and yet the city must fail to attain to the commonest standards of civic art, if there be not conscious decorative effort.

It has been said that modern civic art, in which the practical quality looms large, would require on that portion of the business thoroughfare which is strictly street no erections that have not some other than æsthetic purpose. It would even resist the intrusion, on such precious space, of the purely artistic. But we have seen that in the scientific street plan the areas of unrelieved streets are never large, that even the longest thoroughfares are broken at close intervals by open spaces, by diagonal crossings, focal centres, or at least by architectural accents. Each one of these breaks presents an opportunity to civic art. The open space, the diagonal street crossing, the bridge, the architectural accent,— each calls for æsthetic treatment. Indeed, the last seems almost to involve artistic development, and we have seen how certainly the former call for decorative lighting. Hardly less urgent is their invitation to adornment with fountains or civic sculpture.

Long, in fact, before there was thought of a brilliant lighting of the cities, fountains bubbled in the squares, chiselled heroes were enthroned as masters of the scene, commemorative arches stood at focal points, and bridges were the stateliest parts of urban highways. Years afterwards, but still before attempt was made to render the lighting at such points particularly brilliant or spectacular, the area that could be spared in public spaces had been planted with turf and trees, and later with flowers. The open spaces in the city's heart have thus been inevitably valued from the first as the vantage points of civic art. The most untrained municipal art ideal has seen that these might be the city's jewels. The demand of the modern and trained civic art is that they shall be considered not by themselves, but as components having a direct relation with all the surrounding city plan; that they be embellished, not with reference merely to their own improvement, but with regard to the effect as seen from converging streets. In brief, it would have us realise that the opportunity which is offered by such spaces for the increase of urban amenity lies not in making here a brilliant structural area and there a bit of garden, but in the decoration of the city by the shedding of splendour over humbler adjacent streets. The function of the open space of a city is not, as understood by modern civic art, to surprise with a sudden loveliness that had been hidden until come upon unexpectedly. It is to cast its radiance as far as possible over the surrounding area.

The main dependence, then, of a city for its decorative effect is to be placed on these breaks in the monotony of its closely built-up streets. As the street plan becomes more scientific, the breaks, of one kind and another, occur in increasing numbers. It becomes possible to give an air of splendour, of elaborate embellishment, to the city at large, with no trespassing on the precious space of street. The eye travels from one decorative object to another, finding the thoroughfare only a brief connecting link. The ideal is that of the maker of a beautiful chain, joining his brilliants by links simple in themselves but appropriate to their purpose and rendered lovely by the frequency of the jewels that they unite.

And yet the maker of a chain, working caressingly at his task, will put upon his links such chasing as he can without injury to its function. So the builders of beautiful cities will sometimes be able to bring into the street itself some decoration. There has been noted the effort to make utilities beautiful. We should go further if occasion offers. If the business street be broad in proportion to the travel offering, there may be space even here, without prejudice to utility, for fountain or for statue. So there will be led on to the highway itself the ornamentation of the open space. Or we may find room for a row of small and formal trees that will not be inconsistent with the character of the way, while bringing into it a strip of colour and joining planted square to planted square by a welcome, if slender, stream of nature.

There is much to commend the placing of statues, fountains, and trees on the street, even the business street, if there be sufficient room. Nor are the advantages æsthetic only. The trees, though small and trimmed in formal shapes as fitting the business street, cast a welcome shade when the sun is hot, and soften, it is said, all extremes of temperature. The fountains, if serving to quench the thirst of man and beast,—as will doubtless be their purpose in such location,—have an eminently practical use. They perform also a pleasant function in bringing into the street that sound of running water which,

in its idle play, its music reminiscent of the wood-
land stream and of nature's care-free abandonment,
has in the city so rare a power to charm. It has
been well said that something about us, some lingering touch perhaps of the race's primitive days, gives
to the running water of the city fountain that relation to public life which the fire in the open hearth
has to private life. To appreciate this to the full,
the fountain should be in the square, where there
may be leisure to sit before it. But even in the roar
of the street the fascination of its music is not lost.
As to the statues, the street with its ceaseless multitudes offers, if it has room to offer any site for sculpture, a location that must be full of inspiration to him
who would commemorate in permanent materials
the deeds of great citizens, the examples of national
heroes, the causes for civic pride, and the incentives
to high resolve which are offered by the past.

With double advantage, then, in economy of space
and in effectiveness, the fountain and the sculpture might be combined. And if the joint structure can be thrust back to the building line, given
a place in a narrow corner where an acute angle
would rob a building's façade of serviceability, or
at a point where converging streets make a lot
that is very small, it will give to the way a charm—
grandiose or picturesquely quaint and unexpected—
that civic art must highly esteem. The French and
Italians, in their lavish use of fountains in cities, offer
many an example of a fountain that, placed on the

The Fontaine Molière, Paris. This has been placed in the acute angle formed at the building line by converging streets, a point of great civic significance but one that, because of its slight commercial value, is often an eyesore.

building line, is yet able to change the character of
the street. Of the first effect, the Fontaine St. Michel
in Paris is perhaps the most obvious example; for
the second, a fountain in a corner of the Rue de la
Grosse Horloge, Rouen, will serve. In both of these
sculpture is added conspicuously to the fountain.
Or it may be possible to connect the sculpture with
the architecture of the way. This, in fact, is done
repeatedly, and plainly it may be done with great
success in the case of the public buildings. Upon
them civic sculpture may serve a triple purpose:
adorning the structure and giving to it fitting expression, adorning the city, and conveying, finally,
that public message which is one of the functions
of urban sculpture. An illustration of such use is
found in the beautiful carving over the entrance to
the Doges' Palace in Venice, where a doge in all his
lordly state kneels with reverence and humility before the lion of St. Mark — a reminder that he who
enters serves, and is not master of, the State. So in
the recurring wolf of Sienna and lily of Florence
there were frequent patriotic appeals in the sculptured stone of the Renaissance.

But we have said that a city depends mainly for
decoration, in its business district, after its architecture, on the adornment of its squares and plazas.
Here the sculpture will rise with greatest freedom;
here there is ample room for the play of fountains
and their enjoyment; here trees and shrubs and
flowers and grass have space to flourish; and here

first the city lighting will be brilliant in its power and decorative in its fixtures. Here individual largess will first reveal itself and private taste first embrace an opportunity to stamp its imprint on public property. Nor will it do so, where modern civic art prevails, to the making or marring of the space alone. Its influence will be felt as far on all the converging streets as the open space can be seen.

So it happens that a need is felt, in the decoration of cities, for an authority of expert taste and education to which these matters may be referred, in order that results may be anticipated, mistakes avoided, artistic discernment encouraged, and ill taste curbed. There must be a standard of civic art, by which all that changes the aspect of the way shall be judged — to be condemned if falling below it, to be approved if rising to its height. That standard must be high and there must be authority to enforce adherence to it, but those who have this power must be generous. In public art there should be no bigoted repression; individualism is to be not less feared in the judging than in the creating. The ideal authority would be a thoroughly educated public taste. When there is not this to depend upon, the jury must have much catholicity of sentiment. It must be firmly didactic only in the broadly recognised essentials of art.

Paris solves the problem by calling to her service in advisory capacity the leading artists and architects of the city. Some American municipalities — as New York, Boston, and others—have tried to follow her example by establishing municipal art commissions. But they have been at great pains to safeguard the composition of the commissions and to limit their powers. The act which creates the commission names many of its members by *ex-officio* appointments and closely limits the groups from which the others may be drawn. This is designed to insure the high character of the commission, its broad culture, and its independence of politics. There is then given to it only the negative power of a veto, in order that the art impulse may remain popular and that inspiration may be free. It is told to stand aside and merely to criticise what others propose to do. It has no initiative power. Instead of working with the officials of the city, it may work directly against them. They do not have to seek it in consultation when planning the public works, as in Paris; but they make their plans and then the commission criticises with no power to offer suggestions that will be heeded. It has authority to forbid, but none to advise until requested so to do. The device at best, therefore, is a poor makeshift; but it is a conquest of modern civic art to have recognised the need and, in trying timidly to satisfy it, to have guarded so zealously the publicity of public art, to have feared to take any step that would discourage the close connection that should exist between the people and the beautifying of their city. For modern civic art differs from that of any earlier civilisation in few essentials so urgently as in this: it is democratic.

There is little that is pleasant in criticising a well-meant offering. Especially is this true when a proposed popular gift must be rejected on technical grounds. But we have learned the necessity, if we would have noble cities, of offering such criticism fearlessly and of making an artistic condemnation authoritative. We have perceived that, however unpleasant the task, it is better that the criticism be made in advance, in time to prevent the public mistake, than after the harm has been done. For if an ugly structure be erected, the criticism will follow that might, by coming before, have saved the city an eyesore of which the influence will reach as far as the structure is visible. And the criticism that would have ceased as soon as the proposal had been rejected will now last as long as the structure lasts. If in the decoration of our cities there is a great opportunity for good, there is also a great power for evil. Modern civic art recognises and perceives that it must battle against this.

There is need, however, of the courage that not merely defends, but is aggressive. It is improbable that popular interest in the embellishment of the city would be discouraged by definite suggestions. If the art forces of an urban district could be so marshalled in its behalf that they would as keenly feel the responsibility for making creative suggestions as for repressing the crude and ill-advised, there surely would be a great gain. If they would point out the improvement that might be given to a city, the embellishment that could be advantageously placed here and there, would submit designs for the artistic treatment of the public areas, would designate the proper sites for sculpture or for fountains, popular interest would be heightened rather than diminished. Often the chief bar not only to giving, but to any interest, is the lack of a convincing because concrete ideal.

It is to be noted, in this connection, that the placing of the city ornament is as vital and almost as truly an artistic matter as is the character of the design. The question, too, is one regarding which the public feels less diffidence about asserting its ability to decide than regarding the design, and much less doubt concerning its right to an opinion and to having its own way. The expert commissions of all kinds have learned this to their sorrow. They have had to solve no more frequent or troublesome problems than those concerning the location of structures that are intended to be civic ornaments. For the design that would be artistic and beautiful in one place may be ruined by location in another, where it is out of scale and inharmonious with its surroundings. In the decoration of cities the place for each work of art is as much a question for artistic judgment as is the device itself, and each separate case needs as certainly a separate decision. One may say, indeed, that the question rises also in regard to every public or semi-public building, in regard to every structure that is meant to be an ornament

to the way.   But in these cases there are other purposes to be served as well as those of ornament.
The question is complicated.   There can be, then, no
more distressing failure than a civic monument raised
to adorn the city and failing in that respect, be it
through faulty design, through faulty placing, or
through both.

There are certain general artistic principles that
should govern the placing of civic sculpture, such as
the consistency of placing the ideal in an idyllic
scene, and the sculptured wild animal amid less
civilised surroundings than the business street —
principles that, strangely, are more marked in the
breach than the observance.   There are, again, certain
principles that may be called civic, such as a requirement that statues of only universal or of an especial
national or urban interest shall be placed at an
intersection of important thoroughfares, and that
they must be of undoubted beauty and appropriate
in size.   But each instance will require, as we have
said, a separate decision; and where individual beauty
and scale are factors it is of little use to lay down
"general principles."

This only should be said: in the city, the bridge,
the viaduct, the open space, present unusual opportunities, and this not for their own adornment only
but for that of the streets which lead to them.
Modern civic art here follows in the steps of that of
all the ages.   It is making no experiment, is advancing no new claim; it points for illustrations of its

possibilities to the splendid cities of all times.   If it
has a conquest to make, it is only with regard to
obtaining from the modern bridges their just tribute
to civic decorativeness.   We have lately turned to a
new material in the making of bridges for cities and
as usual its earlier application is strictly practical.   It
happens, too, that iron and steel lend themselves to
beauty of construction far less readily than does stone,
so that there is need of constantly impressing the
æsthetic obligation.   This has been already referred
to more than once.   The point to be made here is
the fitness of the city bridge as a site for sculpture.

The bridge offers in its own construction so
admirable a pedestal, or an architectural background
so excellent, that there is little reason for surprise in
finding it considered in its completeness as a monumental structure.   This is the conception which
created the beautiful Pont Alexander III. in Paris and
to which are due the designs for memorial bridges
in Washington.   Every such case teaches a lesson
and emphasises the appeal that civic art now makes
urgently of the officials of town and city: that in the
making of a bridge-design an architect at least, and
perhaps a sculptor, shall co-operate with the engineer;
and that the structure be classed among the works
of public art to the end that its design, which is to
mean so much to the aspect of the city, shall have
expert artistic criticism before it is approved.   In
the making of the design, too, let there be remembrance that here, where sufficient space can be given

and where no future building can rise to destroy the proportion and harmony now obtained, is one of the most favourable sites for civic sculpture. There is only one location that may be better. That is the square or open space, or the area just before it, where trees and shrubs may give that background of verdure by which some sculpture is improved.

Matters, then, which civic art would have the builders of cities—which is to say all the urban residents — keep in mind, are : (1) the wish for, and even the necessity of, frankly intended artistic embellishment for the city; and (2) the eager desire to make the most of every opportunity for securing this, especially where space can be afforded with no danger of unduly crowding the public way. But it would point out, that on the business street sculpture or fountain can appear as little more than incidental, while in the open space or on the bridge it can be made the centre of a picture of which every detail adds to its importance. Finally, it is necessary that we remember how the artistic factor, not less as to location than as to the design, must be guarded with especial zeal in the case of that which is avowedly intended for a civic ornament. In that specific instance civic art will not forgive a failure. Unless the work is a success æsthetically, its best reason for existence has passed.

In the desire to give to a city the impress of art, there arises a tendency to choose some especially well adapted and conspicuous site in which to emphasise this quality.   The result is the creation of the show place of the city.   Here the municipal architecture is at its best, here sculpture is lavishly provided, here we may even find formal balustrades and terraces. It is like a stage scene, set to represent the majestic city's resources and pride.   Civic art has here full opportunity, and on great days this is the centre to which the people flock.

The tendency is not peculiar to modern conditions. It is, rather, a seemingly inevitable result of popular interest in municipal æsthetics; and, since modern civic art still is young, it is less found to-day than in the days when earlier civilisations attained their glory.   Such a centre was the Acropolis at Athens, such was the Forum in Rome, such were market places in the Mediæval cities.   It is significant, then, of the hold of civic art that there should be a reappearance of the tendency.   In Paris the Place de la Concorde is such a place; in London Trafalgar Square will fairly serve for one, until the completion of the proposed Victoria Memorial as the state processional road shall render a contracted makeshift unnecessary; in Berlin, the Unter den Linden has now been supplemented by the Sieges Allee; in the United States, the "Court of Honour" at the Columbian Exposition was a hint that has had brief following in the temporary creations of a score of cities; and in New York there are indications that the heights of Riverside Drive are to be thus constituted the city's crown.

Considered in the abstract, civic art would with-
hold its unqualified approval. It would fear lest the
city as a whole might suffer from a concentration
of the decorative emphasis. It would prefer a city
beautiful throughout to one that had lavished half
of all its splendour on a civic centre. But practically
there is to be recognised the extreme difficulty of
diffusing the higher expressions of civic art throughout the city, and the wearying and possibly discouraging tediousness as well as the arduousness of
the process — this to be contrasted with the spectacular and prompt results to be gained by concentration. And once such a centre of decorativeness
is successfully established in the city, there is no
question that it has a beneficial influence. It presents a concrete picture that elevates the popular
ideal, for it is understood by the unimaginative. It
stimulates by its examples of what has actually been
achieved. It raises the æsthetic level of the surrounding streets.

An interesting development now appears in the
tendency of modern civic art to transform this civic
centre from a plaza to a street. An ideal location for
such decorative emphasis is, of course, the square
around which the public buildings have been
grouped. No site could be more appropriate than
the town's "administrative centre." But the trouble
with our cities is that there rarely is an "administrative centre," for the public buildings are so seldom
grouped about an open space. Civic art has thus

been unhappily free to choose, and repeatedly it has selected the street or avenue. Berlin confirms the Unter den Linden's suggestion in this direction by the Sieges Allee; New York selects Riverside Drive; Boston an avenue; the new Washington is thus to develop the Mall. Even Paris supplements her Place de la Concorde with the Champs Élysées. The result has at least the merit of extending its field of influence and of stretching out — perhaps to widely different quarters of the town — the decorative effect. The cities of to-day have grown too large to gather around a single little central square, and yet visibly show to their outer rims the influence of its splendour.

In the creation of the Sieges Allee there was a peculiarity which is to be observed. This Avenue of Victory, with its abundant verdure and noble trees, was already beautiful. The Emperor resolved that he would here glorify his ancestors, adorning Berlin the while and patronising the art of sculpture, by giving to the nation thirty-two marble groups of historical sculpture and stretching them along the avenue, sixteen on a side. It should be, indeed, the Sieges Allee. Sculptors were selected and commissioned, and in the course of seven years — at the end of 1901 — the series was completed. The Emperor then made an address to the artists who had served him, and in this he emphasised earnestly the point that may be mentioned here. This was his wish to pose in his imperial capacity as a personal patron of the arts; and to prove, by the success of the undertaking, that

the most favourable auspices for the solution of an art problem are not to be found in convoking commissions or in instituting all sorts of prize juries and competitions, but rather by following the old and approved methods of Classical times and of the Middle Ages—I mean those direct relations between him who gives the order and the artist. . . . A parallel might be drawn between this work and the great artistic achievements of the Middle Ages, or of the Italians, where the ruler and sovereign, who was a lover of the arts and who set the artists their task, did not fail to find the maestros.

Impartial critics have expressed a doubt as to the artistic success of the undertaking having been great enough to "prove" anything. But there cannot fail to be interest in so conspicuous a revival to-day of a characteristic of the civic art of the Renaissance and of "Classical times." In the United States the tendency is strongly in favour of commissions and limited competitions, as perhaps is more fitting for a democracy; but even there one can note the increasing frequency with which individual wealth is identifying itself with one or another phase of art, and how frequently in the smaller towns private fortune becomes the patron of the civic art. The best progress will doubtless be made when the movement gains its impulse from the people. But an artistic Renaissance does not break over civilisation with all the suddenness of a tidal wave. It would be ushered in by just such methods. A few, who are on the mountain heights, will be the first to

The Sieges Allee, Berlin.

see in concrete form the storied "city beautiful." They will commission the artists to picture the vision to the toilers who are still in shadow — down in narrow streets where the dawn of a new day, as it gilds the roofs, is yet unseen. The pictures that these artists paint will educate, reveal, inspire. They are the pioneers; they point out the way; and the people will follow so joyously, so eagerly, that from the people themselves there will come new pioneers. The decoration that can be brought to-day into our cities is thus more than a conquest. It is a pledge of larger victories.

IN THE RESIDENTIAL SECTIONS.

CHAPTER X.

STREET PLOTTING AMONG THE HOMES.

I
N the discussion of modern city-building, we may
now turn from the distinctly business district
to the distinctly residential. In studying the
former, we found that the focal points were first to
be considered. Until these had been selected as
bases, it was idle to give thought to the street plan.
The moment the residential area is entered, these
"nerve centres" become too distant to have great
influence. In their place the district contains no
points of general command. Instead, a number of
local, or neighbourhood centres would tend to have
a disintegrating effect were it not that the business
part of the town still acts as a magnet, holding the
residential area about itself with a firmness that almost balances the decentralising attractions of these
and of the country's spacious beauty. The residential district is thus the battlefield of two forces,
one pulling outward and one pulling in, and as one
or the other is stronger there is crowding or roomy

expansion. This is a contest to be kept in mind, for it makes easier of understanding many urban peculiarities that may properly be traced to these forces.

When the walls of cities came down, the centralising power within had no ally pushing from without; when the lines of rapid-transit were laid, the cords that pulled men to the centre were so loosened as to pull much less tightly; when industrial suburbs were created, counter attractive magnets were established; when the business part of the city increased in brilliancy, fascination, and splendour, the centralising power was in its turn strengthened. So the fortunes of the contest have varied, and even in the case of single cities there is little uniformity in results. Here we find compression and there we find expansion, according as local or neighbourhood factors influence the outcome, until the residential parts of any city, taken as a whole, can be said to have no more than a similar general character.

To make, now, a practical and rational plan for these sections of the city, it is necessary to appreciate the contest of which they are the battleground. But there is a need of doing something more than that. We have to ask ourselves which side civic art will favour, for he who lays out the streets of these districts has it in his power greatly to aid or obstruct either tendency.

Consideration that the residential area is where people are to live, are to build their homes, let their

little children play, and take their own ease when
work is done, removes all doubt of the answer.
Civic art would have as much room, for individual
privacy and for communal beauty, as is compatible
with the impatient demands of the city's workaday
centre. The first question becomes, then, how can
we satisfy the demands of energy and labour with
least sacrifice of the reposeful character of the district ? This must be answered in the street plan.

It is clear, at least, that in leaving the business
district and entering the residential we are confronted by an entirely new problem. Not only is it
possible to imagine a new scheme of plotting, but
the appearance of a new purpose makes it very
desirable to do so; and a change in basic conditions
— through the substitution of local for general foci —
even renders unavoidable a change of method. At
the same time, the one system must be joined closely
to the other so that both rest on a single, solid framework that reduces to a minimum the expenditure of
force in transition from the one to the other; and it
must, further, be possible for the business district to
expand, making conquests in an area that is now occupied by residences, without loss of its own convenience.

In plotting the streets of the business district, we
found that the first essential was to build up the
framework, or skeleton, of arterial thoroughfares. In
that case we had certain focal points for bases. We
lack these points in the new problem; but we may

extend the old framework founded upon them, carrying out the lines until they form the structure of
the new. If we do this, we shall gain the three
objects that we most desire with reference to the
centre: we shall unite the two systems so that
they become, or seem to become, one harmonious
scheme; we shall establish direct lines of communication with the business district as a whole and with
each of the town's great focal points. These lines,
again, as the shortest distance from the residential
arcs of the circumference to the business centre, will
offer the natural routes for travel by rapid-transit or
other means. They will be the great "through
lines" and can be made wide in accordance with
their anticipated usefulness. Incidentally, they will
thus furnish the natural lines on which business may
extend when, outgrowing its present quarters, it
tends to overflow into the residential district — and
so there will be gained the third requisite with reference to the centre.

We shall discover, in further consideration, that
the business in overflowing through these streets
does the slightest possible injury to the character of
this quiet district. In brief, the line of least resist-
ance is become also the line of least harm. Our
framework of radial arterial thoroughfares is substan-
tially, if indirectly, a system of safety-valves to meet
increasing pressure in the commercial district. We
have now adopted that hint for a city plan which,
as Colonel Waring once pointed out, is contained in

the spider's web. In this the quickest way of reaching the centre from any given point is, clearly, obtained; and in the plot of the residential section of the town we have to remember, not as a pleasant but as a primary fact, that time is money.

In the establishment of these radials we gain yet another advantage. There is required in this section the provision of a large number of neighbourhood foci, instead of only two or three great focal points. That is to say, there is a demand for many locally effective sites. The public buildings of the district are the schools and churches, the sub-stations of the post-office, of the police and fire departments, and the branches of the public library. All of these demand convenient situations with reference to the district which they serve, and some of them should have also conspicuous sites, for the æsthetic value hardly less than the serviceability of public structures depends on their location. The radial highways, inevitably cutting the general street system at irregular angles, and themselves the trunk lines of daily travel, will of necessity offer many such sites of prominence. These locations will be, also, convenient of access — not only because they are on the trunk lines, which are broad, direct, straight, and of easy grades, but, since those thoroughfares are designed for lines of through travel, every minor street system will be connected with its own particular artery in the closest and most immediate way. Thus any structure on the radial streets will be easy of

access from the streets on either side of it, in the
district it would serve.

Except for the almost incidental requirement that
there shall be a possibility of effective sites for the
local centres, civic art, in as far as it stands for
the wish for urban beauty, has been as yet very
quiet. Its own first demand in plotting these streets
would be for æsthetic results. It would seek the
restful, lovely, and artistic above everything else.
But municipal art, to gain its ends, must have the
foundation of utility. In fact, art is, first of all,
the doing or the making of the useful thing in the
best possible way. That art which has to do with
city-building, therefore, must be content, when taking up the problem of a street plan for the residential district, to learn first what the requirements
of usefulness are; and then, having put duty before pleasure and having made this provision, it
will do the best it can to stamp the whole with
beauty, harmony, and repose, and to give to refined
individual taste opportunities for expression. If
modern civic art failed to take this course, its own
ends would be defeated. A beauty gained at the
expense of convenience gives no pleasure, and the
urban beauty with which we would surround our
homes has no purpose more pressing than to please:

Happily, the essentials from a workaday standpoint that are required of civic art, in the plotting
of these streets, amount to no more than a convenient framework. They may all be provided without

injuring the attractiveness of the district. Indeed, they have the great artistic merit of giving an appearance of unity to a scheme that now may be varied generously in its details. They invite also the convenient use of themselves as service roads, whither the heavy through travel and the main lines of urban transportation may be thrown, leaving us free in developing the intervening areas to consider such questions as grade and directness secondary at last to the wish for beauty.

At liberty now to seek frankly for beauty, we shall recognise the charm of variety. We will have broad streets and narrow streets, straight and curving ways, and regularly built up districts sprinkled through with open spaces, where there may be playgrounds for children or gardens for the delight of all. And here again there will be certain fundamental provisions, carrying a little farther the framework of the streets. There will be, for instance, at least one broad avenue, intended for wealth and fashion and on which there will be no lines of rapid-transit, and where heavy teaming will be discouraged if not indeed forbidden. There will be, in this avenue, or as supplementary to it, at least one parkway, by which the parks will be suitably approached and the beginning of their charm brought far down-town. There will be system about the provision of the open spaces, their number will be sufficient to give character to the district, and each will be so availed of in

13

the street plotting as to lend the maximum of effect to the streets. This means that there will be arranged such convergence of streets to each of them that it will not find its beauty shut in by building walls, but will be able to spread its pleasant influence far over the surrounding area. Instead of the common appearance of haphazard scattering, there will seem to be a reason for the exact location of every such open space.

The discussion of the treatment of the spaces may well demand a separate chapter; but we have to recognise here the necessity for their generous provision. They are to be the gardens for those who have no gardens of their own; they are to bring into the vista of the street a new and unexpected beauty; they are to vary its monotony, to give room for air, invitation to idleness, to joy in nature, in the bloom of flowers, the song of birds, the play of light and shadow, and the wondrous poem of the season's change on tree and shrub. They are to make provision, in the fundamental structure of the city, and on a generous and comprehensive scale, for the sports and games of the children who will be living near. They are not to be added as luxuries; there should not be need of inserting them, at great cost, vast inconvenience, and with poor effect after the district has been built up. Modern civic art has behind it enough experience to have had their value thoroughly attested; and, when the opportunity arises — as it often must

—to include them in the original street plan, to find for such act not merely ample justification but an obligation that is moral and civic as truly as it is æsthetic.

In this section of the city, too, topography becomes a matter of extreme importance. In the business district, where speed and ease of transportation and communication were primary and all-pervading essentials, difference of level offered only obstacles to that flatness which was to be desired that grades might be almost avoided. Here ascent or descent may be one of the greatest charms of the way. The natural contour of the land becomes so probable and powerful an aid in procuring beauty and individuality, where time and heavy teaming have no longer to be considered seriously, that it has been well said that no precise plan for a residential part of a town which is not absolutely flat can be devised, with satisfactory results, if there be not thorough knowledge of the topography. Nor does this relate only to varying elevations, for every natural watercourse may present an opportunity. To bring out, then, in the street plotting, rather than to repress, the characteristic native beauty of the tract should be one of the first aims when planning the lesser residential streets. And if this be well done, the beauty which is thus given (or permitted without despoilment) to the town will surely stamp it with an individuality all its own.

There is in the exhibition of deference to the

topography, and especially with reference to contour, a further very practical advantage. This is economy in construction. Clearly, the cost of pushing streets with relentless engineering exactness in undeviating lines through a rocky or hilly tract must be much greater than if they were allowed to follow the lay of the land. Nor is the difference one only of construction, for where there are deep cuts or steep embankments the value of abutting property is seriously depreciated, if not almost destroyed, so that it cannot justly be heavily assessed for an "improvement." Even in cases where the established grade departs comparatively little from the actual level of the land, the cost of cutting and filling within the lots, when houses are to be erected, will amount to considerably more in the aggregate than does the slight addition to the length of pavement, curb, walk, and sewer, which is to say of the street, that is occasioned by deviation from a rigid straight line or by following the natural surface. It may be added that filling or cutting very often kills fine trees that might have been saved had the street risen or fallen a little with the natural contour, or that it might be well worth while to swing a street a bit out of line, if so a noble tree could be spared. It will not be necessary always to climb the hills at their highest point, nor to descend to their lowest valleys. With the well-proved charm of the curving street, we may wind around the hill at less cost than cutting through it and with more satisfaction to the traffic than if a shorter distance were bought by a steep gradient. There is too often need of learning that the railroad ideal of directness and an unvarying elevation is unfitted for residential streets, and particularly for those of suburban districts.

The value of the curving thoroughfare where there are hills to be surmounted has been suggested, and its beauty has been taken almost for granted. It will be well, however, to consider with something more of definiteness these claims to æsthetic merit. They are not dependent merely on the circumstance that "the curved line is the line of beauty." That alone would be a point in its favour[1]; but, as the street is occupied, other advantages appear. The houses show far better on a curved than on a straight line. Each advancing step discloses a new view of the façade, and, in fact, more than one face of the house is now in evidence. Conversely, the view from the windows is much pleasanter if the house stand on a curving street, for then windows both on front and side command a vista of the way. Building operations, whether for the poorest class of homes or for the best, are more likely to be successful on an attractive thoroughfare; and not only is there no need for most houses to be built on straight streets, but they will be pleasanter if they

[1] Dr. Charles W. Eliot, in his book on the life and work of his son, *Charles Eliot, Landscape Architect,* quotes Professor William James, the psychologist, as saying, after he had lived for several years at the junction of two curving streets, " that the daily sight of the curve of Scott Street added much to the pleasure of living in his house—or, indeed, in the neighbourhood."

are not.[1] The curving street has the better chance
for picturesqueness, and at any point the curve
brings the lawns and gardens into the vista of the
street, giving to it a very pleasant and appropriate
character for a street of homes, and there is assured
a charming variety in the light and shade. Finally,
it may be noted, that parks and open spaces with a
waving boundary line are more attractive than if
the abutting streets marked them off in straight
lines.

The curved street should, of course, be broader
than the straight one; it presents some sewerage
problems that are not, however, difficult; and if the
curve be sharp the street should not be very long,
lest, instead of pleasing, it annoy by its relatively
extravagant demand on time and space. But with
these warnings the curved street may be approved
for its change, even though a level tract does not
insist on its adoption. It may be noted, incidentally,
that in our imagined plotting of the residential area,
the circle that the latter is supposed to form about
the centre has been already cut into small arcs by
the system of arterial radials. The diversified street
systems would be confined between consecutive
radials, so that the length of curving streets would
be naturally restricted.

Perhaps it will be wise here to turn aside from
the discussion of the theory of street plotting, and

---

[1] Some of the arguments printed here are borrowed from the very excellent
special report of the City Parks Association of Philadelphia (1902) on "The City
Plan."

Manning Boulevard, Albany, N. Y.   Suggesting the charm of the curving street.

Augustus Pruyn, Photo.

to note some examples that concretely illustrate abstract contentions. There is no surer means to weigh an argument.

Of the value of radial thoroughfares, for the main lines of urban transit and direct communication with the centre, the street plan of Vienna offers a conspicuous proof. There are fifteen main radials, and the street railways, coming in by these, centre their operations on the inner Ring. It is said that in Vienna the daily ebb and flow of population takes place with greater ease than in any other large city. The street plans of many municipalities, European and American, illustrate the usefulness of such streets less strikingly only because they illustrate it in part — instead of as a complete system, as does Vienna. Of the broad avenues planned for the residences of the rich and fashionable, of the parkways carrying the approach to the parks far down town, and of the boulevards, there are many examples. Euclid Avenue, a street that early gave fame to Cleveland, Ohio, is a case in point; or better, perhaps, is the lower end of Commonwealth Avenue in Boston, where the double roadway and the broad middle strip of turf and trees is carried so far into the closest built-up residential section that it joins the Public Garden and the Common with the outlying parks, so that one may walk — if he will — from the very heart of business Boston on a *tapis vert* to the parks that girdle the city. Such another example of the purpose is the Avenue des Champs

Élysées and its connecting Avenue du Bois de Boulogne, in Paris.

And from what might have been, but is not, we
can gain a hint of the value of such provision. The
commissioners who laid down the street plan of New
York declared at the outset that Fifth Avenue should
be the middle one of the great longitudinal highways. Suppose they had had the foresight to anti-
cipate the consequent development it would be
likely to have, and had had the courage to provide
for this by making the central avenue wider than
the others,—broad enough for trees, and perhaps for
a strip of turf,—how magnificent a change would
have come upon New York! In Philadelphia there
has been earnest proposal that the present street
plan be rectified in this respect, and a great parkway be cut from Fairmount Park to the City Hall.[1]

As to the squares and open spaces in the residential portions of the city, the plan of Washington
will at once suggest itself. Here, each formal space
of turf,—square or circle, as the case may be,—
flower-jewelled and statue-crowned, is made a centre
of converging streets.

Coming now to curving streets, Vienna, Paris,
Brussels, Florence, or many another ancient city that
has been modernised, furnishes — having availed
itself of the opportunity offered by a demolition of
its old confining walls — an example of long boule-

---

[1] This has now been done, and the results—æsthetic and utilitarian—more than
justify the great cost.

vards circling in slow curve the city area. In the United States the corresponding thoroughfares — as in Chicago, for instance — have been often developed as parkways. There is much to commend the establishment of these encircling streets, offering as they do such convenient routes for belt-line travel, joining radial directly with radial, and forming circles of street pretentiousness and beauty in concentric rings around the urban district. But for example of the more picturesque, because shorter and more sharply curving, streets, it is not so easy to point to thoroughfares of world-wide reputation. These must be, as in our plotting theory, the minor ways. But in England we may note, for instance, the pretty streets of Edgbaston, a suburb of Birmingham; and in the United States those that make so lovely the towns and little cities which constitute the "metropolitan district" of Boston. From Boston, too, we may draw one example that is justly becoming widely known. This is in the long suburban extension of Commonwealth Avenue, now stretching its sinuous length many miles into the country. But aside from the sinuosity of the street, a succession of lovely curves applied to an avenue of stately width and exceptionally long and elaborate surface development, this highway might well demand attention. It is a most striking illustration of a street following the natural contour of the land. It rises and falls with the gentle hills and valleys of the region through which it passes, and discloses at every turn and every changing level a new beauty. There are innumerable small examples of the attractiveness of such street plotting, but here is one so great and conspicuous that it may be cited for all.

There should be consideration now of the width of the minor residential streets. In discussing the plotting of the business district, it was observed that a narrow thoroughfare might be considerably widened, as far as effectiveness goes, by thrusting back the building line. In a district where the construction seldom, or it may be never, covers half the entire building lot, it is very easy to push back this line without injury to the lot owner, and indeed with such benefit to the street as to profit him. This fact makes narrowness on these minor streets, which have no through travel, a matter much less to be dreaded than in the business district, while to recommend it there is the circumstance that a narrow roadway costs so much less than a broad one to construct and maintain that the same expenditure will furnish a better pavement and keep it cleaner. There are, however, three questions to be asked in determining the width of a minor residential street: (1) Is there locally the legal power to establish a building line? (2) Is there a probability that with the growth of the city and the extension of its business centre the street may be required for trade or industry? (3) Would it be desirable, even if there were not that danger, to plan a broader street in order to make a feature of the parking?

The surface development of the street need not be here discussed; but it is evident that a conscientious putting of any one of these questions may demand a wide street. If there be not authority to establish the building line, there is more or less danger that some of the construction will be at the street's edge. This means, if the way be narrow, lack of air and sunshine and a consequent tendency ultimately to squalor. If the business does overflow on to a narrow street, jagged lines will mark the transition. Commercial structures, often of a cheap and undesirable aspect, will be built out to the walk, while the better residences, recessed back at irregular intervals, will be hidden. The full conquest of the street by business will mean serious crowding on the narrow walks and cramped roadway. None of these results can be contemplated with pleasure by modern civic art. All must be averted.

In closing this discussion, a word should be said of its pertinence. While that tendency which is called the modern urban drift continues, there can hardly be found a town or city that is finished. In the business portions of the settlement, growth will generally mean remodelling — a process sadly handicapped by previous conditions, and slow and costly. In the residential portions also there will be some remodelling; but for the most part, as far as street plotting is concerned, growth here will mean addition. There will be free play for theory; and it will be a pity if no beauty is brought into the street plan, through study of the science — the considerate reasonableness — and the art of municipal æsthetics. On the borders of every city, and even within the borders, there is a constant opening of new tracts. These present opportunities by wise plotting for gaining picturesqueness and variety. Often the problem offered by such a tract may be, and has been, solved with better effect, both æsthetically and financially, by giving a chance to the landscape architect than by leaving the design to an engineer. For once the main through lines are laid down, the leading avenues provided, and the open spaces apportioned systematically through the district, the short streets that fill up the little arcs and in the aggregate contain so many houses, should have the picturesqueness and variety of individuality of expression. It should be possible here, where the homes are, to get away from the depressing monotony of a uniform system. Experience is everywhere teaching the lesson of the popularity of this course, by the higher prices that lots in such surroundings bring, and by the better class of dwellings erected in these tracts.

As to remodelling, it is a mistaken idea that an adopted city plan cannot be changed, or that a vast amount of energy is required to change it. The plan is changed constantly. The same power that adopts the map, usually the municipality's legislative body, can alter it by an ordinance, and the result in most large cities is almost a daily changing of plotted streets, or a vacating of those that have been already opened. To make these changes worth while is the harder task, and the task of civic art. It is one, however, to be undertaken not merely with the courage born of confidence, but with an unwonted zeal. For what higher call has civic art than to make beautiful the surroundings of the homes of men; to make refined, lovely, and truly lovable, that environment in which they have leisure for enjoyment or for misery, and where are reared and taught by sense impressions the children who will be the future citizens?

CHAPTER XI.

ON GREAT AVENUES.

TWO great groups or kinds of streets have appeared in the discussion of the topographical plotting of a city's residential area. They are the great avenues, forming the skeleton or framework of the district, and the minor streets that fill in the system's details. Of each group there are subdivisions. The minor streets are of wide variety. The great avenues include the encircling boulevards, the radials that bear the heavy travel to and from the centre, the broad streets set apart for the grandest residences, and, by our earlier classification, the parkways that offer suitable approaches to the parks and stretch enticing suggestions of park beauty far into the busy, workaday sections of the town. These parkways are not, however, to be treated quite as streets. Their very name conveys a hint that in considering the development of the thoroughfares another classification will be now convenient. We shall take the parkways from the group of great

avenues, as having a kinship nearer to the park system than to that of the streets, and give to them a
later study. For the present the group comprising
the principal highways of the residential section may
be considered as composed of the encircling boulevards, the radials, and the finer, in the sense of the
more pretentious, residential streets.

The first duty of the thoroughfares contained in
such a group is to afford ease of communication.
This has been already looked after in the plotting,
and it is mainly by virtue of the excellence with
which they do this that it becomes possible to
describe these streets as prominent. The second
requirement is that they shall have a certain dignified and stately beauty. In the business district,
architectural magnificence and civic splendour of
decoration is largely depended upon to make the
thoroughfares handsome. In the residential quarters,
where the decreased relative importance of the
buildings will not justify the placing of the dependence for stately street effects upon the architecture,
there is need that beauty be brought into the street
itself. To consider how this may here be done is
logically civic art's next step.

The necessity of affording ease of communication,
and of adapting the facilities to comparatively long-
distance travel, has made certain characteristics
obligatory in these streets. These are breadth; and,
in the case of the radials at least, and very often of
the encircling boulevards, a provision for car tracks.

The requirement of breadth is favourable rather than otherwise to the attainment of that stately beauty which is desired. The inner and outer boulevards encircling Paris have an average width of one hundred and forty feet throughout their twenty miles. In a couple of districts, for a total distance of four miles, there is a width of two hundred and forty feet. The Avenue des Champs Élysées is two hundred and seventy-five feet wide. If all this width were required to accommodate the traffic, the condition would be discouraging in the extreme. But the invitation to breadth, naturally and appropriately extended by the present and prospective traffic, is supplemented so earnestly by a desire to emphasise the importance of the streets' relation to the general system, and to render them stately and beautiful, that there is often given a greater width than the necessities of mere transportation require. Land is not so needed for building purposes in the region through which they pass as to make such sacrifice of space too dear for the results obtained. So we find provided, almost as a matter of course on these streets, the breadth which is often desired vainly in the business district, where it might have done so much to accommodate the traffic and to give an air of civic magnificence.

The necessity of arranging for car tracks on many of the streets of this group would seem a less happy condition, but it is possible to provide them in such a way as to involve little injury to the appearance of the street. It should be said that the rapid-transit facilities offered by these thoroughfares will be confined, as far as visible apparatus goes, to the surface. The noisy and ugly elevated railroad will not be suffered to destroy all the potential majesty, or even attractiveness, of the way; and if there be underground construction, there will be nothing of it apparent, save an occasional station which is artistic in design and so situated as not to block the street, or even to seem to do so. For rapid-transit on the surface — which, as the natural method, promises to be always the pleasantest and most popular — we may assume electric power. It has been said that the elder F. L. Olmsted was the first one frankly to accept the car tracks as a permanent feature of the avenue and one that could and should be turned to decorative purpose. On the Beacon Street Boulevard, Boston, he arranged that the tracks should be thrown into a separate turf-planted strip at the road's border, where only the gleaming lines of steel would show upon the greensward. The advantages were not confined to the appearance of the street. They included a lessening of noise and dust, and a possibility of greater speed, and so evident were these gains that the plan was adopted far and wide, and regardless of the location of the strip — whether at an edge of the road, at each side, or in its centre.

The system in use on the Beacon Street Boulevard is the overhead trolley, as we have to suppose — at this writing — that it usually will be on long routes

that are not closely built up. Modern civic art of
course looks forward to the day when, the wires of
the trolley underground or a storage battery in use,
there will be no need of a double column of frequent
sentinel posts to mar the street prospect. Here and
there the vision is already realised, but where its
realisation is delayed, the use of a separate strip of
greensward for the cars can be made an effectual
means of reducing the injury of the posts. They
may then be placed down the centre of the strip,
with an arm outstretched over either track — a device
that substitutes a single for the double row, that does
away with guard wires, and that, by its essential
symmetry, is more favourable to artistic design than
the posts at the track's edge. Or, on this separate
strip, there may be such planting as to make side
posts, when painted an unobtrusive colour, scarcely
noticeable features in the scene. It may be that vines
can be trained over them, or festooned from post to
post to form an effective and pretty barrier between
the carriage road and the tracks, when the street has
left the stone of the city far enough behind to make
such treatment appropriate. Then the posts become
only details of a thoroughly pleasing composition.
And before the vines are thus made use of, there may
be upon the edge of this grassy strip a planting of
shrubs and bushes that will more than half conceal
the posts, and transfer attention from them to the
surpassing beauty of the plants with their varied
loveliness of flower and twig. Until business

marches upon the street and renders incongruous the strip of greensward, and is covetous of the space thus occupied, it were well to give to the tracks of the street railroad such setting as will make them a decorative feature of the street.

It appears, then, that neither requirement which utility may make, in even its most exacting mood, of these leading thoroughfares need prove antagonistic to their handsome development. The great thing is to determine that the streets shall be handsome, that they shall be handsome considered by themselves and irrespective of whatever buildings may be put along their borders. We must take the purely civic point of view and demand that the city in its corporate capacity, independent of anything that individuals may do, shall lay down, as the leading thoroughfares of its residential district, streets that are worthy of the highest development streets can have. We should realise that it is shameful, disgraceful to the high unselfishness of the belief in brotherhood—which may be called the modern religion—that large groups of men should be careless regarding the street on which they occupy splendid homes. When noble houses replete with comforts are erected on streets devoid of beauty, and there is no effort to supply the omission, there is given an evidence that something is the matter with the occupants. The obvious fault of the city in permitting this neglect may reasonably be laid to their own doors. They publish broadcast their lack not of public spirit only, nor merely of civic spirit, but even of neighbourhood, or social, spirit. They live for themselves alone, and with so little foresight as not to see that what one has done for one's city one has done for one's self and one's home.

Assuming, then, a desire to have these streets stately and worthy, we find that the attractiveness of a leading residential thoroughfare, its own lines — as to directness, length, and breadth — having been properly laid down, will depend on the following elements: the pavement and sidewalks; the street furnishings; the use of vegetation, in street trees and turf; the building along the street's borders; and the street's adornment for adornment's sake alone.

It will hardly be called the duty of civic art to determine the character of the street pavement, but there must be requirement that it be well laid and well maintained both as to cleanliness and repair. Civic art will even go so far as to advocate a comparative noiselessness. The glory of the modern feature in our civic Renaissance is that such requirements as these can now be taken for granted. No civic art of other times has rested on so firm and elemental a foundation. Storied Carthage, splendid Athens, kingly Alexandria, imperial Rome, the Florence of Lorenzo the Magnificent, the Bruges and Ghent of the Northern Renaissance — none of these considered the pavement under the horses' feet a prerequisite to their civic art. Even a sidewalk was rare. We, on the other hand, do not begin to talk

of civic art, if we are logical, until the street is paved
and clean.

The walk, since it may become a decorative element of the street, may demand more attention than
the paving of the roadway. The opportunity will
often come when, beneath a long row of trees, there
may be a walk of fine gravel or well packed dirt.
After the hard pavement of the business streets, there
could be no change which is at once practicable and
so pleasant. But commonly, in the damp and rigorous climate with which many cities must do battle, there is need of a footing that is dryer and more
substantial. The prepared stone, or cement, walks
that have lately come widely into use make a humble, but certain, contribution to municipal æsthetics.
One who has written and thought much on town and
city improvement has well said [1] : there is "nothing
more agreeable for eye or foot than long stretches of
granolithic walk, commonly laid with broad margins
of turf on either hand, the smooth, clean light-gray
in beautiful contrast with the velvety verdure. And
there is no surer way to save the precious grass from
trampling feet than to give it such a footway neighbour." In the residential area, even on these leading streets of it, there are no other kinds of walk
to be advocated. If the demand of pedestrianism
be light, these can make for it the lightest provision. If it be heavy, they can be made broad to

[1] See series of articles in *The Century Magazine*, 1902-1903, by Sylvester
Baxter.

care for it. They are easier to the feet than the great
stone flags of the business district; and if the latter were carried into the residential portions, one of
pedestrianism's pleasantest marks of the transition —
the change from stone walks to these softer ways
with their lovely grass borders — would be lost.

Of the furnishings of these streets there is small
occasion to speak now, for civic art's ideals in this
regard have been pointed out in discussing the business thoroughfares. For the most part, the furnishings are the same — the street lights, the street name
signs, the possible poles for trolley or other wires, the
flag-staffs that should be made architectural adjuncts
of the buildings they are erected in connection with
or else frankly decorative features, the fire-alarm
and mail boxes, etc. If it be the ideal of civic art
that these furnishings have artistic design, that they
be made to harmonise with their surroundings, and
be treated, hence, as distinct problems in distinct
portions of the city, there will arise a need, no
doubt, for new designs when we come into the main
avenues of the residential district, but hardly for new
discussion until, by a definite street or city, a concrete problem is presented.

On these avenues, however, there may be wanted
some furnishings that had not been required by the
business streets. Such are seats placed at intervals
along the way. The necessity or advantages of
these will be considered appropriately when we
come to the trees and turf. It is enough now to

note that civic art will not observe their desirability alone, but will be keen to see if they be of appropriate design and colour, so that they blend harmoniously into the scene, and that they are kept in repair. "Out at elbows," as the saying is, is a condition that no town with pretensions to civic art can anywhere permit. In European cities (as Paris) where the provision and rental of some of the chairs on the public way is a "concession" let by the municipality to private contractors, a clause of the agreement requires that the seats conform to a model approved by the administration and be always in repair. The attitude uniformly adopted by civic art to all the details of street furnishing will be one of deep respect. Far from considering these beneath its notice, it will see in them the opportunity to complete, for comparatively trifling sums, pictures that are grandiose in scale but that will never perform their full function until so perfected. Many a noble building, many a lovely square, many a stately street is marred, after vast expenditure, by the lack of that little additional care and that small extra expense that would have finished worthily the decoration.

Coming now to the use that is made of vegetation on the great highways of the residential area, we reach their most distinguishing feature. Nothing at once separates them so markedly from the other streets of the city — in both its business and residential sections — or gives to them a character so instantly and strikingly their own as does this. Few things, also, mark more distinctly the modernness of our civic art. The great avenues will often have turf—even if it be only between car tracks—and rows of trees. Frequently there will be a middle strip planted with the latter. The city that was once forced to shut out the country with wall and bastion throws open the gates and levels the walls, counting now no ornament of its proudest ways more precious than carefully tended nature can give.

The whole conception of the street changes. It is probable that outside of their public squares no parallel is offered in the ancient cities. The way is no longer a mere means of communication. Even the great radials of the residential area, which are so primarily this, find their development modified by the new idea. It becomes possible to class them, trunk lines of travel as they are, with the parkways and noble residential avenues. The new idea is to make an open-air salon of the street; and these thoroughfares that are not, on the one hand, choked with travel and wearisome with the press and din of business, nor yet, on the other hand, minor ways dull with a lack of life and motion,— these avenues, with their constant movement and gaiety, their ebb and flow of passing that is animated but without the rush of desperation, these are the ideal location for the " open-air, public, parlours."

The conception came from the Continent of Europe, apparently, where soft airs and sunny days in

long-continued sequence offer irresistible invitations
to an out-of-doors life. The alamedas of Spain and
her colonies are broad walks shaded with trees,
bordered with carefully nurtured grass, shrubs, and
flowers, with rows of chairs or benches. All day and
evening happy throngs stroll up and down or loll
upon them. No sports or games are here, except
the ever-changing game of life. The smooth, dust-
less driveway that is often part of the alameda is
thronged at certain hours with swiftly moving lines
of vehicles. Their occupants are the players to the
gaily chatting multitudes upon the walk; just as the
latter are, in their turn, the players to these spectators in the carriages. In Paris, and the cities of
France that copy her, men sit at little tables in the
street so long — eating, drinking, smoking, reading
the papers, and watching the life of the way — that
it is impossible to dissociate the boulevards from the
"boulevardiers." And here again, for the pleasure
of the people, the streets are lined with trees, with
now and then a strip of verdure under foot. Again,
too, in Hungary, South Germany, or Austria, no
restaurant can succeed if it have not seats for its
patrons out-of-doors, and there, as in Switzerland
and Italy as well, you will find chairs and tables on
the walks and vine-covered trellises over part of the
public way.

Busier America and cloudier England have not
fully caught the out-of-door spirit in their towns;
but the ceaseless throngs that on holidays and fine

afternoons parade Fifth Avenue in New York, or the Serpentine in Hyde Park, London, and the unanimity with which all the seats in all the squares are occupied, would have given proof enough of the popularity of such avenue provision for enjoyment had there been need of proving it. So we find this new purpose changing the surface development that these thoroughfares will have, and — since they have been already made broad, direct, arterial, and serve well their primary function — it dictates the character of the furnishing and decoration that may be given to them.

In so far as this consists of the use of trees, civic art would urge that the planting be harmonious. It were best, indeed, that the larger, or permanent, trees on any street — or those at least that are between consecutive accents of the street — should be of one kind. They will be far more effective so, and we may then hope for a natural symmetry in growth. The trees should also be cleanly, hardy, naturally long-lived, and of appropriate form. On these broad streets they should have stateliness and ample foliage, and if they be set out in the turf strip their roots will have the better chance of nourishment. The trees, it would urge, should not be left to the care of individuals, nor should their provision be entrusted to private persons. They are here as distinct a furnishing of the way and a public benefit as are any of the street utilities. Considered as the property of the municipality, it should be held

The Champs Elysées, Paris.

responsible for their provision and maintenance, either through the park commission or a city forester. In many cities tree nurseries are already maintained; and in nearly all that are progressive so precious a possession as the street tree is safeguarded by ordinances defending it from the carelessness of drivers and the thoughtlessness of bill posters. Civic art would insist on a very strict enforcement of these ordinances.

As for the strip of turf, or parking, since its sole purpose is to beautify, it will necessarily be well kept. There will be waste receptacles, as inconspicuous as may be, at sufficiently frequent intervals to make easy the maintenance of its neatness, while careful cutting and watering are to be assumed. Flowers will frequently be used. Perennials that do not grow too high may, with proper reservations, be approved; and where there are beds of annuals, conventional or grotesque shapes will be avoided in favour of those straight lines and borders that fit most harmoniously into the long prospect of the street. There should be seats at frequent intervals, far more frequent than is common in the streets of American cities, for we ought to encourage the poor to seek the fresh air and sunshine, and should make it easy as well as pleasant to take care of little children out-of-doors, instead of keeping them in stuffy rooms. Contact with the bustling, busy world may be as good for the caretakers as is the fresh air for the children. There is something to be said, too, for the European custom of supplementing the generous municipal provision of the out-of-door seats by a concession to private contractors which enables the latter to make a small charge for the use of the chairs. This results in the possibility of nearly always getting a seat in the more advantageous positions, and it gives a degree of exclusiveness, which unhappily is sometimes welcome, to this very slight extent, on the public way. The contractors' conduct of their business must, of course, be carefully watched.

From what has been said of the Spanish alamedas, it must not be supposed that the ideal of all these streets, even from the standpoint of pure enjoyment, is a place for dawdling in the open air. If that were all, the park or the planted open spaces were better fitted to serve the end. The special attractiveness of such avenues to the persons who dawdle upon them lies in their brilliancy and animation, in the happy flow of their normal traffic. In our street plan we have imagined not more than one or two of the avenues thus developed as simply a pleasure drive; the rest are arterial thoroughfares, are boulevards, or avenues of fashionable residence. It is the triumph of modern civic art to transform these necessary girdles and girders of the structure of the city into ways of pleasure and beauty. Here the whirr of the electric car, there the rush of swiftly passing motor cars—these are elements of the scene that may count not less distinctly in the

total power to please than does the verdure. For
this reason, the construction which is along the
edge of such streets becomes an important factor in
the scenic attractiveness of both street and town.

The development of the street border in such
cases falls under three general subheads. First, in
the case of the purely beauty or pleasure road, there
may be very little building, or perhaps no building
on one side — as illustrated, for example, by Riverside
Drive, New York, with its extensions secured and
proposed. In this case a lovely view is substituted
for buildings, on one side of the road, with an enor-
mous gain in picturesqueness and beauty. The
opportunity was, however, exceptional. Unless the
road borders a park, or tortuously climbs a steep hill,
— as the road that ascends to San Miniato, Florence,
—or is on a high bluff, as is the Riverside Drive, such
a chance is not presented. If these conditions be not
existent and there still be little building, we have to
assume either frequent stretches of vacant land or
residences surrounded by grounds so relatively
spacious that the gardens count for more than the
structures in giving character to the way. Because
the vacant land is considered a merely temporary
condition it is liable to receive too little attention. A
few cities have now adopted ordinances that prohibit the erection of bill-boards on vacant lots abutting on parks, parkways, or boulevards. This is well
as far as it goes, but the land, whether occupied or
not, that borders a street is so inseparable a factor in

its possible amenity that on these streets at least,
where beauty is so earnestly sought, vacant property
should be strictly governed. The cutting of the
weeds, the general care of the land, and the maintenance in perfect repair of its enclosing boundaries
should be insisted upon. For the private lawns and
gardens there is seldom a need of anxiety. The
wealth that affords a long frontage on such streets
can usually be depended upon to make it a creditable
border to the way.

Second, there are the avenues built up, in varying degrees of density, with handsome residences.
The effects are many. There are the garden-surrounded villas, homesteads, and pretentious mansions
of the fashionable avenue of a city that has ample
room for growth and no great population; there are
the stately rows of closely built apartment houses,
as on some of the proudest streets of Paris; and there
are handsome but sadly crowded residences, as on
Fifth Avenue, in New York. But as far as the
preservation of street stateliness and beauty is concerned, these conditions differ little from those on the
avenue lined with broad estates, where the abutting
property may be safely left in the hands of those
who occupy it, without dictation by the municipality
other than that involved in quite ordinary building
regulations.

The placing of the residences on all the great
avenues, and on the minor streets as well, is a matter
to which civic art would fain have more thoughtful

attention given than is usually secured. The term "placing" of the house, here means both its placing in relation to the street and the development of an appropriate beauty: (1) in selecting the angle at which it shall face; (2) in setting it off with terraces or well planned approaches; and (3) by turning to good account such natural beauty — in tree or rock or irregularity of surface — as the site may have. All this is part of the landscape architect's profession and it would doubtless be well if he and the architect could more frequently co-operate. The vista of many a good street is marred by the needless placing askew of a house.

Finally, on the great radials, which we have imagined as the residential district's main lines of travel, there may be not only the residences which are characteristic of all these streets, but, as we have seen, the public buildings that are the local, or neighbourhood, centres. These should be made worthy of their importance. They become prominent objects of the way, and will gain not a little from the attractiveness of the setting offered by the street. The bareness of the school will disappear as the vines climb its walls, and as swaying trees fleck the sunshine on door and window and send shadows scudding across the walk, like children late to school. The branch post-office and library will have a new and grateful, and here a wholly appropriate, air of domesticity with an outlook on turf and trees and flowers, while the importance of the street is dignified and emphasised by the assemblage thus upon it of the locality's most consequential structures. There come, too, a special variety and interest as post-office, library, school, and church punctuate the building line.

It can be fancied that in the ideal construction of an ideal city the municipality, in laying out these arterial radials, would reserve certain sites on advantageous corners that they might surely be occupied for public purposes. There would be for this the further inducement that because these streets are diagonal, in reference to the street systems they cross, there will be many corners that are difficult of treatment unless more than one lot be included in the tract to be built upon. In that case the site may offer a noble architectural opportunity, while if left in the hands of private owners the small corner lot, now cut down to a triangle, may seem of so little worth as to have scant attention. That this is a real danger and one of serious import to the street appears from the action taken by the influential T-Square Club (of architects) in Philadelphia, when the project for pushing a diagonal parkway from the City Hall to Fairmount Park came before the public. The year's competitions were all devoted to the building problems that would arise from the construction of the thoroughfare. The first of these was to plan "a house on a triangular lot"; the second was "the treatment in elevation of the angle of a private residence" on such a lot. It is evident that there was keen appreciation of a menace to be guarded against, as well as of an opportunity to be embraced.

In the elements of street attractiveness we have now considered, in regular order, the pavement and walks, the "furnishings" of the street, the use of verdure, and the influence of the building along its margin. We have come to the final factor: the adornment for adornment's sake. This must consist of decoration with sculpture, with fountains, exedras, arches, and statues. There is clearly no more appropriate place for such adornment than these great show avenues, with their room to spare. On what other streets could fountains play more fittingly than on these with the flowers and grass; where else than here, where seats are well-nigh a necessity, will the exedra be so natural and useful an ornament of the way; and where but here, with the proffered background of foliage and yet with no "naturalness" of design that must be marred by sudden formalism, can the statue show so picturesquely?

A notable example of such a great avenue, munificently adorned with sculpture, is offered by the little known Paseo de la Reforma in the City of Mexico. This is three miles long and very broad. At each of five places on its length there is laid out that circular broadening that in Paris is called a Rond Point and in London a Circus, but that the Mexicans more aptly name a Glorietta,—the Paseo is a diagonal on a gridiron plan,—and each of these is dedicated to sculpture exalting a national hero. At regular intervals on the road-lawn there rise stone pedestals. They are allotted to the states of the nation, that upon each of them may be commemorated, in a life-size statue, a hero of the state ; while on the far side of the footway — and so facing the avenue — there are numerous monumental seats of stone.

As for the arch, returning to the subject of sculpture on these streets, it hardly rises in one city among a score. But where it does, there would be no site of more theoretical suitability than at the beginning of one of these great avenues, or at its terminus and crown. So, at the beginning of Fifth Avenue, rises the Washington Arch in New York; so, at the entrance to Unter den Linden, in Berlin, is the Brandenburg Thor; and so, at the convergence of avenues, looms the Arch of the Star in Paris.

We speak of the arch as triumphal; but more surely than of triumph is its effect one of pomp and majesty — the two qualities which these avenues are expected especially to stamp upon the town. And as this is said, we should consider the changed conception of civic art. It has become an end in itself. The arch that rose to glorify a conqueror may rise to magnify a city's splendour. The statues that commemorate proud events and worthy citizens are put up the more willingly because they make handsomer a highway. The fountains that had their origin in the need of a public place for drawing water are erected now that they may beautify a street; and the long straight thoroughfares that were laid down as principal lines of communication are broadened to become the salons of the city, and are adorned to stamp it with majesty. Thus are expressed the new ideals of civic art — those dreams that make it modern, because a city's splendour, and beautiful majestic streets, are now desired for the greater happiness and welfare of its citizens.

CHAPTER XII.

ON MINOR RESIDENTIAL STREETS.

A CITY is not all grandiose. Even in an age of industry and commerce, or of ruinous luxury, — according to the point of view, — the city is not all business or all pleasure, nor business and pleasure merely side by side. Earners and spenders have home life, and the city presents no aspect more inspiring, more appealing to civic art, than that of an aggregation of homes. It has no element which invites more earnestly the civic-art ambition and endeavour.

If the town existed merely for business — in trade or manufacture — there would be scant gain in making handsome thoroughfares; and if it existed merely as a rendezvous for the rich, they might be left to seek beauty elsewhere. But the city brings together, as the major part of its population, those who, having to work indeed, are something better than machines — men and women who dream dreams, little children in whose faces the wonder and glory of

Paradise should linger still, youths with love's refining finger on their souls, the aged in whose hearts the vision of the city of God is cherished expectantly. Upon these, the multitudes of the city, rests more than ever before the hope of humanity. They are now the straining vanguard of mankind. "He who makes the city makes the world," for he makes the environment of these, the world's workers. As this environment is lovely and uplifting, or mean and depressing, as it feeds or starves the brains and spirits whose outlook upon earth it compasses, it may be supposed to influence the battle — to help the forward or retrograde movement of the race. So a new dignity, a moral quality, comes into the plea for civic art when it touches the homes of the people.

And is there no yearning for beauty and the comfort of peace and harmony in the home ? We recognise it too well to make the question deserve an answer. The unexplained but long observed and well-nigh unanimous growth of cities to the westward, by the addition to their west side of the homes of those who are able to choose, seems like an unconscious yielding, after the weariness and toil of day, to the beckoning quiet and beauty of the sunset. Is it not the constant repetition of that beauteous sign in the sky, when work is done, that unconsciously calls men thither ?

Civic art has, then, a new and higher impulse when it comes to the homes of the workers, and it finds a field waiting and ready. Its problem is not the collective, civic, and splendid, as on the great avenues; it is not to teach and incite, as in the business district. It is to harmonise individual efforts in order that private endeavour may serve the public end. The exterior of your home, said Ruskin, is not private property. So he stated, boldly and strikingly, a principle that has wide legal recognition — that the outside of the house and such part of the grounds as may be seen from the street are the very real concern of the neighbours. They, indeed, see more of the outside of the house than does he who dwells within it; and if he receives, or would receive, pleasure from their homes and gardens, he should do his share in making a contribution of his own to the attractiveness or beauty of the street. On that firm basis, then, of give and take — a dependence somewhat surer than unselfishness, if not so lovely — rests the inviting character of the minor residential street in so far as it depends on individual homes.

And this dependence is very great. Except a probable row of trees at either curb, the minor street of the older residential area has seldom any feature to give beauty to it save the abutting private property. Even the trees are not here assured. The long bare blocks of New York, the standard "object lesson," are duplicated in many other cities. It may almost be said, in fact, that the normal residential street of minor significance, in the central part of great cities, is a hopeless problem æsthetically except as private property may redeem it. There is need perhaps of reminder, in this assertion, that road, curb, and sidewalk — however necessary and however excellently built — appear as beautiful only to the professional eye of a well-pleased engineer. Yet, if a little variety be brought into their construction, if the colour of walk and grass make pleasant contrast, if the sidewalk in obedience to natural conditions now and then rise a little from the level of the road, or make slow detour in curving line to save a tree, we shall have an effect to which at least beauty is not so foreign as to be denied, should the development on the borders of the street be favourable. But departures from line and level are almost uniformly renounced in the older parts of cities.

On the outskirts and in the newer quarters, where modern civic art has had a chance to alter old conditions, or to create new ones better suited to its taste, there is not only a greater probability of street trees, but it is probable the street plan has been changed. There are streets here of slowly curving lines, and thoroughfares that gradually rise and fall with the natural surface of the ground, to the end that they have elements of beauty in themselves. Yet even here the larger house-grounds, made possible by the lessened pressure at such distance from the city's centre, impose new obligations on the residents of the street. In fact the opportunity of the house-grounds here to mar or improve the street's appearance is thus increased.

As to trees, the subject is a large one. In the

specific instance offered by each city there are a hundred things to be considered. But the general principles applicable to all towns, regardless of whether the natural growth be the palm of Algiers, the linden of Berlin, the acacia of Paris, or the elm of New England,[1] are not many, and such as they are these have been fairly summed up in the preceding chapter. There is only this to add: Since these minor streets seldom have space for more than a single row of trees on each side of the road, the trees should be planted, not directly opposite, but alternately. So with seeming greater frequency there may really be ample room for growth. For these streets, too, where the buildings are not high and are set well back from the walk, there may be chosen trees of large growth and these should be encouraged to grow to their full height. We shall not fear now to seek the splendid individual specimen nor, finding one, shall we fail to cherish it. It may quite properly become here the feature of the view, for the ideal development is no longer that of the strict formalism in other portions of the town. The very abandonment of the engineering standard, in substituting curves for straight lines and permitting grades where levels could have been obtained by simply cutting and filling, invites more laxity in the adornment with vegetation and suggests a tendency towards naturalness. But of course even this prin-

[1] Witness, as testifying to the urban value of these native trees : the Avenue des Palmes in Algiers, Unter den Linden in Berlin, the Avenue des Acacias in Paris, and the frequent Elm Street in New England.

ciple can be called general only in its application to the suburban or less crowded streets. It may still be necessary on solidly built-up thoroughfares, however minor these be in the town's topography, to have small and formal trees.

And finally there is to be emphasised again the value of municipal control of trees. The park board, into whose hands they are very often placed when such control is exercised, has responsibility enough in the squares and parks. In the fascinating problems which are offered by these, and the striking effects that can be secured in them, there is a temptation to overlook the trees or to delegate their care to a superintendent whose work has little overseeing. It is safer at once to vest him with the full responsibility, and for the city to obtain a better officer by making the custody of the trees a distinct department, under the charge of a warden or forester. In the United States this is already decreed by several State laws; and it is an interesting evidence of the foothold of modern civic art that an intelligent provision for the care of these ornaments of the street — pure ornaments as they are commonly thought to be — and details of street furnishing that the splendid cities of antiquity scarcely made a use of, should now be forced upon towns by the laws of states. Even "Antioch the beautiful," whose epithet would suggest a use of the luxuriant vegetation of its plain, depended for distinction on the splendour of its palaces and temples.

There are many other considerations than the æsthetic on which to commend a planting of street trees. Trees not only cool the air, in addition to affording a shade that in itself is cool compared to the sun's direct rays, but they purify it, by absorbing poisonous gases and giving forth oxygen. They also tend to absorb that surplus water in the soil that may make basements damp. It is claimed, too, that they have a commercial value to cities, in that people remain much further into the summer in the towns that are well planted with trees. These considerations, however, re-emphasise, rather than supplant, the entirely sufficient ground of attractiveness on which modern civic art would urge the planting of trees in cities. And having urged their planting, it would urge consistently their care — the safeguarding of their bark, while they are young, with nettings, baskets, or iron guards, and always with stringent ordinances; the proper nurture and protection of their roots; and the defence of their branches from spoliation by linemen, insects, and too vigorous trimming.

Where there are no trees, or where they are so poor and far between as no longer to be a factor, experience would bid us assume the street to be narrow, straight, level, and closely built up — a street in the inner system of a large city. Here the sole dependence for the beauty of the way must be placed on private property. It is a discouraging condition, but it must be bravely faced, and the individual residents,

who certainly have already an inducement to make
their homes attractive, are to be encouraged in the
task,—that conditions may not dishearten them,—
and led so to co-operate that there may be a
harmonious result and that each effect may be
heightened by its neighbours. An enthusiastic attempt to transform one of the solidly built-up blocks
of the borough of Brooklyn in New York into "the
block beautiful" is a recent and an almost pathetic-
ally striking instance of the effort and its courage.

The block selected had barely a tree. The houses
were built in a solid wall, extending unbroken and
with monotonous façade, from corner to corner; and
there was no possibility of lawn or flower-bed. The
plan was to secure a uniform planting of trees, and
by the co-operation of the residents to engage a
gardener who should plant vines against the houses,
and arrange and care for porch and window boxes,
the latter to be placed on the first and second stories.
The moderate measure of success attained amid even
such conditions is rich in suggestion for minor residential streets. In the gay window boxes of German
cities and in those that bring so much beauty to
the dull street walls of London, this lesson is
immensely emphasised.

From such a street as described every change,
while still among private homes, must be one of
increasing opportunity. As the houses retreat from
the walk, there comes a space before them for flowers
and grass; as they draw apart from each other, there

comes a chance for vistas of lawn, for shrubs, and perhaps for beautiful trees on the house-lots themselves. The front fences come down; party fences are abandoned, at least to the building line; and the narrow street is seemingly widened by the breadth of the visible gardens on either side. By degrees these play a more and more prominent part in giving character and beauty to the street's appearance. It is suddenly realised that the individual homes, upon which civic art is here putting its main dependence and for whose occupants it exists, are bearing bravely their part. They are making beautiful a street that in itself had little beauty; and when, at last, the newer portions of the town are reached, and the street rises and falls with the gentle undulation of the natural surface, or winds and curves in lines that are essentially beautiful, it is observed that every changing view-point, every angle, offers a new glimpse of private ground with its opportunity to enhance or lessen the beauty of the street.

In these portions of the city even the minor street will often widen enough to admit of parking. But the dependence on the house-lots will not vanish under such conditions, though it be no longer complete. Until there is the parking — which is street gardening by the community, local or municipal — civic art has no task more urgent than the guidance of private taste, which is to say its persuasion into harmonious action, its æsthetic education, or the instruction of those whose taste is already refined but

A Minor Residential Street,

whose practical experience is slight. Therein lies the opportunity of the societies for outdoor art, and on this need rests their popularity. They are making known the one great modern feature of our civic art which is of a personal concern to every householder. They are teaching the lesson of the use of vegetation, and its use when necessary in subordination to the general weal, that can be learned by no conning of the civilisations of the past. With their every wisely taken step these carry forward the march of modern civic art.

Regarding the lessons to be taught, there must again be limitation here to the most general principles. The local conditions that may properly exaggerate or modify desired results do so too naturally to need a notice, even were it possible to speak specifically of every varying locality with its different flora. It means much for civic art that considerations so abstract and large as "general principles" should have a popular attention, and that the immediate and showy effects of contrasted colours and carpet bedding should be relinquished for those quieter effects which are indeed of untiring loveliness, but which require for full appreciation a more cultured taste, and for anticipation a trained mind. Modern civic art, considered in the abstract, has nothing more pressing to do for the improvement of the minor residential streets than the popularising of those general principles of landscape design that may be applied to the house-lot in the city.

In briefly condensed statement, these principles require the massing and grouping of shrubs in boundary plantations, and the clearance of the lawn thereby of the spotted and unstudied planting which is commonly the first expression of outdoor art ambition. Value is placed on the quiet and beauty of an unbroken lawn, bounded where necessary with belts of foliage that break hard lines by an undulating edge reflecting the varying width of the border plant-ation. This plantation will screen all necessary but unattractive structures, and may take the place of a fence — even of a front fence where privacy is desirable, as it often is. A hedge is better than a fence, but an irregular belt of planting is better than a hedge. The border will have an irregular sky-line, and on its lawn face will taper down almost to the grass — the lower-growing plants being placed in front. This border will have such variety of foli-age and flower as to be a lovely feature in itself. Into its bays or openings a herbaceous or hardy flower border may at times be pressed, while the lawn — left clear, perhaps as far back as the house — will seem to give to the latter a statelier setting and to add no little charm both to street and house-lot. The service yard, at back or side, will be screened from the street; and where the house rises from the ground an edging of shrubs, again in lines of natural irregularity, will break the harsh contrast and hard angle between lawn and structure, wedding them in a lovely union. Now and again, but usually in a place so sequestered as regards the street that it will not affect the latter's appearance, there may be an opportunity for formal gardening. More often there will be a carriage road to provide; but this our landscape designer considers, however necessary, little better than an evil and renders as inconspicuous as possible.

The use of trees, in groups or singly; the utilisation of beautiful or noble specimens which may already stand upon the lot; the planting of vines that their graceful drapery may clothe bare walls, soften sharp corners, or bring new beauty and picturesqueness to piazza, porch, and balcony,—all these are details that will suggest themselves so powerfully in each specific case, and require such distinct decisions, that there is no need to emphasise them here. It is only to be said, as another general principle of landscape art, that the vine should be used with restraint, in remembrance that the architectural effect of a structure should not be sacrificed to the beauty of a luxuriant vine-growth. The vine may be lovely in itself and may bring into the structure a gentleness that the architect failed to secure; but we must not create, as the total of our composition, an apparent substructure of fluttering leaves to support an upper story of stone or brick. Nor can the vine always " be left to grow in its own wilful way." It may need to be watched carefully and trained.

The main points that civic art would urge, in considering the house-lots in their capacity for bringing beauty to the street, may now be summarised. They are: (1) that it is not enough that the house and its grounds be even neat and orderly, essential to street beauty as these qualities are; (2) that in attempt to secure positive beauty there be regard for the elementary principles of landscape art; (3) that with such regard there be some harmony, if not actual co-operation, among neighbours, so that every individual effect may have the support of all the others; (4) and as partly explaining the first and third requirements, that there be remembrance that it is the street, and even the town as far as may be,. which we are to make more beautiful; and thus that the problem of our outdoor art, at this point, is not merely that of a garden, or of shrubbery, or of wedding a house to its site or of giving to it a beautiful setting; but is the larger, more difficult, more virile, and inspiring one of civic beauty. In this, pre-eminently, art must be founded upon rationality and fitness, and its triumph must be democratic.

In those undertakings for municipal æsthetics which have their roots in sociology, there has lately been much emphasis on the "improvement" of back yards. The back yard is a problem that sociology cannot overlook, and even from the standpoint of landscape art it may offer an area equal to that which is clearly visible from the street. If it does, the rules to be applied are not very different. They are modified by the probable necessity of setting aside a portion for a service yard, and by the greater desirability of privacy, with the increased opportunity thus given for the expression of individuality. From the standpoint of civic art, the back yard has significance only on the theory that our municipal æsthetics are something more comprehensive than *art dans la rue;* that they concern not simply the aspect of the city, as the stranger may see it in superficial examination, but that they are to enter into the very structure of the town, refining the home as well as the avenue, and changing the unseen as well as the visible. And of course the back yards of a community do affect the view from the house windows, and so have in them the possibility of adding to the beauty and attractiveness of the city in the eyes of its citizens and the guests in its homes. Here, however, civic art treads close on the rights of privacy, and it would do no more than urge in a general way a study of the principles of good design and a respect, not perhaps for the rights, but for what may be the privileges, of neighbours.

The landscape treatment of a street which has a strip reserved for parking on each side of the road is a problem entirely distinct from the development of street beauty by means of the house-lots. The dependence is not now quite so completely upon them; civic art has before it a task that partakes much more of a community character, since the expressions of individualism should clearly enter but little into parking. The work on the reserved strip is to be done by the municipality through one or another of its

departments, or by the residents of the street acting
as a group, for surely it were a mistake to divide a
section of the public street into parcels and then
abandon each to the whim or neglect of an individual.

There is offered in the centre, or more frequently
on each side of the road between the road and
walk, a strip that is not dedicated to travel. This
should be developed as a ribbon of loveliness that,
laid lengthwise from street's end to street's end, or
as far as the eye can see, will so stamp its character
on the thoroughfare as to make it beautiful. Thus is
parking a new privilege, which has been given only
to modern civic art, and one rich in opportunities.

The long strip on residential streets where travel
is not heavy will surely be planted with turf, and the
most prominent objects upon it will be the trees.
These will be planted here, for their roots will have
a better chance for nurture than where pavement and
walk shut out moisture from the ground. The position of the trees is usually in a formal row, with
regular intervals between—as the commoner ideal for
city planting. But it sometimes happens where there
is parking that they may stand in little groups of two
or three. Especially may this be done when the
trees antedate the street. When such groups are
found, it might probably be that the appearance of
the street would be more hurt than aided by their
removal. This group planting is not as favourable
for symmetry, but it will permit, with its greater
naturalness, the use of several varieties of trees,

while a row requires uniformity for good effect. Much will depend, of course, on the style of the treatment given to the strip of parking. The thing that civic art would note is the opportunity for "natural" development, if this be desired.

In addition to the trees that now rise from neatly kept turf, it will often be well to plant the strip with shrubbery or flowers. Where there is "natural" treatment, the trees may rise from masses of foliage as they so frequently do in nature; and when the treatment is strictly formal, the shrubs or flowers will lend themselves readily to the composition. The streets, however, on which flowers are expected to bloom need to be secluded, and far removed from those sections of the city where flowers are rare, lest their beauty prove too great a temptation and be despoiled. The shrubs, too, are not available except when the strip of parking has considerable width, for it is important that they should not overhang walk or road, and if they be planted too near the curb horses will nibble at them. At corners, also, they must be of low growth lest, by shutting out the view, they invite collisions. And yet, even with these restrictions, they are frequently used, immensely adorning and beautifying the street so that it ceases to seem a public way—a means of public communication only—and appears rather as a lovely avenue in park or private grounds. But the original function of the street is still served admirably — the better, indeed, for the pleasant change in its character.

For what is the function of the minor street in the residential section, if it be not, as far as each individual is concerned, to prove a prolongation, for the public convenience, of his garden walk ? It is the connection between his home and the great arteries of the city; but it is something more than only a line of communication. It is to be as pleasant a line as possible; it is to soothe the tired spirit and delight the eye; to carry the word " Home " far out to meet him when he comes, and to take it with him, with lingering caress, when he departs. It is, in its multiplication, to delight with beauty the thousands in the city who still have eyes to see and ears to hear and appreciation of the beautiful. So its influence is to be refining and elevating, and the little children who play upon it are unconsciously to drink in beauty that will make strong their souls, and that perhaps will repay the city a thousand times in the making of better citizens and the nurturing of genius.

It is a moving, almost a dramatic, circumstance that in the beautiful adjustment to this beautiful end —and is not that the sum of civic art ?—there should be need to put so much dependence upon the people themselves. We have, too, to realise that civic art, even in this its gentler phase, is not sentiment, but is merely the right fitting of this part of the city to its real urban purpose of home making. That fact gives assurance of a success, if men be true to their ideals, that may be hastened, but which we cannot, if we would, arrest.

CHAPTER XIII.

AMONG THE TENEMENTS.

SOCIAL problems are to a large degree problems of environment. This with increasing positiveness is the conclusion of modern scientific study into the depths of sociology. Give to the boy and girl a chance; make it possible for them to work off sheer animal energy in harmless amusements; render homes pleasant, and satisfy the craving of men for brightness, entertainment, and fellowship without throwing them into temptation; let an abundance of fresh air and sunshine into living and sleeping rooms, and the slum will be ancient history and many of sociology's hardest problems will be solved. The Juvenile Court would not have business enough to keep it going; the saloon would have its vigour sapped by a substitute; the hospitals would not require constant multiplication. There would be more of manliness; there would be purer souls, for there would be less temptation; there would be saner minds because of stronger bodies.

And out of depressing social conditions grow political evils. In the city slum smoulders the fire which breaks forth in revolution; in the conditions of the slum are bred those iniquities of politics — or the circumstances which make them possible — that may render revolution justifiable.

Corrective rather than punitive measures have long been the goal of sociology. The ounce of prevention weighs far more than the pound of cure — even if there be cure, which is always doubtful — where there are human lives to be saved, where are concerned citizens, where souls as well as bodies must be fed or starved. Obliterate the slum of the city, and shall we not in very truth see "a new heaven and a new earth . . . the holy city, new Jerusalem, coming down from God out of heaven?"

No two opinions can exist regarding the desirability of the slum's abolishment. The question is whether it can be abolished. We may certainly dream of remedying its worst features, and we must act as well as dream; but when all is said and done, is not the slum, in an improved form, a necessary evil of city life?

Modern civic art, pausing at the threshold of the tenement section of a city, is confronted by that question. It would be sane and practical, whatever the loss of lovely visions; and yet it would be true to itself. In the scientific rebuilding or creation of a city, it would produce a genuine work of art, and can it permit one such blot, such fatal blemish, on its product? The city or town of large population will surely include the very poor. To house these comfortably, to bring into their lives as much of sunshine and innocent pleasure as possible, to keep them in touch with the great pulsing life of the busy city where the might and joyousness of its industry shall reach and thrill them, to give to the children space to play, to the babies and mothers fresh air and quiet, to make the homes not only livable but attractive, to awaken ambition, to encourage the love of the beautiful — would not this, this glorious aggregate, be the first task that civic art would undertake? And behold! The old charm has again proved true; the magic road to happiness seems ever to lead in an oblique direction: we would take the first steps to help the residents of the slum, and before we finish the slum is gone!

Comfortably to house the very poor — this was to be an early step in the procedure. Here sociology joins hands with civic art in most earnest endeavour; but it will find some preliminary steps that it must take by itself. To secure better housing, there must be less crowding, and to gain that result two courses of action are open. Both must be availed of. There must, on the one hand, be furnished a vent that will make it possible for the homes of the poorest workers to cover an enlarged area. On the other hand, some of the workers must be drawn away, if possible, to another centre than that limited district against which the trade, industry, and wealth of the city is forever pounding in pitilessly encroaching waves. For the residue, always the more numerous portion, that still remains, new and better conditions are to be devised.

To enlarge the area available for tenements, there must be cheap rapid-transit. These workers are compelled to live near in time to their employment. From the nomadism of the push cart to the fixedness of shop or fruit-stand, there is requirement that the home of the worker be of quick and easy accessibility. As competition is keener and hours of labour are longer in the descending scale of employment, it becomes more and more essential economically that home and work be near. Civic art must give up any idea, however attractive, of bringing the poor from green fields to daily labour in the city's heart. Either the labour must be removed to the fields, or the workman must be housed in the city in close proximity to his work. He has no time for a long trip and no money to pay for it. The rapid-transit offered, then, must be — to aid the poorest — of the cheapest and most rapid.

There is no means of conveyance as cheap as walking. If this mode of progress can be accelerated by giving direct lines and streets so broad that there are no crowds to obstruct the pedestrian, then, clearly, the area available for the homes of those who must live near their labour has been much extended, and the congestion may be partially relieved. At the same time, the broadened thoroughfares can be made pleasant, cool, and refreshing in summer with the shade of trees and with the air musical with the ripple of running water. The relation of the city plan to the tenement district becomes thus manifest, and there is revealed a need of the same diagonal thoroughfares that were so convenient a feature of the well planned business district and, for pretty much the same reasons as here, so necessary a device for the framework of the general residential area.

Now, if these diagonals through the poorer sections of the city be only those constituting the main urban structure, we shall gain several unfortunate results. First, they will not form appropriately pleasant approaches to the better residential quarters; second, because they are diagonal arterial thoroughfares leading directly to the focal points of the city, they will offer to business so irresistible an invitation that it will sweep through them, probably destroying the trees that had been planted to make them cool and pleasant, congesting the broad walks so that progress is retarded, and, as if each were a main outlet stream from the tumultuous sea of the business centre, bursting the banks and overflowing in rivulets on the side streets, to the increase of pressure against the tenement district and to the wresting of territory from that space which is already so cramped. The probability of this second result is to be considered on those occasions, which will therefore be rare, when it would seem well to purge a degraded district by thrusting through it a broad stream of business traffic.

So advantages accrue in a distinct street system. The framework of this might consist of independent diagonals converging on local centres that will be just off the main lines of the general urban plot but with direct communication with them. These local centres might appropriately be open spaces, developed as playgrounds for the children to whom city streets were else the total of "all outdoors." And, however developed, such spaces would be airwells, deserving the name of lungs in city anatomy, and located precisely where they would benefit the greatest number of people. To streets converging to such centres and independent of the main system of the city, business would be little drawn. The thoroughfares could be made as broad and pleasant as desired, and yet they would form — cutting through this district in diagonal lines and converging on points that are just off the main highways of the city — direct channels of approach to the streets where work is done. The labourer might live much farther in space from his work, while no less near in time, for instead of narrow, crowded, tortuous streets through which slowly to make his way, he could now advance to it by swift and easy strides, unimpeded, and on the shortest lines. So there would be a little more of pleasantness brought into his daily life and a little less of crowding into his surroundings — the latter the first essential to better housing. So, too, this portion of the city would be better adapted to its purely urban requirement, and that is the goal of civic art.

The second step to relieve the crowding was to be the absolute withdrawal of such portions as possible of the tenement population from the necessarily limited area available for its housing in and near the city's heart. Since it is essential that those in the lower scales of employment shall live close to the workshop, the workshop must itself be removed. For many forms of employment, notably manufacture, there are fortunately advantages to the employer as well as to the employee in removal. The cheaper land values, for instance, the pleasanter and wholesomer natural surroundings, the consequent better physical condition of the employees, and the lessened distractions to tempt them (with a resulting greater steadiness in labour as well as capacity for it) offer in the aggregate powerful economic inducements to employers for removal whenever satisfactory transportation facilities can be arranged. As a result, industrial suburbs are now springing up where the habitable area is not closely limited — in short, on the outer rims of cities, precisely where — significantly enough — the British Garden City Association has designed in its model towns to put them.

These manufacturing suburbs, especially when they have grown around a single industry so affording to the humanity and public spirit of a few persons an opportunity to achieve substantial results, are often developed on very artistic lines. Thus they are fraught with much less danger than might be fancied to the residential portions of the town. In the first place, the more exclusive and fashionable quarters will be shunned owing to the greater cost of land. In the second place, the area over which the plants can be scattered is so enormously increased — large establishments may locate as far as twenty miles from great cities — that there is none of the former crowding with its attendant evils. Finally, the taking place of the movement has been coincident with a more scientific regard for town construction, while the very spur to it is so largely found in the wish to secure surroundings that are pleasanter and wholesomer that the factory itself, now vine-covered and garden-surrounded, is less to be dreaded. The homes and street surroundings of the residents, earners of low wages though these be, are rendered attractive and even beautiful. In fact, the residents no longer represent a tenement population. They are that population transplanted, and not merely transplanted but thereby transformed, and their homes are no longer tenements in the usually accepted sense.

The point to be made here, then, is only this: that the act of removal is a blessing to the real tenement quarters even when influenced by economic considerations alone; while frequently it is really an achievement of that phase of civic art which finds its incentive in a sociological impulse. The popular

lectures in England on the housing question, that
were endowed by a legacy of the late Earl of Shaftes-
bury, take, for example, the removal of manufactures
to the suburbs of cities as the panacea they especially
commend.[1] This is also the main hope of relief held
out by Dr. Weber in his exhaustive study of the
growth of cities.[2]

Pressure in the tenement district having been
relieved as far as practicable, both by the withdrawal
of some of the population and by the enlargement
of the available area, we have to consider the improvement of the district's internal conditions that it
may be as little of a blot as possible on the city.
Where there are concentrated so many elements of
picturesqueness, civic art should certainly secure some
contribution to the interest and charm of the city; and
where so large a portion of its population finds a
home,[3] it is under particular obligation, moral and
social, to make life not merely bearable but pleasant.

[1] Striking illustrations may be pointed out of this new industrial movement in,
for example, Port Sunlight, England, with its model cottages, its allotment gardens,
garden plots, and flower shows; in Cadbury's Bourneville Village Trust, near
Birmingham; in the Krupp colonies about Essen, Germany; in the Westinghouse
community near Pittsburg; in the transformation wrought by the National Cash Re-
gister Company at Dayton, Ohio; and in the developments at the Acme White Lead
and Colour Works, Detroit, where there has been adopted the motto, "Take hold
and lift." The success of these settlements indicates that industrial regard for civic
æsthetics is not a concession to sentimental impulse on the part of manufacturers
who are willing, for its sake, to sacrifice something of efficiency; but that it is
a phase of the effort to secure the latter. It is based on a recognition of the fact that
the labourer is a better workman if the environment of home and shop be shorn of
dreariness; if his higher impulses be fed, not starved, and he be made more man and
less machine.

[2] *The Growth of Cities in the Nineteenth Century*, by Adna Ferrin Weber.

[3] It is not unusual in large cities for half of the population to live in tenements,
using the word in even its narrower sense.

It should be understood, of course, that the tenement population is really of as many gradations as that in the other residential areas; and we have to assume in scientific city-building that there has been a constant drawing away, from the small and congested tenement district, of the upper stratum of the population. The influx is at the bottom; the internal effort, so far as it exceeds a mere struggle for existence, is to rise; and the removals are from the top. This is a discouraging condition as far as the abolishing of the slum is concerned, though one full of encouragement in its broader humanitarian aspect. The upper stratum when drawn away is scattered about the city, in a higher grade of apartment houses or tenements, standing by themselves and inhabited by those whose work is in their neighbourhood. It does not create a new tenement district; and thus the reference to such an area is to be understood as applying simply to the section of the city in which are huddled its poorest citizens and where the city's aspect is normally most dismal and depressing. By artificial means of rapid-transit, the withdrawal and dissipation of the upper stratum may be considerably facilitated, pedestrianism being happily not the sole resource. But even with the best facilities there is little chance of more than balancing the inflow with the out-take, and the district is yet to be considered.

A right conception of the municipality's obligation to its residents would insure, as it now is insuring,—

though rather through considerations of hygiene and sociology than those of political justice,— the supplementing of good street planning with improved surface treatment. Broad walks are more necessary here than broad roadways, although this change in conditions is almost never recognised in the street's development. Even the pavement, where so much of life is spent on the street, will be largely used as a floor, and cleanliness is a prime necessity.

In this part of the city, then, modern civic art, largely because it is modern, must concern itself with the rudiments of city-building. A convenient and potentially beautiful arrangement of streets; the broadening of the main thoroughfares in order that there may be easy progress through them, that they may be made pleasant with trees, and that they at least may allow the free circulation of air; the broadening of the walks; and the most improved surface development of the streets — the paving of the roadways with asphalt and their frequent flushing, and the provision when possible of a central strip on the main highways where the trees shall stand and a pleasant walk may pass beneath them — all these quite elementary steps will be the goal of civic art itself and logically will precede the attempts at better housing. As to the location of the reserved strip, it may be well to point out the advantages in this district of placing the trees in the centre of the roadway instead of at the curbs. First, the arrangement is better for the trees. They will have more room for symmetrical development than if placed at the curb, for the houses will be built flush with the street leaving only the walk's width between tree and house; their trunks will be subject to less frequent and less serious injury, while there will be also a better opportunity for the nourishment of the roots, both by enriching the soil and by the ground's absorption of moisture. Second, it will be better for the residents, since trees planted at the curb — if they did flourish — would darken the houses. Third, it will be better for the appearance of the streets, individually and collectively — individually because the trees will grow better, and collectively because open space will be united with open space by a belt of green instead of standing as isolated, disjointed oases without seeming connection or structural naturalness. Fourth, and finally, the centre parking will be better because of its division of the traffic into separate streams of opposite direction, to the considerable increase of rapidity and safety.

On the central strips of this district there need be no attempt to provide turf. They may be great bare playgrounds overhung with trees, and so stretched out that every portion of the area may have one which is readily accessible. Through the middle of them there should run a broad walk, with crown enough to keep it dry, and with seats at close intervals on its edges. If there be surface traction on the street, it should not be suffered to trespass on this middle space that will prove so precious to the children.   Once on the middle strip, they should be as safe as in a designated playground.   Finally, the strip must be well lighted, that it may be as safe at night for adults as in the daytime for the children.

Coming now to the housing question, a subject is approached that has immense importance, an almost baffling complexity, and absorbing interest.   A student of the problem who is also an active settlement worker has written, after a sojourn in England among those who are trying to solve it, that he could not escape a feeling that the country is "a bit hysterical" on this matter; but he adds that undoubtedly "England has no municipal problem paramount to that of housing," and that "in New York and one or two other American cities" the existing evils are not less flagrant.[1]   We have first to remind ourselves, then, that our own subject is not sociology but civic art.   The themes merge again and again — a fact that is the chief glory of the modern conception of civic æsthetics — so that the distinctions have sometimes to be purely arbitrary. We may reasonably assert, however, that civic art need concern itself only with the outward aspect of the houses, and therefore that for such details — sociologically pressing though they are — as sunless bedrooms, dark halls and stairs, foul cellars, dangerous employments, and an absence of bathrooms,

[1] See *Municipal Affairs*, vol. vi., No 3.

civic art has no responsibility, however earnestly it deplores them.

In the first place, it should be observed that in the tenement district mere density of population is not a sure indication of overcrowding — that is, the number of persons per acre may rise without a corresponding increase in wretchedness and, it may even be, with a bettering of conditions. A surer test is the ratio between the population and the floor area. On the broader streets of the district, civic art, recognising that a very dense population must be cared for, will advocate the erection of higher buildings, if there be sufficient fire protection. For the two or three upper floors of a series of tall buildings, or for a very large structure, it should be possible to provide elevator service. The halls on the upper stories of such a series of buildings could be connected so that one elevator would serve them all, and the greater height above the ground would thus involve no hardships that had not full compensation in the lessened noise from the street and the better air. It may be expected also that the large buildings, representing a greater investment, will be better constructed.

On the side streets the dependence will be mainly on strict adherence to a tenement-house building law that has been framed in obedience to enlightened opinions and humanitarian purposes. This will demand that a reasonable proportion of each lot shall be left free from building. Such requirement

gives a chance for air wells and for light. The
method of constructing the "model tenements,"
whether by the municipality, as so frequently in
Great Britain; or by co-operative societies, as familiarly on the Continent; or almost only by private
capital, as in the United States, is not a problem for
civic art. It has to be concerned with the more
serious question of whether these houses intended
for the very poor are really occupied by them, and
not by people of superior means and less need.
There will be danger that the latter, attracted thither
by low rents, comfortable quarters, and pleasant surroundings, may drive out those of greatest poverty
for whom all this had been devised. This is not an
easy thing to regulate; but if the city be so planned
and built up, and its wise ordinances so enforced,
that there are no rookeries, that there is nothing
worse than this to which the poor can go, it still
will succeed in its general purpose. For then, if
driven forth from here, they would only be scattered,
faring no worse wherever they went as far as lodg-
ing goes.

There is, however, one step that may be taken
of which the tendency will be a restriction of residence in the district to the class for whom the district
is designed.[1] And in most cases this designing, we
should remember, is not a theoretical allotment of
space, but will be simply a readjustment, to increase

[1] It must be remembered that this whole discussion is based on the civic-art
point of view. Such a measure as "districting," according to use, is therefore not
discussed.

the comfort of those already quartered there. This step will be based on the circumstance, not less true in London than in any city of America, that the lowest stratum of society is largely made up of foreigners. In the effort not so much to naturalise them as, rather, to conform them to an accepted type of the native poor, the usual depressing effects are secured. The ideal is low; the hearts of the subjects cannot be in it, for it is alien as well as wretched, and only miserable results are obtained. On the other hand, there are in this population extraordinary elements of urban picturesqueness. Representations of the home life of the poor of all the Continent of Europe and of half of Asia may easily be huddled on six hundred feet of street-front in London, Chicago, or New York. In each city, too, there are neighbourhoods given up to the settlers from a single distant land and called foreign "colonies." But all the picturesqueness and as much as possible of the romance have been crushed out of these, and one would hardly know, save for rich complexions, that here was "Little Italy"; and, save for queues, that there was "Chinatown."

Now if, instead of crushing the natural instincts and starving the national longings, these were frankly catered to by the city,—in so far as they violated no broadly conceived laws, or just standards of morality, —there would be developed here altogether the most interesting section of the town. To accomplish this and so to add much to the happiness of the people as well as to the interest of the city, the municipality could well afford to be liberal in the local interpretation of its regular ordinances. And having once developed here the street features that respectively make the German, Italian, Frenchman, and Chinaman entirely at home in the street, there would be much less danger that more prosperous natives would come back to a quarter where they could not feel at home, even though it had been successfully transformed for the comfort of the poor.

Much is said of the necessity of assimilation in a city; but if the ideal of the happy and prosperous classes of their own home beyond the sea be put before these people, instead of that of the lowest stratum of the native population, and the philanthropical forces of the community co-operate in the work, there is hardly room for doubt that better citizens would be made. Incidentally, they would be happier, and that is a factor. It should be said, too, that all the time the city will be impressing its own individuality on the district. On every piece of municipal apparatus even here the city's stamp will appear; and by reiteration there will arise a consciousness and love of that abstract thing, the city, as surely as the love of the concrete neighbourhood. Just as the flag, flying everywhere, comes to be loved as the symbol of the nation, so this insignia will be loved because it stands for a loved city, apprehended by this means as the all-embracing entity. And sentiment, in this part of the town particularly, is the most powerful of forces for social and civic good or ill.

With the housing problem civic art, its attention on the outward aspect of the town, has little further to do. In the quarter or more of the building lot which the law will require to be left open, it may find a chance for the development of a court or back yard; but unless several of these adjoin one another the opportunity will be small and it must, at best, be individual, not affecting the urban prospect from the street. The plotting of the thoroughfares, their surface development, and the treatment of the open spaces upon which they are to focus constitute the proper problems of municipal æsthetics in adapting to its purpose that part of the town where dwell the poorest citizens. The treatment of the squares now alone remains to be discussed.

In plotting the open spaces, suggestion was made that they might be developed as much-needed playgrounds in a section densely populated with children and far removed from the country, or from those roomier portions of the town where private gardens dress the streets with beauty and afford space for play. It was said that, at all events, they would prove breathing places where the people of close streets and narrow quarters might come for air and rest and freedom. The questions now are whether they should be anything more than vacant areas, left bare that children may romp at will, or, possibly, furnished with gymnasium apparatus; or whether,

Seward Park, New York. This open space in a tenement district has been elaborately developed as a playground.

on the other hand, there should be attempts to make them beautiful; and, in the latter case, the kind of beauty to be sought.

If it be assumed that the plot of the tenement district shows a number of open spaces separated by little distance, there will be much to recommend variety in the treatment. The district will include people of a variety of taste in recreation, and while at least one open space may be developed as a playground and furnished with swings, outdoor gymnasium apparatus, a wading pool, and a public comfort house, and with numerous seats for the mothers, another, with equal reasonableness, may have a band-stand as its dominating *motif,* while a third, perhaps no less popular and certainly no less loved, will be a garden spot gay with flowers and beautiful with stretches of greensward and great trees.

The first two types of development hardly require pleading or apology. If there be fear that the third be not quite worth while lest it be not fully appreciated among the tenements, assurance may be drawn from facts and figures collected by Jacob A. Riis, the most sympathetic of tenement students, and one thoroughly reliable. He refers in one of his later studies, the story of the " Ten Years' War " to better social conditions among the poor of New York, to a finding of the Tenement House Commission. This showed " three hundred and twenty-four thousand persons living out of sight and reach of a green spot of any kind," surely an evidence of unwise city planning, and a condition for civic art to shudder at. When an open space had been created among the huddled homes of this population, he describes the significant spectacle of children "gazing in rapt admiration at the poor show of a dozen geraniums and English ivy plants, in pots on the window-sill of the overseer's cottage," adding that "they stood for ten minutes at a time resting their eyes upon them. In the crowd were aged women and bearded men. They moved slowly, when crowded out, looking back many times at the enchanted spot." Referring to a playground in Chicago, Riis suggests the civilising influence of a bit of nature's beauty. "The police lieutenant," he says, "has had a tree called after him. The boys that did that used to be terrors. Now they take care of the trees. They plead for a low limb that is in the way, that no one may cut it off." In the aristocratic portions of the town, few would care if a troublesome limb were removed, and the citizens would not think to name a tree for their hero.

For such truly appreciative spirits as these should civic art's republic be created. If there be inducement to bring beauty into the city for the sake of those who may find it by travel if it be not around their homes, how much more is there inducement to provide it for those who hunger for it and have no other place to seek it; for those who, having hungered, feast upon such as is given, finding a banquet in crumbs! And how much more than merely sense satisfaction they gain from it ! The assertion is made (by Dr. L. S. Rowe [1]) that "at the present time the attractiveness of the saloon is greatly enhanced by reason of the uninviting appearance of the streets in certain of our large cities. . . . The distinction between good and bad citizenship runs parallel with the line of division between the wholesome and injurious use of leisure." The opportunities in cities for the elevating and healthful use of leisure ought, then, to be readily accessible and abundant.

The square that is given over to planting for beauty's sake should have many seats in it, that its enjoyment may be encouraged. It should be well lighted, for light is the best policeman, as Emerson said, and that depredations be not too easy perennials should here be used as freely as possible. But in such planting in this quarter, brilliant effects are to be sought and there must be a sequence of bloom, so that from the first violet and earliest crocus to the latest aster no week may lack its blossoms to gladden drooping spirits and brighten dull surroundings. From this point of view, the distribution of seeds and bulbs among the poor, that they may have window boxes, is of interest to civic art for other than merely the decorative effect of the blooms when seen from the street.

As to the band-stand, the Bethnal Green improvement in London offers a suggestion not merely for the placing of the stand but for that convergence of

[1] University of Pennsylvania.

streets to the open space as a focal centre, which was to be a feature of the topography of the area. Here the band-stand is in the centre of a space an acre or more in extent. The area is encircled by a street, and from this belting thoroughfare seven streets radiate, connecting the area closely with the general street system of the district.[1] These new streets were made forty to sixty feet wide, taking the place of old eighteen-foot streets. The band-stand is on a terraced mound, secured by dumping the earth obtained from digging the foundations of the neighbouring municipal tenements, with a result not only artistically effective but much more economical than if it had been carted away. Here, when the band plays, there is a great outpouring of people from all around; and it may be doubted whether, even among the music-loving Italians who throng the Piazza St. Marco on a music night and make it "the gayest scene in Europe," there is more of real enjoyment than among these poor East-enders of London when, a stone's throw from their homes, they sit among the flowers and listen to a band.

It has been a reproach hurled often against our modern cities that they have a tenement problem; that the conditions of modern industry bring to the city far greater numbers than can be comfortably handled there, so that men and women and children are huddled together like animals, all the beauty

---

[1] The Bethnal Green improvement, it should be remembered, was not on the original plot; but was a late transformation of a badly congested district, requiring an artificial connection with its surroundings.

crushed out of their lives, and no sunshine left to them save such as God had put into their hearts. But this crowding of the poor is not a new evil of urban life. In the multiplication of cities it is more far-reaching than ever before; but there has never been a city that did not have it. The civic art of other times has closed its eyes to this condition. Let us make the municipality fair and great, it has said, stately in those showier parts by which men judge of cities. Here let the poor take their ease and, forgetful of the wretched homes they leave, rejoice in the prosperity they may see but cannot touch, and be proud that they are citizens. Because that former civic art was thus aristocratic, because it sought to provide beauty for the few, to the neglect and disregard of the many, there was coincident with it much of iniquity in the lower circles of urban life and of corruption in the higher. To be enduring and effective, in the best sense of those terms, civic art must be democratic, and the desire to be that brings with it the problem of the tenement district.

Modern civic art may not have solved the problem, but it has a dream of doing so. It has dared to acknowledge the existence of, and then has had the courage to try to remedy, that evil which the civic art of other times did not admit. Until the municipality is beautiful in every portion; until there is a complete adaptation to purposes and functions; until its citizens, the lowly as well as the rich, are rendered as comfortable as municipal science and humanity can make them, modern civic art will scorn to call its conquest complete. That is why a discussion of the tenement district is necessary now as well as possible in considering civic art, and that it is discussed is the highest glory of that art.

THE CITY AT LARGE.

CHAPTER XIV.

COMPREHENSIVE PLANNING.

IN the development of an artistically built city, problems have appeared within problems. It has been found necessary to divide the city into parts, according to the purposes it serves; and each of these parts has presented a question of development by itself, while the great, all-embracing urban problem has proved to be the co-ordination of these into a single scheme comprehensive and harmonious. We come now, in the building and placing of certain large institutions, to a series of problems that are most attractive and interesting. They stand by themselves, unhampered by requirements of close conformity to conditions around them, asking only — for the city's beauty's sake — that they have the loveliest and stateliest solution that may be found.

There is evidence of progress in the perception that the problems are collective—in a recognition that their sum is far more than an architectural question.

For merely to build with an eye to beauty, while itself a forward step, is the first one to be taken; but first to place well and then to build well shows a yet further advance. "Man," says Bacon, "comes to build stately sooner than garden finely, as if gardening were the greater perfection"; and John Addington Symonds, writing of the Renaissance in Italy, remarks, "Architecture is always the first of the fine arts to emerge from barbarism in the service of religion and of civic life. A house, as Hegel says, must be built for the god, before the god, carved in stone or figured in mosaic, can be placed there"; and council chambers, he continues, "must be prepared for the senate of a state before the national achievements can be painted on the walls."

With this suggestion before us of the evolution in the art of building, we shall do well to observe in what stage of progress various cities and parts of cities are, and under what conditions there is realised that degree of advance involved in seeking to supplement good architecture by a lovely and appropriate setting.

When the Pantheon in Paris, the Royal Exchange in London, the Bulfinch State House in Boston, had stood for many years with bare interior walls, there were interesting and successful efforts to beautify them with mural paintings. The structures, in brief, having been completed, "achievements" were painted on the walls. The later Criminal Courts building in New York and the Court-House in Baltimore were hardly finished before the municipal art societies took steps to adorn them with wall paintings. The Boston Public Library, the National Library in Washington, the little Appellate Court-House in New York,—each locally a later construction still,—had the decoration of their interior walls planned with almost as much original certainty and confidence as the adornment of their exteriors. There was immediate co-operation between the architects and the painters and sculptors. From the first step, then, of a demand for an outwardly beautiful as well as convenient structure, we can observe in modern civic art an advance—slow and tentative at first, but finally confident—to a demand for a building beautiful within and without. The second step is at last taken with assurance.

The buildings which stood for its taking, it may be noted, were representative also of intellectual endeavour. The persons responsible for their planning were necessarily men of culture in that term's broad sense of a taste naturally refined as well as educated. But even the buildings erected at their behest and with their recommendations covered each its full lot. They had no architectural setting and much less the advantage of gardening. Considerations of economy may have discouraged such a demand, just as they once discouraged interior enrichment and, before that, exterior embellishment,— until these things came to be considered as essential. The third step still remained to be taken.

18

Here and there, on the outskirts of cities, villas and palaces had been rising for hundreds of years, set so consistently and harmoniously among their gardens that house and estate made a single lovely composition. But these, raised for the gratification of individuals, were private, not public, art. Architecture, "the first of the fine arts to emerge from barbarism in the service of civic life," was accompanied now in many public structures by decoration within doors, but not yet by gardening. Even the universities, rising building by building and gaining steadily in resources and visible splendour, scattered their new structures hit or miss about their grounds.

There has been, until the last few years, no system, no orderliness, no idea of gaining an aggregate effect that should be more impressive than any series of individual results could be. Even now, the co-operation has appeared only spasmodically, and almost wholly among the richer institutions as if the creation of a general scheme for harmonious development were a luxury, and not a bit of economy far more needed by the poorer college than by the rich university. The latter will be imposing from the very multiplicity of its buildings and the magnificence of some of them, however improvidently they may be scattered ; the former has need to foster its every incidental opportunity and to gain all the effectiveness it can by so economical a means as merely making every structure a support to every other, and the tract in which they stand a favourable staging.

The movement's first permanent conquest in the United States was probably in the University of California, but its beginnings as a factor in modern civic art reached back at least to the Columbian Exposition at Chicago. That (1893) was the great popular object-lesson in the value of extensive co-operation, in the placing of buildings and their landscape development as strictly as in their architectural elevation. The lesson was international in its effect, exerting an influence that has appeared over and over in many lands, but nowhere more dramatically than in the case of the University of California. A rich woman who had done much for the institution proposed to add to her benefactions a mining building, in memory of her husband. The question of site and style of architecture at once arising, the lack of a definite scheme of development that should be a guide and assistance in such matters was realised. The woman who had proposed to give a building made a much nobler gift as a first step to the former, for she authorised an international competition for a fixed and beautiful ideal toward which the institution should advance with every step that brought completeness nearer. She paid all the expenses of the competition, including the prizes of thirty thousand dollars. The first jury met in Antwerp and the last meeting was in San Francisco, where (in 1899) the award was made.

This showed a plan of which the full carrying out will require many millions of dollars and perhaps, even in the western part of the United States, generations of time. It set a goal to be striven for. It did not simply ameliorate the past ; it projected far into the future a scheme toward which each improvement of the present might be a step. Its tendency was to encourage improvements, for it guaranteed the present at the same time that it guaranteed the future,— by giving an assurance that every step taken now, in accordance with the ultimate vision, is wisely taken and will not have some day to be undone. It substituted for a present-day ideal, toward which the past was to be advanced by the bettering of old conditions, an ideal of the future, as far beyond the present as is the present beyond the past.

There was much to induce immediate appreciation of such a plan, and on a less ambitious scale its widespread adoption by institutions. In the development of their restricted acreage and the harmonious placing therein of a few paths and buildings, the problem would not be complex; there would be no embarrassment by private interests to destroy a hope of achieving results promptly and with completeness; and the advantages, both in economy and in effectiveness, of such comprehensive designing would appear at once to men and women of that social and mental equipment to be expected among the managers of educational and philanthropical institutions. So, among the universities, we now find in the United States many illustrations of its success. At Harvard, beautiful memorial gates and a handsome wall have shut in the scholastic " yard," and a landscape architect has planted the shrub borders and chosen the sites for new buildings. At Yale, when a great deal of new construction was to mark the bi-centennial, experts were called upon to draw a plan toward the fulfilment of which each new building would be a step. Columbia, rising on the heights of upper New York, creates there, in conjunction with her neighbours, "the Acropolis" of the city. Princeton ; the University of Pennsylvania ; and new Chicago, with her red roofs contrasting with the gray stone of the Tudor architecture—these, and many less prominent institutions that are now undergoing a similarly complete artistic development, have lessons for the towns or cities in which they are. They test the project of original comprehensive planning, and in their conspicuous object-lessons prove its efficiency.

But even before they suggest a course for the community to follow, they make addition, in so far as their own considerable area is concerned,— and a strong addition,— to the present beauty of the town. The tract which an institution occupies is one of those problems within a problem that go to make up the great, enclosing, urban problem. It is, in fact, not only one of them, but a type of many of them. If the buildings that comprise the visible part of a university be harmoniously grouped and artistically placed in relation to their landscape, and thereby make a lovely and fitting whole, why should not similar care be exercised in placing the philanthropical, penal, and religious institutions, and then such individual buildings as schools, libraries, and churches — when the latter stand alone ? In the aggregate, these form an important portion of the town, well deserving of separate thought in consideration of how to obtain a greater urban beauty, and perhaps having all the more influence because they are widely scattered. The injunction, then, of civic art, as regards the building and placing of institutions, is that the general urban plan should be supplemented by a plan for each of these, equally systematic and complete within its own subject, and toward which the institution may be developed by harmonious steps just as the city as a whole will be developing —the faster because of these plans — toward a larger scheme of ultimate and beautiful completeness.

The striking examples of what the conscientiously æsthetic development of its institutions may mean to the aspect of a city are offered, of course, by Oxford and Cambridge in England. The universities dominate the towns, and because they are so beautiful in their many quadrangles and buildings — as if each "college" were a separate institution — the cities are beautiful. It may be objected that these universities had no original comprehensive plan to work by; but at the pace at which we build to-day we do in years what would have then meant centuries.

Gate to the " Yard " at Harvard.

We have not, or do not take in construction, that leisure which is so favourable to refinement and harmony. Building at slap-dash speed, unless we have a plan to guide us we shall build awry. But when Oxford rose, it has been said, "the pointing of an arch was like an act of worship and the fervour of religion found expression in an exuberance of fair handiwork." We have not the patience now, nor the same high consecration; but we have ambition, great wealth, and the models of the past to point the way. Oxford may not have needed a general plan of development; but to-day we do need it, and if we have it and it is good, modern cities too will find in their institutions adorning features.

The quadrangle of the English university has been adopted, with such local modifications as may be needed, as the elementary unit in the development scheme of most of those later institutions that have sought at the start a complete plan. The system has the advantage of affording variety at the same time that it gives an appearance of unity, and it fairly invites harmony. It offers, too, a conveniently close grouping of associated structures, and gives an air of dignity and reserve, even of seclusion and peace, that is at once desirable and fitting. The passenger on the city street, gazing into the quadrangle, beholds there the repose of an institution going quietly, and with no friction or waste, about its work. There is that clothing with beauty of adaptation to purpose which is the strong desire of civic art.

The examples that are offered thus by institutions — of the successful and strikingly practical application of that poetic dream which had wrought the brief glory of an exposition — cannot fail to be broadly instructive. The pertinence of the dream, it may be said, was not even in the first place only for institutions. It was more obviously, indeed, for the subsequent expositions — all of which it has affected. Then its suggestion of permanent results was recognised most promptly and most cordially by institutions. Next, and with a long forward — though entirely natural — step, comes the grouping of the public buildings of town and city and the development of a civic centre. After that, and as a yet more thrilling and magnificent application of the example, came the appointment of an expert commission, representative of those fine arts that must be combined for the highest adornment of a city, to consider and propose plans for the improvement of the city of Washington.[1] At last there grows out of it a widespread demand for expert advice, by commissions or by individuals of professional training, regarding the artistic development of tracts and towns — from the great city of New York, with its multitude of problems, down to the village, or a portion of a village!

[1] In this commission, architecture was represented by Daniel H. Burnham and Charles F. McKim; landscape architecture, by Frederick Law Olmsted, Jr.; and sculpture by Augustus St. Gaudens. Mr. Burnham, it should be added, was Director of Works at the Columbian Exposition in Chicago, and the effective co-operation of the architects and artists who then and there gave to American art both a new direction and a tremendous impetus had been largely secured and maintained by his executive ability. The commission continues, though time alters its personnel.

So the interdependence of all the arts that go to make up civic art is realised as it has not been before. There is seen the possibility of their mutual helpfulness in creating a comprehensive scheme that shall be harmonious throughout, and the necessity of obtaining such a plan in advance and from those upon whose judgment there may be complete reliance. It is realised, as possibly the highest and final step of civic art, that the town or city, or tract in town or city, of which it is hoped to make a beautiful composition cannot be left to chance growth; that corrections subsequently made are as much less satisfactory as they are more costly than would be faithful adherence to a good original plan.

It costs little to get a good design or map, and acceptance of it involves no special outlay. It simply gives assurance that all the money that would normally be spent each year for improvements will now be spent with far-sighted wisdom. It promises that each public work will mean certain progress toward a final splendid goal,—which will have become, not a vague dream, but a concrete vision, a pictured reality that all may see and comprehend and wish and work for.

In the composition of such an expert commission it would be well—since city-building is a science as well as an art—to add to the representatives of the fine arts an engineer, and one member who would stand not for engineering alone, nor for architecture alone, nor for landscape design alone, nor for sculpture alone, but for all of these together and comprehensively, as one who has made a special study of the general science and art of city-building. And so there would be created an expert commission of five, to put before the community a vision of what its own town might be and should be.

The thought is a great one; the programme is so loftily conceived, so broadly and unselfishly worked out, and looks for its results so completely to the future, that it is surprising to find so wide and prompt an acceptance of it. But the programme means much for civic art, giving to it at once a firm basis, and raising it in promise above the need of makeshift improvements,—its ideal, beyond the danger of destruction by the death of any individual; its achievements, beyond the menace of a disorganised confusion,— to a plane of system, reason, permanency, and calm artistic judgment.

In devising such a comprehensive plan for a city's development, it might be well to designate the style of architecture that shall be employed in the strictly public buildings. One hesitates to speak of this, for the occasions when it will prove of thorough practicalness must be so rare that the suggestion is liable to have a visionary sound. It has been suggested, however, that in Washington the government buildings be "monumental and serious in type, and preferably of the so-called Classic style," with the understanding that the number of stories in a monumental building should never be more than four and should be limited to three if possible.[1] An advantage in such designation would lie in the assurance of harmony among the official buildings of the town, and in the tendency to restrain eccentricity and a violation of purity of design in that construction which is fraught with most danger to the community's æsthetic charm. Private dwellings exemplify, indeed, all sorts of queer tastes, but they are not as conspicuous, nor considered so justly representative, as are the public buildings.

In the construction of the latter, also,—for their various purposes,—it is not unlikely that the democracy of the twentieth century will find its chief architectural expression. This will naturally tend at first, as it already has, to a *bourgeois* type. But the beautiful Gothic constructions of the citizens of Flanders, when they too came to raise town halls in free cities, show that the highest art need not be despaired of. This example suggests, too, that it would not be wise to limit the choice of architecture to a style that is alien in period and clime. To do so might be relatively "safe," but the safety would be that of a timidity that took no chances of great success. The lesson, rather, to be taught, is the old, earnest one of fitness.

It has been estimated that during a few particular but recent months in the United States, the gifts for public libraries exceeded twelve and a quarter

[1] "Grouping of Public Buildings and Development of Washington," by Cass Gilbert, F. A. I. A., in "Papers Relating to the Improvement of the City of Washington," Senate Document No. 94, Fifty-sixth Congress, second session.

millions of dollars. During the same period there were great sums given, and officially appropriated, for the construction of hospitals, art museums, town halls, and school-houses. All of these structures, because they were designed to serve the public, had a purpose that, since the fall of Rome, has become almost new in architecture. They contained, in the aggregate, not only great possibilities for improving the aspect of cities, but they offered to architects a superb opportunity for doing really original creative work, in adapting the buildings to this new purpose and so giving to them the beauty of fitness of expression. Libraries, for instance, should now stand not for "elegant storehouses of books" on the old traditional lines, but for working institutions or for home-like reading-rooms, as the need may be.

There is to-day, then, an opportunity that is immense, both from the architectural and civic standpoint, in the construction of public buildings and institutions, but where the comprehensive plan for the city touches their architecture with dictation it should touch very lightly. It might find, from the examples already existing in any given place, expediency in recommending adherence to a general fixed style, if that be not too alien; but it would grant all the freedom possible within those limits, once there had been insistence on sincerity and chastity — on a calm and careful draughting that makes no straining for bizarre effect.

Among the school-houses in particular, scattered

through all parts of the city in visible expression of the dominating system of public instruction, and serving the like purpose in the like way, there would better be uniformity than attempt at variety of aspect. Each school should have a playground, and each should have a garden, as they now so generally have in Northern Europe and are rapidly coming to have in the United States. Nor does modern civic art have need of apology for including in its scrutiny details that are as educational and sociological as these. It observes that by the school garden will be most widely disseminated that popular love of nature and practical experience in her ways that can do so much to vest with beauty the streets and homes of a city. In themselves, also, these school gardens, many times repeated and each with its structure forming a complete and harmonious composition, may be important factors in adding to the pleasantness of the town. Throughout it all no private houses and no other such numerous public structures can more appropriately be models, both in their own development and in their adjustment to the street. They should be little centres of wholesome influence regarding civic duty.

So, to sum up the chapter, three conclusions appear in considering a comprehensive general planning of the city. They are, as most important: the great need — the need too little realised — of obtaining one underlying plan, which may touch lightly on the public architecture, but which shall weld together in a harmonious system the street plotting of the different districts, shall mark the course of present and future improvements with entire assurance, and shall put before the people a tangible goal to work toward — the picture of what their own city may be, and should be, made; as of next importance, the advantage of comprehensive plans for the future development of all the public or semi-public institutions, that these problems within a problem may have no haphazard growth but may go forward by sure steps to that ideal of fitness and of dignity that will make them ornaments of the city; and, finally, the propriety of giving a degree of recognisable uniformity to those structures of the town that have a like public character and perform a like public function and are built from the public means — the advantage, in short, of considering any public structure not by itself, when adopting its plan, but in its relation to the community as a whole and to the other structures of its type. That is the secret at the root not only of comprehensive planning, but of civic art.

CHAPTER XV.

OPEN SPACES.

THE open spaces of a city are, or should be, its ornaments. This is a new rule in city-building, a requirement that was not made in the old days of civic art when the creation of an open space meant the establishment of an outdoor market. In those times, when the sun got high and the little booths, their morning's work done, were folded away silently as the white umbrellas that had probably covered them, the square became a bare and lonely place unless — as was likely to be the case — a fountain bubbled garrulously in its centre. Then the fresh running water established a social rendezvous, and about it there was gossip enough to explain the laughter and muttering of the fountain long after the town had gone to sleep. On rainy days a new value appeared in the open space, for people scurried across it like leaves before the wind. Usually they hugged the sides of the square, where there were arcades or awnings to keep off the sun, shop windows to look into, and plenty of friends to talk to; but when the rain came and there was reason to hurry, the square offered short cuts that were eagerly availed of.

There were some who thought that the open spaces of a city ceased to be a necessity when the markets were driven indoors or to especially designated areas, when fresh water was carried into every house by underground pipes, and the square seemed to have no value save that of occasionally offering a means to shorten one's journey, if one were in a hurry. It did look forlorn and dreary. Then there were planned new cities and parts of cities without open spaces.

But vast areas of regularly plotted streets became dreadfully monotonous. It was seen that even a deserted square served many a useful purpose: it brought variety into urban topography; it transformed building lots on the boundary streets into valuable sites, for now they had an assurance of light, the conspicuousness that belongs to a vantage point, and they offered a chance for perspective to aid appreciation of good façades. And the square afforded an excellent location for civic sculpture. It shortened distances, too, and when the citizens wanted to gather out-of-doors it made a place for them to come to. Then arose the wish to beautify cities, to bring stateliness into the business district and the soft touch of nature into the regions where the homes were. The opportunities of the square for this were perceived and seized.

Place de la République, Paris.

Noble buildings were gathered around it where they could be seen. Sculpture adorned it. Brilliant lights made it gay at night, and if the fountain had lost the power to establish a social rendezvous, a band might play here on a summer evening and it would collect a crowd. Pageantry found here its opportunity; turf was sometimes planted in the spaces between diagonal paths,—that had been left, in order that the square might still be useful in the shortening of distance,—and when the space was ample there were flowers and seats and trees and bushes. The square entered again into the life of the people and they loved to gather in it. But it did something else, for now it added to the visible attractiveness of the town. Here a bit of public garden, there a sculptured vestibule to architectural masses, there again a playground (for adults or children), and here a broadened thoroughfare crowded with the criss-cross travel that must have congested a street,—the open space served many ends of which the sum was this: the better adaptation of a city to its countless purposes. Then it became a problem for civic art.

In the mere running over of its various developments, many types of open space appear. There are those in the crowded business district, most frequently before a public building, which are arranged to set off the abutting architecture, making with sculpture and brilliant lights a dignified approach to it and for the city a stately ornament. There are those most naturally before a focal point — such as one of the entrances to the town — of which the special purpose is provision for converging traffic. There are those in the tenement district, serving various ends; and there are those, finally, in the general residential quarters, established deliberately to be areas of beauty or children's playgrounds, or spaces which, though formed by the seeming accident of an irregular angle where streets converge, have been turned to good account æsthetically.

One would think that so useful a feature of the urban structure must have been made long since a part of the science of city-building, with the distribution of the spaces and the principles underlying their development reduced to general rules. But so distinctly is recognition of their value an achievement of modern civic art that, be it observed, they have not as yet even a generic name, unless it be that cumbrous and indefinite title, "open space"— which might be street, or river, or back yard, quite as well as the thing that is meant. We take them, too, as we find them, usually three-fourths of them not purposely created but found existent through fortunate miscalculations or irregularities in urban topography. And then they are developed as the whim of the moment dictates — perhaps to be changed after a decade in cases of some success, perhaps to make us wish other treatment before the work is done. For we fill in our open space as if it were a blank area on a wall that we were attempt-

ing to " decorate " or " treat " without a thought of
the wall around it, without regard for its possible
harmony, for its purpose, for its connection with the
building. If that were actually done, there would
be danger of clapping a poster where there ought to
be a mural painting, of painting delicately where a
passage is to be, or of leaving bare a space in the
middle of a thickly figured wall. The like of all
these things is too often done in treating the open
spaces of cities. They are sprinkled over the street
plan without system or due proportion; and they are
developed, each by itself, with little thought of
relation to the boundary streets and none perhaps
of their relation to the city as a whole.

If the problem were the original plotting of a
city, the position of the open spaces would clearly
demand an attention coincident with that given to
the street plan. Neither the one nor the other could
be arranged with entire satisfaction by itself. It is
essential for the best results that in the location of
each such open area there be a certain obvious appropriateness and naturalness — that is, since their
boundaries are streets, they should seem, whether
circles, triangles, or squares, to grow out of the
street lines, rather than appear to be placed upon
them. In the distribution, also, there should be
comprehensive planning that their many purposes
may be fully served, and that each section, in proportion to its needs, may be equally provided. But
because appreciation of open spaces at their full

value is a late chapter in urban science,—though Penn placed them generously on his gridiron plan for Philadelphia, and Sir Christopher Wren made the provision of geometrical open areas a feature of his plan for the remodelling of London,—there is very little such advantageous planning at the start. We have to make the best we can of the spaces that happen to exist upon the plan; and when, at great expense, we put in new ones, we have to choose the neighbourhoods that need them most and locate them at the nearest practicable point to that situation which would be ideal. In the placing of modern urban squares, therefore, there is much of makeshift, though in their treatment a freer rein is given.[1]

Of the development of those squares that are in the tenement district, there has already been a discussion. To those (mainly in the business district) adorned with sculpture and ornate fountains and made gay with brilliant lighting, there has been a reference in the chapter on city adornment with fountains and sculpture. It was there pointed out that the opportunity offered by such spaces for the

[1] In many cities — most strikingly in London — where land values have become so high as almost to discourage municipal purchases for the creation of open spaces, and where the crowding is so severe that there is excuse for fear that an arbitrary reduction of the habitable area in a given section may increase rather than diminish suffering, but where, on the other hand, that very crowding and the pushing of the urban boundaries into a distance that the poor cannot traverse make pitiful appeal for public open areas, there has been a utilisation of ancient graveyards. They are transformed, with excellent sanitary effect, to serve as breathing places, garden spots, and playgrounds. But their location as regards the street plan is obviously without system.

increase of urban amenity consisted not in surprising
with a sudden splendour, that had been hidden until unexpectedly come upon, but in casting their
radiance as far as possible on adjacent streets. In
the treatment of such a space, then, there is to
be regard not merely for the space itself, but for the
effect as seen from the streets that lead to it. This
consideration may even determine the scale to be
adopted in the monumental construction that perhaps
dominates the area.

But in planning these, as all, open spaces, the requirements imposed by the vistas from the streets
that approach them are little more than hints — very
helpful in particulars, but leaving much of detail
and even of general plan for local decision. Three
things, with respect to this, are to be considered:
the accommodation and convenience of the travel,
civic art having its base in civic utility, for this may
determine even the location of the sculpture and the
amount of ground it occupies; the character of the
surrounding neighbourhood, which will determine
the whole nature of the treatment of the space, that
monotony may be relieved and charm increased by
the break; and finally what is required for the harmonious setting of such of the abutting architecture
as may be deemed fairly permanent.

Such architecture quite probably includes some
public or semi-public building, for in the Old World
at least the open space is likely to have been first
a market's site, and the latter would have been

selected with reference to the strong and permanent
popular attraction offered by a structure of Church or
State. In the setting of the architecture something
more than harmony may be sought. Often the area
will give an opportunity for terracing or for balustrades, that will make an imposing approach without trespassing too severely on precious space.
While this is a result that especially affects the building, it should be recalled that in the embellishment
of cities architecture and its setting are factors upon
which much dependence must be put.

Nor should the enhancement by the square of
surrounding architectural effects be allowed to cease
with approaching darkness. It is a boast of modern
cities that in their business sections they have no
night. We have seen that a community's first
efforts toward decorative and brilliant lighting are
almost sure to be at such show points as its open
spaces, and that these at evening, even more than in
the day, may be centres of light and gaiety. The
"*ville lumière*" offers proof enough of that. But
there is still something more to be accomplished, for
the square would lose much of its glory if night's
dark mantle were suffered to hide the beautiful public buildings that front upon it, they being as much
a part of it as the statue in its centre. Should
no architectural provision be made for decorative
lamps as parts of the structures, surely hidden lights
might throw upon the façades a glow sufficient to
bring out mouldings, carvings, and proportions, and

so secure to the square at night its architectural
setting of the day. Where it is surrounded by private houses, with which such liberty may not be taken,
the open space is more likely to be planted; and then
what witchery may be given by a wise arrangement
of the lights!

Now if the application of these principles to a
few famous "squares" be considered, their significance is more easily perceived.[1] Trafalgar Square in
London, which was described by Peel as "the finest
site in Europe," is one of the most travelled squares
in the world. Yet there are two huge fountains and
something like half a dozen statues besides the great
Nelson column. But the fountains stand back from
the maelstrom of converging traffic, and against the
terrace, so that they take no space that is needed for
travel; the Nelson shaft, which occupies the centre
of the square, is tall enough to dominate the whole
busy scene and be visible as a landmark from afar,
and yet its base is not so large as to trespass — the
natural convergence of traffic being before, not
around, it. Finally, the smaller statues are placed
so as to be decorative adjuncts — in purpose, at
least — which are constructively incidental as far as
the topography goes. Here, then, is a great space
singularly well utilised. It may be considered as
having three divisions: the first, a vestibule crowded
with criss-cross traffic and therefore left clear ; the
second, a richly ornamented setting for the enthroned

[1] See articles by the author in Nos. 5, 6, 7, vol. ii. of *House and Garden*.

architecture; the third, the terrace upon the top of which the public building stands. There is illustration here of how important an accessory to its architecture a square may be made without loss of its own independence. And in the midst of a vast city, walled by great buildings that are pierced only by busy streets, the roar of traffic pulsing over its every inch, there is no attempt in Trafalgar Square at incongruous "naturalness." The whole treatment is richly urban, frankly artificial, and yet unique in its superb decorativeness. The very fountains are sculptured, their basins enclosed in geometrical copings. Their streams are thrown high into the air with a music that is very grateful, and on their broad calm bosom many little Britons sail craft that are make-believe frigates, beneath the shadow of the Nelson monument!

The Piazza San Marco in Venice is almost bare, only the Campanile and the ornate flagstaffs before the cathedral having trespassed upon it. In its way it exemplifies that neglect of vegetation which is the typical original sin in the cities of garden-like Italy. But in the Piazza San Marco the sin is pardonable. Space is too precious, there is too little room for careless walking to have justified the transformation of this one broad square into a garden-court. It is the chief focus of the city, and "keep off the grass" signs would here have robbed the people, water would have mocked them, while the merely decorative pavement sets off the architecture

Trafalgar Square, London.

and is stranger in its breadth, in Venice, than a garden would have been.

In the handsome Piazza del Popolo in Rome there is one of the most interesting examples of the square deliberately planned for city embellishment. The whole view from the top of the Pincian Hill, which overlooks the piazza, the bridge beyond, and the background of modern buildings, is a lesson in the science of modern civic construction. The piazza is old, and the obelisk that stands in its centre has been there for more than three hundred years, but the treatment of the space is essentially modern, forming the fitting vestibule to new Rome. Into the square comes the broadened Corso; from it diverge great radial thoroughfares. With the ancient "Hill of Gardens" rising on one side, and tall trees leaving on the other only the vista of the bridge, there is verdure enough in the surroundings to justify a purely formal and architectural arrangement. This includes a geometrical placing of single lamp-posts and candelabra, and curved bounding walls adorned with sculpture. The whole space is something larger, perhaps, than is needed to-day; but the fast growth of that section of the city across the Tiber, of whose traffic this piazza is the natural distributing point, makes its size appear a wise provision for the future. The lesson of the square is not so much in its hint for other communities—the situation being peculiar— as in its illustration of how perfectly, with what results in nobility of aspect, in harmony to surroundings, and in convenience to the neighbourhood, an open space may be treated if only the problem be given sufficient thought. Potentially, its spaces are the city's jewels.

There is a strong temptation to continue the discussion, by examining many squares in many cities. There is the fine Place de la Concorde in Paris, for example, of which there has been purposely no mention, because, even as Trafalgar Square, it is far more a state than a municipal creation, and because its position with relation to its surroundings is so exceptionally favourable as to render it fairly discouraging as a model. And then in New York there is Union Square, which, with some good features,— as its use of vegetation in Manhattan Island's dreariness of stone and iron,—is at this writing an example both of ineffective and of positively wrong planning. Putting aside such sins against civic art as the incongruous "cottage," there is not even adaptation to civic utility, for the paths wind circuitously, to the destruction of the square's value for short cuts, and the portion that is paved as a plaza is the wrong portion. It has the bareness of an island where streams have parted, while at the other end of the square their confluence in relatively narrow quarters creates serious congestion. But enough has been said to show that the open space to which an architectural treatment has been allotted is a problem full of complexity and one requiring strictly individual decision. When it is ably solved it has a magnificent power for the embellishment of the city and for the increase of urban stateliness.

Among the open areas in the business district of the city, there are some of which the primary purpose must be the facilitation of congested travel, or at all events the added convenience of travel. Such are those spaces likely to be provided at the formal entrances to the city. But of these there has been discussion.[1]

Passing, then, from the crowded business district, where the demands of traffic are insistent, we come to the residential sections of the town. Here, except as rarely when the area is set apart for a playground, the first duty of the open space is to increase the attractiveness of its neighbourhood. Here, then, we shall welcome trees; here there may be flowers and grass; here there may be invitation to idleness and loitering; and here, among the homes and gardens of the citizens, there may be the public garden, provided by the municipality for the common pleasure of all.

In the landscape designing of such a space it will be wise to adopt the formal style. The space will almost certainly be geometrical in outline; it will be crossed by paths that serve to some extent as highways; and if it be not large enough properly to be called a park, it is too small to shut out the city. Even if no architectural or monumental construction gives the keynote to the square's arrangement, the

[1] See pages 66 to 75.

city's buildings will peer over all its boundaries and the noise of traffic will be heard in its quietest corners. To attempt, then, to imitate the country here, with naturalness of effect, were absurd. It is best to accept frankly the urban conditions and to make the square a decorative adjunct of the street, since here we have opportunity to bring to the aid of the street such powerful factors for city beauty as flowers and trees and running water. These must, however, be used with due respect for the architecture, for we must take care neither to conceal that nor to violate good taste by lack of harmony in the setting provided. We have to remember that the beauty of the space itself is not the goal we seek, but rather the addition, by its support, of the beauty of the city.

To gain this end, not the spaces alone but the spaces and their surroundings are to be considered as the pictures, and are to be developed — however ornately or simply — with consistency and completeness. That is to say, it will not suffice if — as to-day in Copley Square in Boston — the architecture be safeguarded by legislation that prohibits the erection of dwarfing "sky-scrapers," and a protecting coping be put around the precious space devoted to flowers and turf, while hideous trolley poles are permitted on the boundary sidewalks. There then results only a pathetic failure. Nor will it do, again, to suffer an ugly telegraph pole to rise incongruously from a bed of flowers; nor to arrange the reserved space, upon

The Square and the Place Darcy, Dijon, France.

which beautiful and dignified architecture looks with placidity, in beds of bright-hued flowers laid out in fantastic contortions. Where this has been done, in a certain notable case, we have the effect of a civic skirt dance between a lovely library and church, all the reposefulness of an architectural base destroyed. Elsewhere, there may be an area beautifully developed in itself; but above its charming surface treatment wires cross and recross, the sun throws the shadow of a graceless lamp-post athwart the turf, and beyond a border of blossoming shrubs a trolley pole rises in black barbarity.

In the better residential parts of London one comes frequently upon a square surrounded by an iron fence. There are great trees within, and pretty natural gardening; but on the four sides there are closed gates that separate it hopelessly from the barren highways. Yet the garden makes an attractive outlook from the surrounding houses, that rent the higher because of it; and there is illustration of the lines,

> Around it is the street, a restless arm
> That clasps the country to the city's heart.

The square owes its existence to the landed proprietor to whom the region belongs. He has plotted it and maintains it because of the better rent he gets for his houses, and only the occupants of these houses have keys to the gates. This, then, is not civic art. It offers a convenient example of what the municipally created square ought not to be. It is not a beautiful bit of London, but a piece of "created ornament" superimposed.

The ideal for the spaces here, as for those in the business district, would be to make them glorified parts of the street — parts which have a special adornment because the street has suddenly widened sufficiently to admit of such adorning. In practice, however, it is less easy where vegetation is used, than where the treatment is architectural, to avoid a line of distinction between street and square, for unless the street have parking the difference is decided. To conceal it by bringing the street into so complete a harmony that the two seem to merge, should be the endeavour; when this is not possible, we should accept frankly the distinction and attempt to create, within boundaries as little forbidding as practicable, a bit of formal gardening that is suited perfectly to its surroundings.

A number of the "circles" in Washington illustrate so well the adornment of the street that their provision is regarded as a conspicuous merit of the Washington street plan. Nearly every one of these circles possesses a central architectural *motif* in a bit of sculpture. This is on the axes of the streets that meet at the circle, and for long distances is a factor in their decoration — the open space not shutting the sculpture away within itself. In Baltimore's Washington Place, and in the Wilhelm's Platz, Berlin,— to cite a European instance,— the like excellent result is shown. In these cases, too, it is to be noted, the open space gives an opportunity to furnish the sculpture with a background of verdure, without concealing it. The Baltimore square is formed by the street's widening so that the roadway, dividing, encloses the reserved and formally ornamented space. The statue is in the centre. A line of trees, planted along each side of the middle area, prolongs the street's vista, which is further preserved by the absence of conspicuous screens at the ends of the square. Another interesting detail is that, while the walks curve in apparently luxurious indolence, their curves are so adjusted to one another that the hurried pedestrian, leaving the street walk and traversing the square, need barely deviate from a straight line in so doing. He can loiter if he wishes, but he is not obliged to do so.

When, for one reason or another, it is not practicable thus to make the open space seem part of the very structure of the street, we have to make the boundaries as inconspicuous as possible while creating within them a bit of formal gardening. The section of the town in which the space is, together with the size of the space, must be largely determinate of the exact treatment adopted. Often bright flowers, that will flood an otherwise gloomy bit of city with the country's sunshine, will be advisable, and almost always running water will give pleasure. The fountain is probably the most satisfactory device for the latter; but the playground's shallow pool, where children may wade and sail their boats, gives pleasure in its way. The playground is not an æsthetic factor, as a rule, but the pool's grateful contrast to hot and dusty streets contains a suggestion for ornamental open spaces. Indeed, a round pond, flower-bordered, was adopted as the feature of Bowling Green, New York. In this unexpected placidity rushing Broadway terminated. There was enough formalism to retain the urban character of the spot and enough tranquillity to recall the Dutch origin of the space. When tall office buildings crowd around it the contrast may become too violent, so that even history will not excuse such incongruity; but generally in a quiet residential section, far from any natural body of water, this treatment should prove very charming. It should be said, too, of the playground, that the privacy which this ought to have, as regards the street, may be secured with screening shrubs. These by their beauty may make it a strong, though incidental, æsthetic factor.

The opportunity of the open space should be utilised to add to turf and flowers and idling or dancing water one other potent factor, none too easy otherwise to obtain in the development of city beauty. This is true especially of that larger area which the less crowded portions of the city can usually spare for purposes so good and pleasant. The factor in mind is the clustering of great trees — that beautiful effect which is absent from even the tree-lined thoroughfare. The trees are not only lovely in themselves and gratifying for the shade which they

afford, but most acceptably do they close the vista
of a street or make a beautiful screen to separate distinct sections of a town. For the best effect, the
space should be large enough to include without
crowding a goodly number. Boston Common is so
large that a more encouraging example is found in
the equally well-known Madison Square, New York.
Here, as on the Common, the trees are the principal
feature, and after that the directness and convenience of the paths (especially in the Common)
which make the spaces really useful.

Yet both of these areas illustrate, also, the invitation to outdoor living — to loitering in the open air
and finding pleasure and the possibility of rest when
out-of-doors — that the open spaces of a city may so
well extend. By most of its chute-like streets the
city summons us out-of-doors only that through
their means we may pass from one interior to another. We may have poor rooms to sit in, with
foul air and little sunshine, but if no business calls us
forth we remain indoors rather than dally in the busy
street. The parks, with their songs of birds, their
waving boughs, their long, peaceful vistas, are far
away; if the city does not furnish oases of beauty
in the desert of its streets, and with numerous well-
placed chairs or benches make practical and urgent
its invitation to a leisurely enjoyment of the beauty
thus provided, civic art will waste its fragrance and
prove untrue to its social impulse. To-day, this impulse must be earnestly reckoned with. Modern

civic art desires the beauty of towns and cities not for beauty's sake, but for the greater happiness, health, and comfort of the citizens. It finds in the open space an opportunity to call them out-of-doors for other than business purposes, to keep them in fresh air and sunshine, and in their most receptive mood to woo them by sheer force of beauty to that love and that contentment on which are founded individual and civic virtue.

It is a higher purpose than had the square of other times. Not to gossip with one's neighbours, but to commune with nature; to draw inspiration, instead of water, from a common source; in the midst of the busy city to find an isle of peace, where the scent of flowers, that are yours as much as any one's, is in your nostrils and the music of childish laughter is in the air; where the sunshine has to filter through the trees to find you; or where the darkness and the moonlight weave a spell of mystery and romance, as if prosaic streets were far away — this is the call of the planted open space in the city of to-day, so far as it is right to think of it apart from the street that it adorns.

Hudson Park, New York. This square illustrates an unusual and interesting development, but one lacking relation to the streets it should adorn. The fencing of the greensward also is to be regretted.

CHAPTER XVI.

PARKWAYS.

T HE necessity, when we would consider parkways by themselves, of removing them from
the group of city thoroughfares into which
they had naturally fallen, is an evidence that even in
theory they have much in common with the boulevards and avenues of a city. In practice the line of
demarcation is still more uncertain. A street precisely similar will be called in one city an avenue, in
another a boulevard, and in a third a parkway.
Originally the boulevard was a street or walk occupying the site of demolished fortifications. Most properly, therefore, it tends to encircle the town. But
even the *Century Dictionary* has already bestowed
on it a broader application, by defining it as "also"
a "street which is of especial width and given a
park-like appearance by reserving spaces at the side
or centre for shade trees, flowers, seats, and the like,
and not used for heavy teaming." An avenue —
usually, but not necessarily, understood as built up

with pretentious houses — may in its turn have the same peculiarities. Both are quite likely to lead to a park; and while that circumstance may be incidental with them, it is not easy, the attribute being provided, to tell whether it is essential, as in the case of a parkway, or fortuitous, as with an avenue or boulevard.[1]

Considered closely, however, the parkway may have a development that belongs to neither boulevard nor avenue and that justifies its separate discussion. In speaking of the former thoroughfares, it was noted that the first requirement was that they should afford ease of communication and that the second was that they should have a certain "dignified and stately" beauty. When we come to the parkways, there is no restriction as to the kind of beauty that may be given. It may be as picturesque, gentle, and softly winning as we please. And while it is necessary that a parkway should have connection with a park, — either leading to it from the city or joining park to park, if it be not acting in itself as a park, — yet there may fairly be reversal of the old order of requirements. Now the beauty of the way is the first essential. There may be a hundred means of approach to a given park, and from necessity the parkway cannot be the shortest from all portions of the town. There may even be electric cars on other

[1] "The Philadelphia Parkway Project," for instance, might be accurately defined as a scheme to build a magnificent avenue, or even boulevard, from the centre of the city to Fairmount Park. Because, however, suitable approach to the park is its *raison d'être*, the thoroughfare is properly called a parkway.

routes, so that it may not be possible to say that the bulk of the travel is by this thoroughfare. But it can be said, if the parkways fill their mission, that no other approach will be as pleasant as by them. Entirely accurate, therefore, is the suggestion in their name: they are related more closely to the parks of the town than to its street system; and ever in the parks sheer directness — mere facility of communication between distant points — is of less account than is pleasantness in the way of going.

The relation that the parkways have to the street plan is based on their duty to transform separate parks into a park system, and to unite this to the street system. Repeatedly the latter task is relinquished to existing avenues, and often these are so well fitted to perform it that there would have been no justification for assuming the vast expense of thrusting a parkway through a closely built-up area. But in such case, the care of the avenue thus utilised may well be transferred to the park authorities, that its development may be rendered consistent with its new function and that it may be appropriately maintained. An excellent example is found in Boston's Commonwealth Avenue, the success of which in carrying — in conjunction with the Public Garden and the Common — an entrance to the park system into the very heart of the city has been already noted. When this function of the avenue was appreciated, its care was turned over to the park commissioners; there was no need of building a special parkway leading westward, and Boston's example of a parkway becomes a lovely, winding, almost sylvan road that follows the Fens and joins park to park rather than park to city.

A parkway's relation to the street plan is, then, about that — modified æsthetically by the strong influence of the parks — which is borne by the arterial thoroughfares that lead to, or unite, the urban foci. When these focal points are centres of business, the highways that lead to them, or connect them, are business streets; in the plotting of the parkways, when public pleasure grounds or reservations of beautiful scenery are substituted as the focal points, it is natural that the character of the arterial approach should also change, and that, while it serves relatively the same purpose as the arterial street in the business district, a first essential now should be the requirement that it have a beauty consistent with its terminal.

From that higher and juster thought of a city as an aggregation of homes, instead of merely as a mart or exchange, it is as important that there be reservations for public enjoyment and that they be made easy and pleasant of access as that there should be facilities for doing business. The one is as indispensable as the other to a well-rounded city. But because appreciation of the value of parks is a very late product of city development, and the necessity of relieving the park from that appearance of "added ornamentation" which is the abhorrence

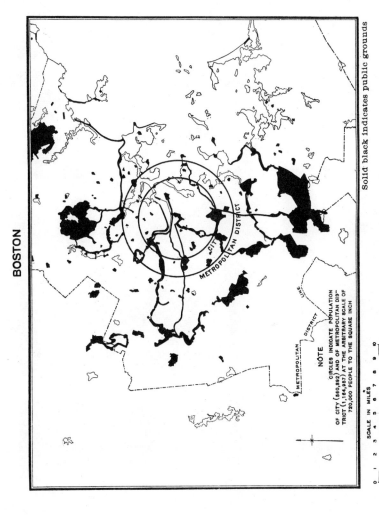

BOSTON

NOTE

CIRCLES INDICATE POPULATION OF CITY (560,892) AND OF METROPOLITAN DIS-TRICT (1,184,867) AT THE ARBITRARY SCALE OF 720,000 PEOPLE TO THE SQUARE INCH

SCALE IN MILES

0 1 2 3 4 5 6 7 8 9 10

METROPOLITAN DISTRICT

CITY

METROPOLITAN DISTRICT LINE

Solid black indicates public grounds

Chart Showing the Public Reservations in the Metropolitan District of Boston. Note how the outlying parks are connected with the areas of densest population by means of parkways.

of art is of yet later perception, the parks usually
are in fact added to the city plan, and the parkways
are completely omitted from it until close building
has supplemented street plotting. For that reason,
a discussion of the genuine parkway (as distinguished from a utilised avenue or "boulevard"), in
its function of an approach-road from the city to the
parks, appears more academic than practical. But
when we remember the splendid Fairmount parkway,
Philadelphia, and the frequency with which there are
now demands for a suitable connection of outlying
parks with the city, the theory of the parkway appears still pertinent. It gives an ideal to work
toward — even when avenues have to be utilised.

There should at once be recognition that there
may properly be two kinds of parkway — that which
unites park and city, and that which joins separated
parks. A third may be developed from these, to
serve the ends of beauty and attractiveness alone;
but even for the former there must be distinct consideration if they would have appropriate adjustment
to their purpose.

It may be noticed that Philadelphia's Fairmount
Parkway, which is of the first group, is a straight line,
making the shortest possible distance from the City
Hall to the park and cutting the city's gridiron street
plan with a diagonal. Several local considerations
entered into the selection of such a route, but the
value of directness in a parkway which is the approach to the park from the heart of the city may as

well be recognised. The advantage is akin to that of directness in the arterial thoroughfare that leads to any other focal point, enabling persons to reach it in the shortest possible time. But when the purpose of the parkway is simply to furnish a pleasant approach for those who drive, this necessity will not be so obvious. Whenever car tracks are not provided, the way is practically such a drive, for it will be little used by pedestrians; and then detours, undulations, and natural curves, if they add distinctly to its beauty and attractiveness, need not be feared. In Minneapolis, for example, there is a very lovely park approach, in Kenwood Parkway, which, with the pleasing and natural irregularity of a winding brook, carries the charm of the parks close to the homes of many of those who can be independent of the cars. This is why sheer directness cannot be said to be a first essential in all the parkways even of this group, though obviously it may very often be desirable.

Where there are cars, the approach may well be made direct; and it is worth while to note that a provision for car tracks is an entirely appropriate development on this thoroughfare. Indeed, from the standpoint of the city as a whole, it is difficult to see that the parkway has any higher or more urgent duty than that of affording swift, cheap, easy, and pleasant access to the parks for "the masses" of the city. This can be done only by giving to it sufficient breadth to accommodate — in addition to roadways and walks — separated car tracks. That they may be added without injuring seriously the beauty or safety of the way has already appeared in the disposition of the tracks on the great avenues. There is in thus facilitating the rapid transportation of city crowds to and from the parks a further advantage. Not only does the parkway do real service to the crowds by this means, but in removing the heavy travel from the ordinary city streets, which otherwise must be used as the main approaches, and transferring it to a highway that has been especially designed and set apart for the purpose, it relieves residential streets of the noise, confusion, and danger consequent on the handling of extra traffic.[1]

Thus, even for the parkway which serves as an approach from the city to the park there may suitably be two types of development. It may be broad, straight, direct, with car tracks on it, and so be like one of those arterial avenues that unite the broad residential belt with the business centre of the city. Or it may be luxuriously and indolently roundabout, sacrificing everything — breadth of roadway, directness, and a provision for moving large multitudes — to the one end of beauty, so that it carries the restful peace and loveliness of the park far into the city.

---

[1] A suggested breadth and its apportionment for such an approach road is one hundred and twenty-five feet, this allowing thirty-five feet for the electric railway, which is to be on a shaded strip of turf, and on each side of it a roadway thirty feet wide, a planting strip seven feet wide, and a sidewalk eight feet in breadth. This, or five feet less, is pretty nearly the minimum for this kind of parkway. The width can be increased to two hundred or even three hundred feet, and be wholly utilized with good effect by screening the cars with belts of shrubbery, adding bridle paths, etc.

For the parkway of which the function is to transform isolated areas of park land into a coherent system, by uniting one to another, the latter development alone is suitable. The parkway that joins them must be in the seeming, however narrow, a strip of park. In driving, walking, riding, or bicycling from one portion of the system to another, there must be no need of recourse to city streets. There is to be desired no break of unwelcome contrast, but by continuing park roads and park-like scenery a persistency of beauty throughout the system. This, clearly, is the ideal; and if, repeatedly, the cities — induced by the economy of large recoupments in the high value of building lots on these linking roads — transform them into avenues or boulevards, they are not wholly true to the civic-art ideal. If they still call them "parkways," they only make confession of the knowledge of their guilt. The true way were to lose in a mystery of planting the narrow borders of the tract.[1]

It is fitting that the parkway which unites outlying parks should partake of the character of its termini. And we have observed that civic art would

[1] Those roads that follow, under the titles Fenway, Riverway, Jamaicaway, etc., the Fens of Boston illustrate a compromise that is interesting because unusually successful. Here a meandering stream, with a broad shallow channel and charmingly planted banks, sets the winding course for a park road on either side, with walk and bridle path. On the far border of each road, often at varying level from it, and separated very widely from their counterpart across the stream, — perhaps even "planted out" as respects the other shore, — there are building sites. Now and then a structure rises so prominently as to mar the prospect and to awaken dread of the time when such buildings will be more numerous, but on the whole the sacrifice has as yet involved small loss.

The Sumac Drive in the Park and Pleasure Drive Association's Holdings, Madison, Wis. A suggestion of how outlying parks that have been developed in the natural style can be suitably connected.

permit much latitude in the development of the road, approving of picturesqueness, of natural or formal beauty, or of architectural pretentiousness, according to the conditions under which it is laid out and the nature of the termini. Because outlying parks, however, are generally large parks developed in the natural style, it were usually better to have in mind — as the ideal — a country lane with its tangled flower-decked border, or a wood road with its dark vistas and twinkling sunlight, than the city avenue's stately elegance and precision. Then there will be no discordant jar in the progress from park to park, but even the addition of a new, harmonious, charm. As fittingly, however, the formal park will be approached or left by a formally developed parkway, in which the architectural and purely artificial character will have emphasis. Or it may be that in its linking of reservation to reservation the parkway will have to pass over a portion of the city on a viaduct — for the parks are likely to include high ground. It would not be practical to give a semblance of naturalness to such a road, nor would there be art in the insincerity. The outlook would be over the housetops of the city,—than which no prospect could be more urban,—and we should now develop our parkway on frankly architectural lines, finding the keynote in the huge structure of the viaduct itself.[1]

The thought of the fascination of the outlook

[1] A convenient example is found in the northern extensions of Riverside Drive, New York.

from a bridge — whether we look on idling streams, into dark ravines, upon freighted ships, or over house-tops — is a reminder of the apt assertion that a bridge is the most attractive of parks or promenades, in proportion to its area. Witness, the temptation to linger there, exhilarated by the broad view and the free air. If the function of the parkway were, like that of the park, only to give pleasure, there would often be justification for such construction when the necessities, and even the convenience, of travel did not require it. And the parkway is coming to have this third function, is being constructed now and then not to lead to anything in particular, not to join park to park or park to city, but solely because of its own possible beauty and the pleasure it may give.

The development was not surprising, for a road of which the first requirement was beauty and only the second communication; and no discussion of parkways can approach completeness if it do not take into consideration the existence of a group tending to serve this purpose. It will not be easy to define the group with accuracy. Again and again, parkways that belong in it will merge into the boulevard or stately avenue. Riverside Drive, New York, is a fair example, with its terraced bluffs and its miles of noble views across the Hudson. But one side of the Drive is built up with houses, so that the thorough-fare has already invited discussion as a splendid residential street. Summit Avenue in St. Paul occupies a similar position, on a bluff overlooking the Mississippi; but it is built up on both sides, and cannot be thought of save as a magnificently situated avenue.

As a rule, however, the appellations are used too loosely to serve as guides, and in seeking to distinguish this type of parkway from boulevard or avenue, we shall have to look narrowly for the purpose of the construction in each separate case. If Riverside Drive, for example, was created primarily to secure for public enjoyment the beauty of its view; if this was the object (as it surely was) of Duluth's splendid "Boulevard" Drive, skirting Lake Superior at a height of four or five hundred feet above the water; or of the eight-mile shell road along the seashore at Mobile,— to note an example separated by the length of the United States,— or of the Ocean Boulevard in San Francisco, then we shall do well to call them "parkways." For the parkways of this group may be described as elongated and greatly narrowed strips of park—which will mean that they were constructed for the same general purpose as that for which parks are established — used also as means of communication. With this definition, the drive may lie through a ravine shut in by walls of natural beauty that give no hint of adjacent boundaries, it may traverse fields, may include brook or river between its divided ways, or it may be reduced to barely a road's width — with a view beyond.

Recognition of this third type of parkway invites

the inclusion in it of that luxury of urban development — the speedway. This too is a road designed for no other purpose than to give pleasure, and it may be claimed for the speedway that the pleasure it gives is by no means confined to the drivers of fast horses. The great numbers to whom, as onlookers, its free exhibitions afford keen delight suggest that as a pleasure-giving drive the speedway — which is certainly not to be classed among the thoroughfares that are integral parts of the street plan — may rightly be grouped only with the parkways. And yet there is this distinction to be noted: the special object of the parkway is beauty, and it belongs by inherent right to municipal æsthetics. To the speedway there may be given the beauty of clear-cut lines, of long straight reaches, of engineering exactness; and the stateliness that comes from mere breadth of firm, clean roadway; of long perspective marred by no breaks in its continuity; of formal rows of regular and stunning light fixtures and perhaps of trees. But such handsome treatment will be, quite as on the business street, secondary to the first function of the speedway. The road would seem then, in the building of the city, to stand almost by itself — a luxury (in that its one purpose is to give pleasure) which civic art will not require, as it may require the parkway, for complete topographical development; but which, given, civic art will turn to the best advantage that it can — levying upon it contribution to the stateliness and dignity of the city, as it makes levy of the great avenues and even of the tenements.

In this chapter it will be observed that in so far as the discussion has been concrete, rather than of parkways in the abstract, cited examples have been from the United States to the exclusion of European instances. This is not that Europe has no beautiful drives as municipal possessions; but it may be doubted whether it has any better than those of the United States, or whether it has as many of them to offer. In parks and park development America has little to learn from across the sea. Perhaps this is because it has had to begin at the beginning and in a few years do everything, while in the countries of ancient cities many a park is a growth of centuries, and many a lovely urban pleasure ground is crown property that owes most of its charm merely to having been left alone for generations. The result may be fully as attractive to the eye of the citizen of to-day, but the process cannot be as favourable to the development of a science or formula of city beauty.

There is, also, this difference: in America where the cities are newer the parks tend more than in Europe to be, in semblance at least, indivisible parts of the cities themselves — to enter into the urban structure as elements of beauty that are inseparable, not accidental or added, ornaments. To emphasise this character is one of the first functions of the parkway, in its transformation of isolated pleasure grounds

into a system and the union of this system with the
street plan of the city. From the broad standpoint
of civic art, which would find scant satisfaction in
the development of a beautiful park to the neglect
of the remaining urban territory, this function is
of extreme importance. There must be not conjunction, but combination; not addition, but change.
If the park, in its skilfully emphasised natural beauty,
be the æsthetic treasure of the city, the parkway
must be the proper approach to it, the setting of that
jewel worn with entire propriety on the fair — the
richly adorned — city's breast.

CHAPTER XVII.

DISTRIBUTION AND LOCATION OF PARKS.

A YOUNG landscape architect, who subsequently became in the achievements of his short life one of the leaders of his profession in the United States, has expressed conveniently the difference in purpose of the city park and "square."[1] He said:

> Smaller spaces can satisfy many of the desires of the crowded city people — can supply fresh air and ample play room, and shade of trees, and brightness of grass and flowers — but the occasionally so pressing want of that quiet and peculiar refreshment which comes from contemplation of scenery — the want which the rich satisfy by fleeing from town at certain seasons, but which the poor (who are trespassers in the country) can seldom fill — is only to be met by the country-park.

The refreshment that the "park" as distinguished

---

[1] The man was Charles Eliot, and from the long story of his life and work that has been given to the public by his father,— *Charles Eliot, Landscape Architect,* by Charles W. Eliot,—many suggestions for this and the succeeding chapter have been drawn, as henceforth every writer upon city parks must draw from it. The article to which reference is here made was published in *Garden and Forest,* October, 1888.

from the "square" is designed to give may be defined, then, as that of relief from the excessive artificiality of city life, and from its strain and striving. A large public park may serve, of course, a variety of purposes; but this one of them will be more prominent, more necessary, than the others. If there be ever a conflict in the requirements of the several purposes, the others must be sacrificed to this, or none will be successfully realised and the result will be scrappy and confused. The dominant *motif* must be that of change from the normal conditions of town life — from some of its unnatural pleasures as well as from its cares and its artificiality of outlook.

So the modern city in its large public park has as distinct and definite a function to perform as in any other portion of its structure. How modern this is; how entirely it is due to the pressure at which we live and work to-day; how it serves an ethical, a sociological, even a hygienic end, as well as the æsthetic purpose; and so how naturally attempt to satisfy it becomes a phase of modern civic art, will appear on very slight reflection. There is no need of explanation; but we should note that civic art will be playing its old rôle — gaining its own, peculiar end, of urban beauty, by merely the fitting of the park to serve best the purpose for which parks are wanted. Indeed, this form of civic art is almost the first to be recognised popularly, and approved. And this is because it is so unmistakably clear that only by æsthetic development, by the greatest possible

View in Seneca Park, Rochester, N. Y.   Note the invitation to loiter and enjoy the view.

increase of charm and beauty, can the parks best serve their end.

The park becomes, then, for the purposes of urban study that public reservation which has been set aside to soothe tired brains and hearts and wearied nerves by the quiet restfulness of its beauty. Because this is so definitely the modern conception of its duty, there has come to be a curious notion that it may be possible to determine the proper park acreage for a given community by a mathematical calculation that need be no more intricate than that by which a physician estimates the amount of sedative he would administer. Given the number of people, how many acres of parks shall we provide? It is a common question, as if the science of modern city-building could reduce to a fixed ratio the proper relation of park area to population. To discover this ratio there has been a great deal of figuring and compiling of reports, for it would be a convenient thing to have. But consideration of the park's purpose should show the futility of even hoping to discover a law.

On the one hand, the community's need of the park will vary according to the pace at which it lives, the density with which the town is built,— that is, the frequency of private gardens, the number of open spaces, and of streets with trees and parking,— and finally upon the parks' distribution and accessibility. Thus some communities have much more need of parks than have others of equal population, just as different patients need different doses. The "average man" is familiarly recognised physiologically as a myth. It is idle also to seek suggestion in the statistics of cities. In the United States, among cities of one hundred thousand or more population, the number of people per acre of park has been found to vary from twenty-seven and five-tenths to eleven thousand four hundred and sixty-six. And in the single city of Chicago there is an acre of park in one portion of the town to every two hundred and thirty-four persons; while for another section of the population the city affords only an acre to four thousand seven hundred and twenty. The latter proportion affects a vast number and is very much worse than the showing of the average allotment for the entire city.[1] But it proves, for the difference in some cities would be more striking than in Chicago, how poor a basis of judgment the "average" record is, because of the factor of distribution.

Observe, also, that the success with which a park will serve its purpose depends more on the topography and the natural character of the scenery than upon the number of acres comprised within its boundaries. A long, peaceful view is a powerful element in giving that sense of repose which is desirable in a country-park. Where the land is flat, it may be necessary to include many acres in order to secure such a prospect without break or jar; where there is a hill, a little area on its crest may give the

[1] *American Municipal Progress,* by Charles Zueblin.

result in an outlook over peaceful, private farmsteads;
or a few acres spread in a thin line around the margin
of a lake may enclose so complete a picture as to
produce with ever so little land the desired impression.

So there is properly no law to be enunciated regarding the ratio of area to population, although it
has been suggested that a minimum should be established of one acre of park (and city square) to two
hundred people.[1] This has been figured out not
only with reference to a possibility of crowding,
which obviously would defeat the purpose of the
park, but with regard to an appropriate per capita
charge for construction and maintenance. Doubtless its chief value from the standpoint of civic art
would lie, not in proportioning original park acreage
to a city, but in suggesting the increases in the existing provision — supposing that to be precisely
adequate to-day — which would be fairly commen-
surate with a continued growth in population.

It is to be predicated, if park requirements seem
to have been considered with some exactness, that
civic art feels in the development of the parks the
thrill and inspiration of a great opportunity and the
incentive to make the very most — at whatever cost
of painstaking — of this powerful element in the
aggregate of city beauty. As a municipal possession
the parks are peculiar to modern times and are

---

[1] *Park Census Report for 1901,* of the American Park and Outdoor Art
Association.

326 Modern Civic Art.

therefore the special problem and special chance of modern civic art. It is because of this fact, however unconscious its apprehension, that the park problem is generally grappled more intelligently, and with more thoroughness, at the awakening of civic-art ambition, than any other of the problems of municipal æsthetics. There is almost uniformly recognition of the necessity of expert guidance, not merely in the engineering features of the park, but, with increasing frequency, in its original location, and almost completely in its artistic development. Any politician will be allowed to pass upon the beauty of a lamp-post long after the community has decreed that all the politicians together shall not have power to designate the location of a single shrub in the park. This dependence upon expert taste is a very happy condition, representing the attainment in one phase of urban development of that popular attitude which is to be the ideal for all — and so long the vain ideal.

The location and distribution of the parks must seem, of course, a much more humdrum and prosaic affair than the development of their beauty. The preparation of the canvas and the selection of the block of marble are never as interesting to the observer as the painting of the picture and the freeing of the marble-imprisoned figure. But these acts are elementary. They are so fundamental that upon the excellence with which they are done is dependent any ultimate success. From that point of view they are more thrilling even, in the sense which they should give of responsibility and of opportunity, than is that subsequent development which might, if proved a failure, be undone.

Consideration, then, of the requirements of the parks, from the side of the parks and of the community, brings us to these common-sense and simple conclusions: the country- or rural-park—as it is called to distinguish it from the city square—should contain sufficient acreage to include a complete natural landscape, where the boundaries will not be obtrusive. The multiplication of such parks or landscapes should continue until the community is sufficiently served, both as to numbers, so that it may be possible to find secluded spots however popular the parks, and as to distribution, so that all portions of the community may be served with an equality based, in the ideal, upon their needs. Thus will be created—if not by the municipality alone, by the co-operation with it of the surrounding towns or by the united action of a whole county—a park system, parkways uniting the separate parks. For it is not to be supposed that one plot would have, or could have, such geographical position and extent as to be equally satisfactory to every part of the community.

But into the question of location there enter other than sociological considerations. The relative cost of various plots must always be a factor locally; and because the park is to be, pre-eminently, a tract of movingly beautiful scenery, developed on natural lines that it may present the greatest contrast to the town's artificiality, the landscape possibilities of the area have to be carefully regarded. And in this we come to principles that may be of general service.

Charles Eliot, in addressing the Metropolitan Park Commission of Boston, criticised the tendency of many towns to select their park lands with reference to " a certain inherited pre-conception " of what parks ought to be—borrowing their notion from the " deer park," the grassy land dotted with great trees, that is the common English concept of the word " park " He then laid down three principles of selection. The first was that the land should possess, or afford opportunity for the creation of, interesting or beautiful scenery, of one type or another. The second was that the land should generally be a tract that was ill adapted to streets and buildings. The third was that it should be related with as much symmetry as possible to the district that it was desired to serve. The second principle is important as affecting the probable cost of the land. It has been elaborated by the secretary of the Essex County (New Jersey) Park Commission to include land " difficult to use for any other purpose and dangerous to the public health," which shall, in its conversion into a pleasure ground, have its unsightly and menacing character eliminated. In this, clearly, there would be a great gain. Not only would cheap land be secured, but an unsanitary area would be

made to contribute to the health of the community
and an eyesore to its beauty. To these principles
one other may be added — or it may be conceived as
an elaboration of the first: preserve to public enjoyment the most striking natural feature, be it the
finest view or the best scenery, of the region in and
about the town.

Out of the principles there comes a rule that
applies so often that it may be laid down almost
as a principle: reserve for park development the
stream banks of the community. This acquirement
is nearly sure to be picturesque, potentially if not in
fact, and has certainly the relief of variety; it is quite
likely to be distinctive; and it is frequently, until
thus taken charge of, a menace to the health of the
community, for it is low, often swampy, and probably made a dumping-ground if not an open sewer
for the neighbourhood. On this account also, while
possessing perhaps the district's greatest chance of
beauty, it is a source of ugliness until redeemed.
But the ridges of its rising banks are likely to furnish
a convenient natural boundary to frame a landscape
picture to be here created, while the trans-water
view, which is always charming, adds the width of
the stream to the apparent park area without removing an equal tract from the slender tax-lists of
the town or from the habitable area of the crowded
city. The reservation affords, too, public access to
a sure current of fresh air, and possibly to a place
for water sports. In short, no inland space equally

contracted is likely to serve well so many ends. The one serious obstacle to such location is the possible commercial productiveness of the banks. On this account it often proves impracticable to obtain more than isolated areas, of mere "open space" extent, and the community has still to go for its country-park into the environs, unable even to approach it by a stream-bank parkway. Fortunately, however, if also unhappily, more towns and cities might establish parks upon the banks of their streams than dream of doing so.

This is especially true among the smaller towns; and with them, it should be noted, the park requirements are not quite the same as with the larger cities. There is, for example, very little real need of providing carriage-drives, for it will be easy to reach innumerable pleasant country roads, which spread from the town in all directions and for distances that would be the despair of a park commission. The tendency of the town to follow the example of the city has caused this condition to be widely ignored, although it is so plain that it should be recognised at once. And the park of the quiet country town may often cater more frankly to the entertainment of the people than it is proper for the rural-park of a city to do. The stream or lake, in the opportunities it offers for boating, skating, etc., may thus give here the keynote to the attractiveness of the whole pleasure ground.

Having determined the general location of the

park and its approximate acreage, there rises a nice question as to the precise location of the boundary line.   A shifting of this a few feet to one side or the other may make more difference in the park's appearance than is commonly realised; and civic art, as we have seen, must be at least as scrupulous in its efforts to secure the maximum of beauty for the park as for the smaller open space, for the lighting apparatus, or for any other detail in the furnishing and adorning of the city.

A leading firm of landscape architects, writing some years ago to a park commission which employed them, thus aptly summarised the commoner treatment of the boundary problem:

It is generally easier to acquire the whole of a given parcel of real estate, though half of it is not really wanted, and then to omit the purchase of any of the next parcel, though half of that is sadly needed, than it is to acquire a part from this and a part from that for the sake of obtaining what is essential, and omitting what is of less importance, to the landscape of the domain to be preserved.   There are few public grounds which are not grossly deformed by the imperfections of their boundaries.   Almost everywhere the immediate saving in time and trouble for the surveyor, the conveyancer, and the commission concerned has worked permanent injury to public interests in public scenery.

It is only too true that those who should be the champions of civic art are thus often careless.   They do not insist upon a strict adherence to the ideal in a matter that seems a small detail, but that actually may affect seriously the beauty of the park and the relation of the park to the town.

The suggestion that the acreage of a given park would best include a complete natural landscape sets down the general position of the boundaries. They should enclose a topographical unit. Half a hill-slope, half a pond, half a glen will not suffice, nor will the whole do unless this include the unit's natural frame. If an arbitrary frame be apparent, the charm of the scene is lost, for to the city dweller no small element in the park's attractiveness is the impression of spaciousness, the feeling that here there is plenty of room. An obvious circumscribing of the area, as by securing, for example, land that reaches exactly to the top of the hill,— where private construction then defines park limits,— immensely reduces the pleasure that might have been given by pushing the boundaries over the crest of the hill, so that the wilderness should seem of indefinite extent.

Those sides of the park, which in time may become all sides of it, that touch the town can best be bounded by streets — not necessarily by straight streets; indeed, preferably by those of waving lines. The park gains by having as its boundary a publicly controlled highway instead of individuals' back yards that may be neglected. The community gains, because the park, instead of being shut away behind private lands and to a large extent concealed, is brought into visibly close proximity; because it makes a positive and great addition to the beauty of the street it touches; and because by its relation to the street it creates attractive, and therefore valuable, building sites. Finally, the arrangement is better for the individuals of the community. On the one hand, gardens that adjoined the public domain would be much more subject to trespass than if there were a street between; on the other, there might well be a sense of injustice in the maintenance at public expense of a beautiful natural park separated by no visible line from an individual's private garden, so as virtually to be added to his estate.

To carry the boundary over the ridges of enclosing hills; not to be hampered by private boundaries, but, rather, to deviate from straight lines if so a great boulder, a clump of noble trees, a face of rock, or a lovely watercourse can be included to complete the landscape picture; and, where town and park adjoin, to make a public way the boundary — these are rules that will serve for guidance when, the general location and approximate acreage of the park determined, its exact limits are to be laid down.

In the development of the boundary street, the community is under certain obligations to the park. As the park enhances the beauty of the street by securing for one side of the highway a beautiful and undespoiled landscape, so the street should make sure that park views are, at least, not ruined by hideous structures on the thoroughfare or at its edge. It should guarantee that the bill-board will not scream its message across the quiet scene, and that the harsh though necessary contrast of urban construction will be softened and made to blend as far as possible with the park's scenery by the half-concealing foliage of trees. If it be well to put a street popularly used as a park approach into the hands of the park commissioners, that it may be suitably maintained, there would seem to be equally good reason for making the like disposition of the boundary streets. The action possibly has yet to be taken for the first time, but the defence of park boundaries from bill-board attack has already become fairly common in American cities.

It ought now to be clear, from considering park requirements, that mere space alone will by no means satisfy the need. Something more than acres are wanted for the public reservations of town or city for the requirements, so many in number and so various in kind, become explicit in their aggregate. Because this is true, it is very important, for the securing of good results, that the location of the parks should be fixed at the earliest possible time. They ought to be planned, indeed, at the start, with the streets and the squares; but unhappily very few cities have been built up from an original ground plan since people's parks came to be recognised as urban necessities rather than as luxuries.

In the old world it has been possible to make good use of many a royal pleasure ground or nobleman's estate, originally chosen because of the natural beauty of the site; made easily accessible by its long years of use, and now perhaps surrounded by the town; and showing internally that beauty of de-

LONDON

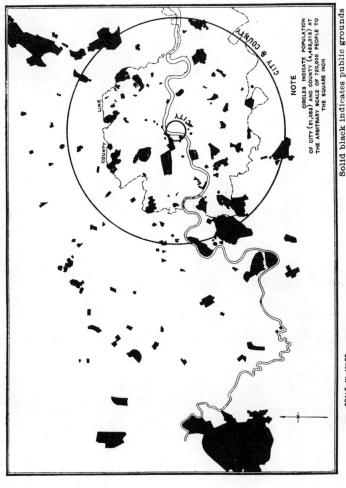

NOTE

CIRCLES INDICATE POPULATION
OF CITY (31,083) AND COUNTY (1,483,018) AT
THE ARBITRARY SCALE OF 720,000 PEOPLE TO
THE SQUARE INCH

Solid black indicates public grounds

SCALE IN MILES
0   1   2   3   4   5   6   7   8   9   10

Chart Showing the Distribution of Public Reservations in and about Metropolitan London.
This may be compared with the chart showing the reservations in metropolitan Boston, where a
"system" has been developed.

velopment which comes with centuries of loving co-operation between man and nature. In the moats that surrounded old city walls many of these towns have had, too, the chance — since walls have been torn down — of joining park to park, and of belting the city, or its more congested inner portions, with a circle of park that is at least impartial in the distribution of pleasure-ground space. Except occasionally, therefore, the park problems of the cities of Europe — especially on the Continent — have been less pressing and less difficult than those in America. Nor should they ever in the future be anywhere as hard as in the past.

Now that the necessity for parks is recognised, and their distribution, location, and boundaries are perceived to be questions really concerned with the science of city-building, — not merely a matter of finding room and utilising any tract, — the position of the parks should be plotted and their sites secured as speedily as possible. There should not be delay until money is available to develop them. A public reservation will serve the purpose that gives to it a name before it has any "development." And promptness in such action will usually mean economy, both in the price of the land, and in the need subsequently of having to undo much less when restoring it to a condition that is natural in suggestion if not in fact.

Secure at once the most striking scenery of the district, preserve as much as possible of the shore line or watercourse for public enjoyment, and then supplement these holdings with areas so distributed, so apportioned, so extended, as best to serve in the total of the system the various park requirements of the community. This, in a nutshell, is the course to be approved.

CHAPTER XVIII.

PARK DEVELOPMENT.

THE distinction between the location of a park and the park's development is not as that between a street's plotting and its surface treatment, its planting, etc. The street is laid down that it may serve a special purpose, and we have to do the best we can under circumstances that are possibly very unfavourable. The site of the park is chosen and its limits determined — in a measure at least — by the natural picture already existent. The task is not to transform that, but to preserve it and even to emphasise it. We have the lovely problem of making a grand or beautiful scene more unmistakably grand or beautiful, so that no one, however dull or untrained, can fail to be conscious of its possession of the qualities of beauty or grandeur, or to enjoy them. As compared with the embarrassment in other parts of the town, æstheticism is here almost unhampered. Modern civic art, in its most charming development, here has a full opportunity.

22

The larger opportunity involves a greater obligation and a larger responsibility. There is need that
he who directs the work have at once naturally refined taste and professional training. Nor must he
be an artist only, who would preserve and dare to
emphasise the beauty of nature; he must be the
lover, content to lose in his work his own identity,
to serve Nature without assertion of himself, but
with that love and understanding which takes the
loved one's point of view, apprehending the un-
formed wish, and reading in the suggestion a command. Though this involve a long course of action,
he will obey it joyfully, bearing criticism with patience, and he will be undiscouraged by the slow
process of the years. His mind must be on the distant picture that Nature has sketched and that he,
with her aid, shall finish — not to-day, or to-morrow,
but in the years to come, when at last his lifework,
in the completeness of beauty, shall stand for generations. Far more than student, more than artist, more
than blundering lover, he must be student, artist,
lover, all in one — united by high consecration. For
his is "the most interesting of the arts; to poetry
and painting what reality is to a description, what
the original is to a copy"[1]; and its purpose is of the
purest and sweetest.

The park superintendent and commissioners
should have had a voice in the location of the
park, that the district may be adequately served

[1] Girardin, 1777.

The Glen in Minnehaha Park, Minneapolis. Minn.

and its most distinctive scenery secured. So the canvas is stretched, the marble selected, and we come — in the park's development — to that fascinating task, the making of the picture.

It may be well to note at once the restrictions. There are certain things that must be done to make possible the enjoyment of the park by large numbers of people and its necessary connection with the city, that are handicaps to an ideal development of scenery. They are essential, however, and may as well be planned for at the start. These hampering necessities include most strikingly the roads and paths and definite boundaries, for the few needed structures may often be "planted out" or may be made even to contribute picturesqueness to the scene.

As to the boundaries, it has been already suggested that, by putting them just beyond the landscape's natural frame and concealing them with heavy planting, any appearance from the park of a hard line will be lost; indeed, that there may be obtained that seeming indefiniteness of extent which will prove an additional charm of the park to city dwellers. Where there are entrances, however, it will be advisable for various reasons to mark distinctly the breaks in the boundary line. In planning these, the greatest care should be taken to make their location convenient, for just because each entrance adds a difficulty to idyllic treatment, by the formality which it may require and the convergence there of roads and paths, it will not do to multiply them indefinitely. And even in the theory of country-park development, as well as in convenience, there is excuse for the conspicuousness of an entrance. The entrance to the park from the city is also the exit to the city from the park,—the exit from the natural into the artificial and formal. It is not improper that this should be indicated to those who are in the park. On the side of the town, a stately and formal entrance is much more harmonious—even consistent and appropriate —than would be a seemingly casual break in a natural border of undergrowth and trees. On the country side, the like requirement is not as pressing, but there is reason enough. Though the park will turn to the best use it can any peaceful or romantic views over country not included in the park area, the point of egress from park to real "country" should still be definitely known, since there one passes out of the area that is reserved for public enjoyment and where the beauty of every detail may be rightfully demanded.

In some cases, very notably in Hyde Park, London, and in Prospect Park, in the borough of Brooklyn, New York, so striking an architectural entrance as an arch of commemoration or triumph is provided. Hyde Park is not really a country-park. There are large trees and meadow-like stretches of turf, but there is very little effort to make the visitor forget that a great city is beating against the perfectly evident fence, and in its broad and conspicuous roads

there is much of formalism. Prospect Park is country-
like and yet a massive arch surmounted by a glorious
quadriga marks the entrance. On its street side there
is a broad, paved plaza to which various streets and
surface transit lines converge. A plaza here, thus
treated topographically as a focus, is an excellent arrangement. It emphasises the importance of the
park entrance and tends by increasing the park's
accessibility — through the ease, convenience, and
rapidity of its own distributing power — to bring the
park nearer to the people.

In regard to park roads and paths, it is clear that
these are necessary for the enjoyment of the park by
many persons. There are a few who with delight
and profit might enter a pathless wilderness, and
climbing, wandering, guideless there, would find for
themselves the vantage points, the half-hidden beauties, and who at their wish could return with ease.
But there are many who will drive, and many who
will ride on horse or bicycle, and many who, though
walking, would be lost without the path, or unable
to discover or to reach the view-points and secluded
pictures without such aid — physical and mental.
For all of these, and even for the preservation of the
quiet beauty of the scene, in which contemplating
thousands are to be scattered inconspicuously and
harmlessly, it is necessary that there be drives and
paths. For park development is the most liberal of
arts and, as Wordsworth says, no servant of such an
art aims to gratify merely an individual or class;

"the true servants of the arts pay homage to the human kind."

Not merely, then, to lead from point to point is the duty of these park paths and roads; but to lead by the most attractive way, to reveal as many as possible of the landscape beauties, and at the same time so to lead that while every view from the way itself is lovely the way shall be as slightly noticeable a feature of the park as possible — almost unobserved until required, and a non-intruding guide to those who use it in solitary commune with nature. Here directness is not a factor. No one is to be in a hurry here. To soothe the spirit and calm tired nerves with peaceful outlooks and beautiful views, the roads and paths may wind and turn. They must be built well, so that there will be pleasure in the mere act of travelling, but more important than their construction is their location. If at the beginning there be no money with which to build elaborate roads, yet their position should at once be plotted — they should be placed where they ought to be, and improved subsequently, as occasion comes.

Finally, even the trolley can be brought into the park. There has been a great deal of hesitation as to this point, and on the whole it is creditable that there should have been, for what more natural than to fear that admission of the means of rapid-transit would destroy tranquillity and conventionalise the park, and what more commendable than to defend the tract, though at the cost of public convenience, from an intrusion of such effect? But the narrow line of rapid-transit need do no injury. It may be fully screened, by grading and by planting, and even made by such bordering a way of beauty in itself. This once granted, the thought of the duty of the park to the community—to woo to its beautiful serenity the city's workers in the greatest numbers possible — should carry a conviction that urban transit facilities need not be halted at the gates. They may well be brought close to park vantage points.

With the borders arranged, the entrances chosen and marked, and the drives and paths laid down, those probable drawbacks which are truly essential are known, and there remains the task of extracting from the scene the maximum of beauty, in completeness and consistency, that potentially may linger there. And this should amount to much, especially if the plot has been chosen because of its natural beauty.

The unity will be already existent to a considerable extent in the natural picture of the selected tract; the harmony will be brought out by the breadth of the composition and the naturalness of the treatment; the variety, in the picturesqueness of the details. Over all will be thrown that evident fitness to its purpose — here of refreshment to the city-wearied — that is the final, all-enveloping quality of beauty and of art. There will be frequent necessity for regrading. In the treatment of the water surfaces and their margins, that they may not give an air of formality to a scene which is meant to be natural, both the taste and training of the landscape artist will be required. In the planting there must be often clever exaggeration of the suggestions of Nature, lest the inexperienced overlook the niceness and fineness of her distinctions and lose a charm of the park. But all these are professional questions. They are the local problems of each separate country-park, and are general only in their universal repetition in an infinite variety.

The great things to be remembered, the thoughts that are to solve these problems when they arise and that are to determine each detail in the work to be done, are two: first, that purpose of the park which may be called psychological, in its proffer of refreshment by means of peace and beauty, that, "under the spreading branches of the trees, we may take the benediction of the air." From this point of view the park, it is suggested, serves to the modern crowded industrial city such a spiritual purpose as the architectural grandeur and loveliness of a cathedral served to the comparatively rural population of the Middle Ages. The park is the cathedral of the modern city. The second, the park's purpose to preserve to the people, and even to enhance for their enjoyment, types of the existing natural beauty of their neighbourhood.

From the latter standpoint, park commissioners

In Genesee Valley Park, Rochester, N. Y. "The park is the cathedral of the modern city."

should be considered as trustees of scenery. For some of the parks of cities, indeed whenever a tract has been selected especially on account of its striking beauty, grandeur, or picturesqueness, they are primarily this. And so there enters into civic art, into the art even of *city* beauty, the preservation of distinctive natural scenery. This is not incongruous. The purpose of municipal æsthetics is simply to bring into the lives of the city-bound the greatest possible amount of beauty, to secure for them the beauty that should rightfully be theirs, to defend from wretchedness their homes and daily outlook, and to make sure that where there are brought together the greatest number of persons — with what powers of enjoyment and aggregate of sensibility!— their higher cravings shall not be starved; but that, rather, it shall be possible for them to draw from their surroundings the inspiration on which is founded the progress of the race. With this thought, can civic art afford to neglect whatever is most noble or most beautiful in the natural scenery of the region in which the town is situated? If it has dared to neglect it in other times, the reason is the essential difference between modern civic art and any that has gone before — the difference between an ethical and a purely sensual standard, between an art to make men and an art man-made.

Unless there be public reservations for park purposes, we have to consider to what an increasingly narrow and artificial life the population of cities would be condemned. The larger the community, the more completely, and for the greater distances, will the naturally beautiful points of the surrounding region be turned into private grounds, and the more impossible will it become for the people — who are ever "trespassers in the country"— to get close to nature. But through its means they come to the knowledge and so to the love of God; while without it there is lost the true sense of proportionate values, and the temporary and human are vaingloriously magnified.

When the popular function of the park is examined thus from various standpoints, there is reached an attitude of mind which makes it easy to judge regarding certain more or less incidental questions in park development which yet recur so frequently as to be well-nigh universal perplexities. Such for example are the buildings that are put in parks; the sculpture that is thrust into them; the efforts to transform them, or parts of their area, into zoölogical or botanical gardens; and finally,— and rather on the other side of the matter,— the tendency to use the cemetery as a public park, if no distinct pleasure ground has been set aside.

Consideration that the park is developed in the natural style in order that it may present the sharpest contrast to the artificiality of the city, should make it clear that buildings are to be admitted to its area in only the chariest way. The fact that the design is to accommodate comfortably, and for periods of many hours, large numbers of people, will necessitate some buildings. These may properly include not only shelters from the sudden storm, but restaurants where light and inexpensive refreshments can be obtained. We have, then, antithetical requirements which can be harmonised only by making the buildings as few as possible, as inconspicuous as may be, and in form picturesque additions to the scene. All public institutions — museums and galleries — should be barred out. They have no business in a rural-park; and if they are put there because the land costs nothing, the people pay more for the site — in the loss of the ground occupied by the structure and its approaches, in the marring of the landscape vista by the intrusion of formalism upon its naturalness, and in the defeat of the park's purpose in at least the portion thus occupied — than they would have paid for a site on the grandest avenue. It is a payment, too, that must be made every day and every year in an increasing sum. If the structures are placed here that they may have a beautiful and advantageous setting, their gain is the park's loss. We must believe that in a wiser planning of cities there would be furnished enough sites of inherent dignity, stateliness, and beauty to make it possible to accommodate such buildings without trespassing on the park.

As to statuary, of which the purpose must be decorative, educational, or commemorative, it is difficult to understand how so much was ever admitted to natural parks. The statue itself will probably look well with a green background of soft foliage, but it is so incongruous in a "natural" scene that only the narrowest artistic view could have excused its admission. With regard to the other functions of sculpture, people do not go to the park to think. Statuary has properly, then, no place in rural-parks.

The use of some of the park area for zoölogical or botanical gardens is more easily understood. These require large tracts of land; and if the botanical garden does not necessarily destroy the beauty of the park, even replacing with some addition of interest the naturalness that it may endanger, the zoölogical garden — which is incompatible with the maintenance of a calm and perfect landscape picture — is certainly very attractive to the people. It will undoubtedly draw to the park many who otherwise would seldom visit it, and it will effectually refresh them with scenes unlike those of the city. It is even true, probably, that a majority of the visitors to a large park on a holiday would prefer some artificial attraction, some positive amusement, to the soothing contemplation of lovely scenery — and here is an amusement that at least will do them no harm. So the gardens open a large question — a question of circular railroad tracks, of whirling horses, of a thousand artificial forms of amusement. There is only one answer to make —

the answer to another question, "Is this what the country-park was made for; is it for this the striking scenery was reserved?" There is so little beauty in the zoölogical garden, and beauty is so incidental a factor in the botanical garden, that civic art need no longer concern itself with them. But in leaving the subject, it may say that—from a sociological, not a civic-art, standpoint—there might fittingly be provided among the "parks" one that should be frankly a public pleasure ground, with zoölogical and botanical gardens and all the recreative gewgaws of the hour.

Finally, the community's use of the cemetery as a park is simply a pathetic confession of the public need of park reservations. Speaking artistically, the cemeteries have lately shown vast improvement. From a type originally comparable to stoneyards, they tend to become more and more park-like. As the beauty of grading and planting increases and monuments become less prominent features, the effect is less depressing. It is restful and like that of the park. We should note, too, that in selecting the site of the "God's acre," there is likely to have been that reservation of particularly lovely natural scenery which is one of the factors in the park's success. But the great significance of a community's park-use of the cemetery is the proof of the need of parks. It is a use to be encouraged and approved, until the park is provided, for all the reasons for which parks are approved.

A word should be said as to those reservations
that may be state or national in origin, but which
are municipal in the use that an adjacent community
makes of them. It is a word of explanation. From
the standpoint of civic art, the relation of such parks
to the nearest community is the same as the relation
of state and national buildings, squares, and bridges
to the city in which these happen to be — the
relation of the Capitol to Washington, of the Place
de la Concorde and Alexander III. Bridge to Paris, or
of the Sieges Allee to Berlin. Civic art asks no
question as to origin. It is satisfied if the city be
adorned, be rendered more fitted to its purpose,
fairer, more worthy of itself. In studying the subject, these state-created ornaments may be valuable
for illustrations, while of little use as examples to
other cities whose citizens must generally depend
upon their own resources. But in studying the
completed picture, instead of the process of its creation, they are not to be distinguished as factors in its
beauty from those that are municipally established.
All act together to make the city beautiful.

There remains one point to speak of in regard
to park development. It is the encouragement that
should be given to the people to visit the parks.
"Democracy," says Walt Whitman,[1] "most of all
affiliates with the open air, is sunny and hardy and
sane only with nature." And then, speaking of
American democracy in particular, he notes that this,

[1] Autobiographia.

in its myriad personalities, in factories, workshops, stores, offices,—through the dense streets and houses of cities, and all the manifold sophisticated life,—must either be fibred, vitalised, by regular contact with outdoor light and air and growths, farm scenes, animals, fields, trees, birds, sun-warmth, and free skies, or it will morbidly dwindle and pale. We cannot have grand races of mechanics, work people, and commonalty (the only specific purpose of America) on any less terms. I conceive of no flourishing and heroic elements of democracy in the United States, or of democracy maintaining itself at all, without the nature-element forming a main part— to be its health-element and beauty-element.

And not merely should there be encouragement to go to the park, but to linger in it for considerable periods at a time, that its full beauty and influence may be leisurely absorbed. There is no other way to appreciate the park to the full except in leisurely fashion. Its contrast to the city in bestowing a sense of repose is dependent on a willingness to take time, on a feeling that haste and urgency do not enter here. In fact, much of the enjoyment of the park is forbidden to those who drive through it, and the speeding bicyclist has only a blurred, vague sense of beauty, as has the motorist.

So in developing the park there should be frequent invitation to loitering. There should be facilities for hitching horses; attractive footpaths should lead enticingly into mysteries of planting that appeal resistlessly to the instinct for discovery. There should be secluded nooks and recesses; it should be possible to walk everywhere, to lie upon the grass; to drift all day if one wishes, without additional expense, upon the sheet of water, or to paddle beneath the mirrored trees, and in sequestered nooks to anchor for a morning or afternoon. There should be seats for those who fear to use the ground, and everywhere the invitation to those idle day-dreams that may be the most profitable dreams we have. In the ground cover there should hide the sweet surprise of unexpected flowers, to woo the careless to a more thoughtful study of their surroundings. There should be many places where the music of rippling water, of singing birds, and of the far-away laughter of little children shall be so secure from interruption by grosser sounds as to attract the listener and hold him with its lovely charm.

For all of this there will be need of many little shelters from the storm; of many waste receptacles, that no untidiness may result from the eating of luncheons out-of-doors; of ample and convenient facilities for getting drinking water; and of, finally, efficient police protection. But these things can be provided quite inconspicuously, so that they shall not be apparent but shall, in almost subconscious recognition of their presence, substantiate the alluring invitation of the park.

And its invitation should be not that of the summer only, but of the year. The beauty of the snowy meadows, the broadening of the vistas when the leaves have fallen, the hide-and-seek of the water in the half-frozen brook, the dark tree-trunks silhouetted against the snow and throwing blue shadows on the

white fields, the etching of bare branches against
the sky — these are winter beauties of the park that
should be understood.   Then comes in spring the
never tiring miracle of the awakening to life of every
plant — the peeping of the flowers above the snow,
the bursting of the buds, the unfolding of little
leaves, the uncurling ferns, the tender green that
spreads over hill and dale; and when at last the
glory of the summer wanes, there yet is gorgeous
autumn, with the lingering, wailing death of the
year, just when it has flaunted most proudly its
splendour and the rich ripeness of its success.   This
is the annual story — even drama, of the park, to
which the people are to be summoned from the city
streets.

For the park has not a passive, but an active,
function. It is not to stand aloof, a treasure of
the city, beautiful, still, reserved.   There is nothing
among all the achievements of modern civic art that
is created merely to be looked at, and the park is no
exception.   It is, to be sure, beautiful.   From the
standpoint of sheer beauty there is no other urban
possession comparable to this; but life must pulse
through all of civic art.   If in any city belonging
there be not intense human purpose, if it have not
a duty to perform, civic art disclaims it.   So the
park, with the warmth and strength of love, — of
love of all the working world, of tender pity for its
weariness and long restraint, — should hold out its
arms to city dwellers, should invite them to itself,

23

until its naturalness and beauty enter into their lives and become as distinct a part of the city's relation to its citizens as are the streets and squares. Only then has the park fulfilled its mission **as a phase of** modern civic art.

CHAPTER XIX.

TEMPORARY AND OCCASIONAL DECORATION.

TO enter into the life of the people — this was to be the duty of the park as a component of that modern civic art which exists for the people's sake. To be itself a product of their life, to owe its very existence to their emotion, its strength to their fervour,—that is the condition, even the privilege, of temporary and occasional decoration in the city. In the intimacy of this connection, there is proved the right of brief and fleeting decoration to be included, for other reasons than its spectacular effect-iveness, in the discussion of civic art. It is born of the people's emotion. It is the outward manifesta-tion of their sentiment. As the song in the music-ian's heart leaps forth upon the keys, as the vision in the painter's soul is transcribed upon the canvas, so the impulse of the people displays itself upon street and square. They are the artist, and the decoration —refined or crude—is their handiwork. The ropes of laurel, the rows of snowy columns, the flower-twined masts, the fluttering banners, the myriad lights, the procession marching to the heart-beats of a nation — these will be indeed, if rendered beautiful, a phase of civic art. They will be the freest, most spontaneous, of all civic-art expressions.

To be sure the decoration is transitory. It is as short-lived as the beauty of the rose, as the festival of the stars in the pageant of a night. But when we read of the urban glories of the past, do we forget the colour-crowded streets of those old towns of Burgundy, where the fountains tossed red wine and white, and where musicians played from within a pastry; do we forget the solemn ecclesiastical functions that were wont to transform for a season the warring cities of Italy; has the stately Roman triumph passed out of mind; and has the grace of the Athenian procession been forgotten? All these were fleeting; but so much were they a part of the life of their communities that they are now as inseparable from the memory of the cities as are the marble palaces that would then have seemed the more permanent phase of civic art. It is not the duration of a beautiful thing, but its essentialness, its intimate connection with the thought and feeling — with the life — of the people, and hence its urban utility, that counts in giving to it a place in civic art.

The temporary and occasional decoration, however temporary and however occasional, is thus one of the opportunities to be availed of in the building of the city beautiful. There should, certainly, be no self-consciousness about the impulse. The wish to decorate must come from a full heart, spontaneously; but just as the artist, without prejudice to a later inspiration, will study rules of art, so may we, in the tranquil hours between the great waves of emotion, contemplate those simple rules that underlie expression and give to it effectiveness. For the one purpose of expression is to produce effect. When a popular emotion sweeps over a community and so stirs it that the very house-fronts bear its emblems and the business streets lose their matter-of-factness in passionate portrayal of feeling, then, with no sense of self-consciousness or restraint, there will be observance of such rules as may be known to increase the effectiveness of the expression. So there will be a fitting to purpose, and the requirements of civic art will have as usual utilitarian as well as æsthetic value.

It will be well to examine first the conditions that make possible and even give rise to temporary and occasional decoration. They are: (1) an emotion; (2) an emotion so general as to be well-nigh unanimous.

The latter factor invites co-operation. When all the residents on a block feel so strongly on a certain subject that they all wish on the same day to deck their houses with flags, or to drape them with the emblems of sorrow, why should each one act by himself alone ? They choose the same time for expressing their sentiment; they make use of like materials and methods, for the feeling is common; what, then, could be more awkward, more constrained, and actually unnatural, when unanimity of emotion tends to draw men together, than for each household to act by itself? And co-operation, with its inducement to harmony and unity in results, is one of the steps to a popular realisation of civic art.

Yet this has proved a most difficult thing to secure in temporary decoration. Until as lately as Queen Victoria's "diamond jubilee," there appeared to be in recent times no general effort toward it or even for artistic direction, as far as the householders were concerned. It has been said that on that occasion there was literally not a street and hardly a house in all of vast London that had not some attempt at decoration. Gilded lions and unicorns, crowns of imitation jewels, the entwined letters V. R. and the numerals of the dates, intricate illuminations in gas jets and coloured glass, rows of little fairy-lamps, the flags of the empire, were the materials, rich in artistic possibilities, that a prosaic and unimaginative people, without direction or co-operation, transformed into a confused and jumbled splurge of loyalty. A witness of the celebration, who could be perhaps as little suspected of thoughts of civic art as any describer of the event, wrote of it:

The decorations were not beautiful, and with the exception of those in St. James's Street there was no harmony of design nor scheme of colour, and a great opportunity was lost. There was probably no other time when so much money was spent in display with results so inadequate. Had the government put the matter in the hands of a committee of artists, much might have been done that would have made the route of the procession a valley full of beauty and significance; but, as it was, every householder followed his own ideas and so, while the loyalty displayed was quite evident, the taste was most primitive. It was the same sort of decoration that one sees on a Christmas tree.

At the time of the reception to Admiral Dewey in New York, which was only two years later, the National Society of Mural Painters devised a beautiful scheme of house-front decoration. The society's own efforts were confined to eight important blocks; but it made public its house-front suggestions, urging that on separate blocks of the line of march the householders should co-operate so that results might be harmonious. The requirements were simple: a restriction of the mass of decoration to the third-story windows; a use of leaves, flowers, rugs or tapestries, and of the colours of the navy (which were blue and white) with accents of gold, in addition to the national colours. An appeal was directed to the public spirit of the people; it was suggested that if there were harmony within single blocks and the third-story accent were adhered to generally, the blocks might differ as much as desired; and it was perfectly clear to every one that the suggestions were sensible and would produce if carried out effects much lovelier and much stronger than the usual straggling, irregular display made up of unrelated splotches of colour. But there was little response to the appeal. Either the public was incredulous as to the possibility of co-operation, or each household, wishing to greet the hero with a triumphant song of welcome, preferred to sing its own particular tune in its own key instead of uniting in a mighty chorus. This at least was very much the effect, and it measures somewhat more strikingly than did the event in London, since here there had been given a chance for better things, the loss of power through failure to act together.

A few weeks afterward, at the Dewey reception in Boston, certain streets were assigned to different artists and it is said that "a variety of colour schemes were carried out with considerable success." At New Haven, two years later still, on the occasion of Yale University's bi-centennial celebration, a scheme that had been designed by a prominent decorative artist[1] was quite widely adhered to. So, as the ideals of civic art reach farther and are better understood, co-operation is, in fact, secured with increasing frequency. The conditions in New Haven, it may be explained, were of a type very different from those in New York. The streets were full of verdure with many and large trees, and the houses, seldom exceeding two stories in height, had gardens or lawns before them. There was thus requirement of an entirely new plan. The dominant features of this were a band of green, to extend across the front of each dwelling just above the first row of windows. The entrance or other conspicuous point

[1] Louis C. Tiffany.

on the house-front was emphasised by a massing
of evergreens, and over these fluttered the flags of
the university.

Now, if the co-operation which should give ideal
results is still secured with sad infrequency, there
should be recollection that modern civic art has
made progress in an occasional taking of that long
step which is marked when artists are asked to
devise plans for popular decoration that shall be
suitable and beautiful. There is a bridging even of
centuries in this, to times when the procession was
considered, as it should never have ceased to be considered, a work of art; a looking back to such glorious
days for municipal æsthetics as those when Cecca,
the gifted engineer and architect, arranged the pageants of Florence, and brought saints and angels into
narrow streets whence all of sombre grayness and
austerity had fled before a flood of banners, of roof-
ing drapery, and gay carpets.

The first step is, obviously, to get the good,
artistic, and reasonable plan. The next will be
general adherence to it — and that is co-operation, if
not by a pleasanter name at least by a probably
easier route. The swift advance that the last few
years have witnessed in the control of decoration for
popular festivals — which is only a return, after a
period of extravagant laxity, to the saner methods
of earlier times — is thus one of the impressive
evidences of a Renaissance in civic art.

In considering a plan of decoration, the first

question to ask is the nature of the emotion. The whole meaning of the decoration is to express a sentiment, and that sentiment may be one of joy, pride, reverence, or grief. This the decoration as well as the pageant must unmistakably indicate. The open-air dancing in the squares of Paris on the night of July 14th, the fireworks in American cities on the night of July 4th, the tossed confetti and frolic of the masqueraders in the carnival cities — could anything be more joyous, or more typical in its expression of joyousness, than those popular celebrations ? The exuberance should be expressed with equal clearness by the decoration; and when the bands play funeral marches, and flags are furled, and a slow and solemn tread takes the place of gaiety, the change must appear as surely in the dressing of the streets and house-fronts. Thus is the first question the nature of the sentiment. Its framing is another way of asking the impression which is to be conveyed. The latter query, however, is broader, for sometimes there will be a desire to make a show of might or power for reasons that appeal to the intellect rather than to the heart. A very long procession of voters, for instance, may be designed to affect the onlookers by sheer numbers, and householders, by evincing their sympathies in decorations, will emphasise or lessen the procession's effect. The decorations would be here traceable, indeed, to sentiment, but they would spring not so much from excess of that as from a wish to impress which has been formulated by reason. So we may change the form of the first question and make it, "What is the impression to be conveyed?"

The second question concerns the conditions under which the display is made. Will it be seen mainly at night or in the daytime, on land or on water, in a region of sunshine and abundant flowers, or where storms are so frequent that stands must be designed with roofs and where it is not safe to plan the exposure of rich stuffs? This question, if not as unescapable as the first, may affect the result as keenly, and it shows the utter futility of attempting to frame rules for occasional decoration that will apply generally.

Yet, out of even the few examples already noted, there are lessons to be drawn for the householders. The importance of co-operation has been observed, to the end that in the decoration of a city there shall be adopted a civic unit — which is to say, a street or block — and not the false or irrelevant unit of the individual. There has appeared the artistic necessity of harmony and even of evidence of a substantial unanimity — philosophically justified by the thought that the display is one united people's expression of a common feeling. This has been the motive, indeed, for the co-operation. To give this appearance of an underlying connecting unity, there has been seen the value of establishing a definite accent. This, by sameness of colour and position, will join all parts of the display, however much

these differ in harmonious detail. The householder
has thus secured, after all, a good deal of helpful
suggestion from the examples, for he necessarily
started with the two main questions answered: the
impression to be conveyed, and the conditions under
which the display is made.

The conditions will be a very important factor.
Examples may be noted. When Cecca planned
the street decorations and pageants of Florence, he
had little need to fear storm; but he had to consider
the pitiless heat of the sun that would beat upon
spectators and actors, once the narrow streets were
left and the broad, shadeless plaza had been entered.
We read, then, that the whole Piazza del Duomo was
roofed with a cool blue drapery on which were
stitched coats of arms and golden lilies. Its fitness
and utility formed one of the beauties of the decoration. For the inaugural celebration in Washington
in 1901,— probably, and significantly, the first at
which there was a serious attempt to obtain a general effect in the street decorations that should be
harmonious and beautiful,— it was necessary to provide many stands and to roof them, lest the weather
be inclement. Their designing was given to architects instead of to carpenters, and the very pillars
that supported their roofs and the roofs themselves
became decorative features. A group of these stands
or pavilions, symmetrically arranged, uniform in size,
attractively finished in front, painted white and decorated with vines, transformed a bit of street as effect-

ively as had the Florentine's cloth sky, and for very much the same reason its beauty gave an intellectual pleasure.

In Venice any strictly popular festival must take place on water, and the wedding of the city to the Adriatic, in the republic's proudest days, became probably the most well-known of all her fêtes; but in modern times, when the picturesqueness and romance of the city show best at night as kindly shadows aid the imagination, Venice, still making use of the water, decks herself for strangers after the sun has set. Then from the towers and domes of her countless churches, from the balconies of her palaces whence their number is doubled by the mirroring canals, glow the lights that transform her from a city of memories to one of dreams. This illumination is possibly the briefest of all modern civic decorations, but while it lasts a song comes over the water to lull you to sleep, that you may not know when it disappears. There is reason back of this, and to the abundant loveliness of the scene there is cleverly added that element of attractiveness which is in the unattainable and the pathetic.

The Van Dyck celebration in Antwerp, in 1899, was organised by the artists of the city. It took place before the Hôtel de Ville, in that Grande Place that scarcely needed extra decorations to frame worthily a Mediæval pageant. For, in a late year of the nineteenth century, the festival was Mediæval, because its subject was of that time. In the procession marched the nations and the arts — the Gothic a joyous group singing a hymn. Then there were floats showing the Dutch artists and the subjects of Van Dyck's paintings, and finally the representation of Van Dyck himself, with the cities London, Genoa, Venice, Rome, Paris, Vienna, Munich, Dresden, The Hague, and Antwerp grouped around him in admiration. There was an address by a cardinal in scarlet, and just after him came his monseigneurs in blue silk, while the burgomaster might himself have stepped from a Van Dyck portrait. There was historical appropriateness in this celebration.

The carnivals, be they in Rome or New Orleans, are rather great urban frolics than examples of civic decoration; and the beautiful festivals of flowers, be they in sunny California or on the shores of the Mediterranean, are the festivals of little towns — the floriculturists' harvest home — rather than the pageants of cities. But they have, with the carnivals, this significance: they are natural and therefore distinctive, as distinctive as the old Venetian celebration of the wedding of the sea. And the factors that go to make them a success, human light-heartedness and abundant flowers, are found at hand. In their way they are thus as significant in their expression as the stately Roman triumph of a Cæsar, or the Labour Day procession of a modern industrial town. Thus the influencing conditions are not climatic alone, nor merely natural ; but temperamental, economic, and perhaps historical.

Broad Street, Philadelphia, Temporarily Transformed into a "Court of Honour" for a Pageant.

When there is to be a civic pageant of such importance as to suggest a general dressing of houses, there is nearly always a demand that the occasion be made a holiday, to the end that the almost ceaseless labour of the town shall be for the time suspended. As a matter of theory, there is much to recommend the fixing of urban celebrations for the night.   There will then be little disturbance of work, the streets are clear, and, as in Venice, only that need be illuminated which will add to the beauty and appropriate effectiveness of the scene, while there is much of picturesqueness and decoration in the very lights themselves.   But taking the city as a whole, the end of a day means weariness and rest appeals more than even play.   The recent appearance of illuminated " courts-of-honour," that are simply business streets transformed in the evening, does not probably indicate, therefore, that because of our better control of lights and increased lighting facilities we are to turn our urban pageants into evening festivals.   No civic celebration can be a really splendid and popular success for which the occasion has not been made a holiday.

To the consideration, then, of the householders' part in the city festivals,— even regarding these in an abstraction which is discouraging to definite conclusion, where the cases to be treated are so many and varied,— there have now appeared from the selected typical examples some further suggestions of value. Not only should there be co-operation, in the

common expression at one time of a common sentiment; not only must that expression precisely fit the
sentiment; and not only may the co-operation between the householders manifest itself with best artistic results in the establishment of a uniform accent
in the decorations, and the maintenance of civic
units, but the manner of the celebration should be:
distinctive; suited to time and to various local conditions; in its larger aspects not decorative merely
but reasonable, and it may even be with an underlying
utility — i. e., the selection for decoration of that
which is necessary or convenient for the pageant.
In addition, it should set before the people an ideal of
beauty or picturesqueness that is locally pertinent,
however unattainable; and the occasion should be
made a holiday.

Do these conclusions seem trite? They tend
to the following suggestions that certainly are not
familiar in the observance: they suggest that in the
decoration of the structures of a town the national
colours are not always pertinent. The adoption of
a city flag, a city colour, or a city emblem,— not
necessarily more elaborate than the Venetian lion of
St. Mark's or the lily of Florence, — that can be used
on many strictly local occasions would be far better.
Patriotism is good, but in hardly one festival in a
year does the show of it express accurately the
festival's sentiment. They suggest that for towns
so situated as to have a body of water as the leading
highway, there should be no conventional cramping

of the pageant into city streets. It should be put upon the water. This will nearly always mean a gain in picturesqueness and in the provision for spectators. It will mean, besides, adaptation to local natural conditions and thus distinctiveness. The conclusions suggest, further, that there should not be the incongruity of elaborately decorated buildings, with rude and undressed stands before them. The stands, as a necessary adjunct to the pageant, should be made a dominant *motif* in the decoration. And they suggest that the householders instead of acting individually, each trying to make the greatest splurge, should relinquish the advertisement point of view and should adopt the really decorative, to the end that on a block or street they should act in harmony to give to that space the beauty which perhaps they may not hope to see in permanent results, but of which they happily may dream.

As to the pageant itself, there are not many kinds of play. Play is real life in counterfeit, with a veiling of the serious. We march in procession to play at war — in a light-heartedness that restores to the race its boyhood; we dance, and so return to the old "leap" of earliest Latium and Hellas; we masquerade, and feel the kinship of the earliest peoples when in the skins of goats and sheep they also "played"; we make music, and in our melody there is an echo of the pipe of the herdsman on mountain side or starlit plain before any cities were.

24

From these universal, simple, time-worn elements, to devise the distinctive, expressive, beautiful, may well demand the genius of the artist. The picture that he evolves — the visible song or poem perhaps more properly, so definitely and yet so briefly does it speak — is with accuracy to be considered only as a work of art. He will do much by combination. We march or dance as we masquerade; and we would do well to sing as we march.

Inevitably, as there is grasped this higher conception of the possibilities of the civic festival, there will be felt the need of making decoration and pageant complementary, that each may supplement the other. The municipality, festooning laurel or flowers from upright to upright, or setting Venetian masts, flower-garlanded, banner-tipped, or martial with arms and shields, along the way, has an opportunity as conspicuous as that of the individual householders greatly to emphasise the expression of the formal spectacle. When in New York, for instance, the artists combined to erect the Dewey arch of triumph, with its victory-crowned and laurel-hung approaches, they gave to the parade at that particular point an added expression such that the ovation seemed to culminate in the arch.

It is noteworthy that there was a co-operation of artists in this work. There are times when a work of art is to be born of the dream of a single artist, lest a composite product show self-consciousness. But in devising an expression of popular sentiment,

as we must do in occasional decorations, it were well
for artists to combine that they may represent more
accurately the various shades of emotion of which
the aggregate alone constitutes popular sentiment.
This is an idea almost as new to-day as is modern
civic art itself. But we may observe its growing
power in that artistic progress which marks the
greater public festivals of America, for it has been
recently applied with increasing confidence and completeness: first, the Centennial in Philadelphia; second, the Columbian Exposition in Chicago; third,
the Congressional, or National, Library in Washington — not, indeed a "festival," but as strictly public
art and to almost a like extent an expression of popular sentiment; fourth, the Dewey Arch in New York.[1]
This idea, though it seem new to-day, had its test-
ing centuries ago, in the co-operation which made the
artistic guilds of the Middle Ages so notably successful, and in the cathedrals that were building through
generations. The test has served again in modern
times. Almost the only feature now remembered
of the Dewey celebration is this work which the
artists did together; and of the Columbian Exposition, the exhibits drop out of mind while there
lingers, as strong as ever, the vision of the harmoniously grouped and proportioned buildings. A
"dream city" men called it then; but the dream has
outlived all else.

[1] These "steps of progress" are borrowed from an article in *The International
Monthly*, January, 1900, by Charles DeKay, in a discussion of "Organization among
American Artists."

When the Dewey Arch had served its purpose, there arose a demand that it be made permanent. There was recognition that in its hasty sculpture much might be improved; but the demand for a naval arch of generally similar character became insistent and clamorous. It was not quite strong enough, however, to raise the vast sum of money that was required, and the project failed. A few years earlier a like demand, for the perpetuation in marble of a temporary arch that had been erected as a feature of the decoration for the Washington centennial in New York, succeeded. This stands to-day as one of the public art treasures of the city; and there is shown the practical advantage of having the decoration, though it be ever so temporary and occasional, set an ideal before the people.

But in the planning of the city's festivals these ulterior and very conscientious purposes are not to hide the real object, which is pre-eminently and necessarily temporary. The festival's whole excuse for being is in the occasion which it expresses. And further than that it tends to become, in a world that is ever working harder, the one really public recreation. In England and America, without free theatres, and where people do not play without excuse, this is now virtually the case. The park, in offering quiet and rest, invites to a negative method of recreation; there is only the festival, the celebration of one kind or another, to urge to positive, active recreation. What this may mean with its sudden relative freedom, its exceptional colour and gaiety, to lonely foreigners and especially to those who come from the south of Europe, cannot be readily imagined. These are not always fitted to gain from the quiet beauty of the park that tranquil pleasure which the park is designed to give, or if gaining this to find in it complete satisfaction. Thus the recreative element in the temporary entertainments is never to be lost sight of. Furthermore these, as the only really civic, in the sense of *public,* occasions, and as events that have also a larger and deeper pertinence than the pleasure of an idle hour, may well demand that the municipality throw itself with enthusiasm into their planning. The city should regard them with a seriousness that they seldom have in these days that are so fearful of frivolity. It should resolve to make of them the utmost possible, to secure in pageant and decoration the most beautiful effects, and so to impart by their means popular lessons in art — lessons that will be the better learned because loved.

Incidentally, it is no secret that a beautiful celebration is good "business." The best economy is to add to the appropriation that will create an ordinary spectacle a sum that will make it extraordinary in its beauty and attractiveness. There are too many examples of this, and the principle is too well understood, to need elaboration or explaining. It is known, too, that decoration "pays" in a modest way, even when it is not very artistic or very pretentious. On the several occasions when there has been, for some special reason, a brilliant illumination of a few blocks of business street or their transformation into a "Court of Honour," there has followed with perhaps not a single exception a request by the merchants that the decoration or lighting be continued beyond its appropriate time, so beneficial has proved its effect on business. A few weeks before this was written, a street-improvement club of San Francisco decorated the thoroughfare which they had made their special charge with greens for the holidays. The ugly trolley poles were hidden with evergreen; festoons of it were draped from pole to pole, and an arch of boughs spanned the sidewalk where a rubbish chute descended from a building that was being remodelled. It was not a very impressive effort; little money was expended; there was simply a co-operative and harmonious utilisation of the means at hand. But the Christmas spirit so entered into this street that the shoppers thronged it and the enterprise "paid" abundantly.

In another, and somewhat smaller, city a residential street about a half-dozen blocks in length has a middle strip of turf on which are planted magnolias at regular intervals. The trees have attained large size and are healthy, so that when they are in bloom the street is one of "the sights" of the town. It is now proposed by the residents to celebrate annually among themselves magnolia-blossoming day. In this suggestion civic art finds strong appeal; in pertinence, distinctiveness, and picturesqueness, it is worthy of the best traditions of civic art's concern with the temporary and occasional.

And how near this is, how eagerly it embraces the opportunity for including the frankly artistic and decorative in a city's aspect and for bringing into the city's life the playfulness, gaiety, joy, of art, is so obvious as to appear without the need of reflection. We have only to learn that we should embrace this opportunity with a seriousness and earnestness that would see in it not the temporary only, but the abiding; not alone the briefly smiling faces, the clapping hands, the idle jesting of a crowd, but also the satisfaction of the primal yearnings of humanity, the brightening of many lives, the most effective mode of popular education. We should consider the temporary and occasional decoration an art opportunity and an art problem, and as such should study it and apply to it art principles.

Into this, the most transitory phase of civic art, there should, then, go the high-minded earnestness that properly belongs to the whole great effort. The total of that may be now defined: it is the adjustment of the city to its city needs so fittingly that life will be made easier for a vast and growing portion of mankind, and the bringing into it of that beauty which is the continual need and rightful heritage of men and which has been their persistent dream.

INDEX.

377

Index. 381